服部幸應／服部津貴子
［監修］

こどもくらぶ
［編］

What is 和食 WASHOKU?

〈英文対訳付〉

ミネルヴァ書房

和食というのは、日本の気候・風土・歴史のなかではぐくまれてきた料理のことです。わたしたち日本人は、自然のめぐみを活用し、素材のもち味を引きだす調理法を発達させてきました。また、和食は、日本人の慣習や行事とも密接にかかわっています。つまり、和食ということばは、料理そのものだけをさすのではなく、日本の伝統的な食文化をさしているともいえるでしょう。

この「What is 和食 WASHOKU?」は、つぎのように4章で構成し、和食をさまざまな面から取り上げていきます。

第1章	一汁三菜とは	和食と日本文化
第2章	郷土料理を知ろう	日本各地の和食
第3章	懐石料理を知ろう	和食とおもてなし
第4章	和食からWASHOKUへ	世界にひろがる和食

さらに、各章のパート2では、家庭でたのしくつくれる和食のレシピを紹介します。実際に料理をつくって、食べて、和食のすばらしさを実感しましょう。

この本を読んで、みなさんが和食を身近なものとし、日本の食文化について興味をもってくださることを願っています。

Introduction

"Washoku" is a Japanese cuisine developed in the nature, geographical features and environments, the climate and the history in Japan. Japanese people have utilized blessings of the nature and have developed the cooking techniques and methods to make the most of the tastes of ingredients. Washoku has deep relationships with Japanese customs, festivals and ceremonies. Washoku can be said as not only being the food itself but representing Japanese traditional food cultures.
"What is 和食 WASHOKU?" consists of 4 chapters, and covers many aspects of Washoku.

Chapter 1 **What is "1 Soup and 3 Dishes"?** Washoku and Japanese traditional cultures
Chapter 2 **Japanese local foods** Washoku in each local region
Chapter 3 **What is "Kaiseki cuisine"?** Washoku and Japanese hospitality
Chapter 4 **From "和食" to "Washoku"** Washoku spreading all over the world

Some easy recipes of Washoku to cook at home kitchen are introduced in the latter section of each chapter. Cook Japanese foods by yourself, eat what you cooked, and realize the wonderfulness of Washoku.
Hope this book will make you more familiar with Washoku, and many people become interested in Washoku.

もくじ

第1章 一汁三菜とは 和食と日本文化
chapter 1 What is "1 Soup and 3 Dishes"? Washoku and Japanese traditional cultures

パート1 知ろう！ 調べよう！ Let's know it！ Let's research it！

- 伝統行事と和食　Traditional events and Washoku … 8
- 一汁三菜とは　What is "1 Soup and 3 Dishes"? … 10
- ごはんについて知ろう　What is Gohan: Rice? … 12
- 味の決め手は「だし」　"Dashi" is the key to Japanese taste … 14
- 乾物について知ろう　What is dried food? … 16
- 汁物のいろいろ　Various kinds of Japanese Soup … 18
- みそとしょうゆについて知ろう　What is Miso and Shoyu (Soy sauce)? … 20
- 和食の調理の基本は「切る」こと　"Cutting" is the basic technique of Washoku … 22
- 調理の五法　5 cooking methods … 24
- 季節感をたいせつに　Emphasis on seasonality of Washoku … 28
- 和食の食事作法　Table manners of Washoku … 30

パート2 つくろう！ 食べよう！ Let's make it！ Let's eat it！

- 夏の一汁三菜　1 Soup and 3 Dishes in Summer … 34
  - 🟢 枝豆ごはん　Edamame Rice … 34
  - 🔵 アジのつみれ汁　Minced Horse Mackerel Ball Soup … 35
  - 🟢 とり肉の照焼　Chicken Teriyaki … 36
  - 🔵 タコの酢の物　Vinegared Octopus … 37
  - 🟢 焼きなす　Grilled Eggplant … 37
- 秋の一汁三菜　1 Soup and 3 Dishes in Autumn … 38
  - 🟠 きのこの炊きこみごはん　Mushroom Rice … 38
  - 🟣 とん汁　Pork Miso Soup … 39
  - 🟠 サンマの塩焼　Grilled Pacific Saury … 40
  - 🟠 菊花びたし　Boiled Chrysanthemum … 40
  - 🟠 肉じゃが　Braised Beef and Potato … 41

第2章 郷土料理を知ろう 日本各地の和食
chapter 2　Japanese local foods　Washoku in each local region

パート1　知ろう！調べよう！　Let's know it！Let's research it！

伝統行事と郷土料理　Traditional Events and Local Foods	44
北海道の郷土料理　ジンギスカン　Local food of Hokkaido—Genghis Khan Barbecue	46
秋田県の郷土料理　きりたんぽ　Local food of Akita—Kiritampo	48
宮城県の郷土料理　はらこめし　Local food of Miyagi—Harako (Salmon roe) rice bowl	50
なべ料理について知ろう　What is Nabe (hot pot) cuisine?	52
新潟県の郷土料理　のっぺ　Local food of Niigata—Noppe soup	54
長野県の郷土料理　おやき　Local food of Nagano—Oyaki	56
千葉県の郷土料理　イワシのごま漬け　Local food of Chiba—Salted sardine with sesame	58
三重県の郷土料理　ハマグリ料理　Local food of Mie—Hamaguri clam dishes	60
山口県の郷土料理　岩国ずし　Local food of Yamaguchi—Iwakuni-zushi	62
すしについて知ろう　What is Sushi？	64
愛媛県の郷土料理　タイそうめん　Local food of Ehime—Somen noodles with sea bream	66
長崎県の郷土料理　卓袱料理　Local food of Nagasaki—Shippoku cuisine	68

パート2　つくろう！食べよう！　Let's make it！Let's eat it！

北海道の郷土料理　イカめし　Local food of Hokkaido　Squid Stuffed with Rice	70
長野県の郷土料理　おやき　Local food of Nagano　Oyaki	72
岡山県の郷土料理　ばらずし　Local food of Okayama　Bara-zushi	74
長崎県の郷土料理　ぶたの角煮　Local food of Nagasaki　Simmered pork cubes	76

第3章 懐石料理を知ろう　和食とおもてなし
chapter 3　What is "Kaiseki cuisine"?　Washoku and Japanese hospitality

パート1　知ろう！　調べよう！　Let's know it ! Let's research it !

懐石料理とは　　What is "Kaiseki cuisine"? ·· 80
懐石料理の基本は一汁三菜　　The basics of Kaiseki cuisine is "1 Soup and 3 Dishes" ···· 82
煮物わんから焼き物へ　　Simmered food bowl and Grilled dish ······················ 86
預け鉢とは　　What is "Azukebachi"? ·· 88
八寸とは　　What is "Hassun"? ·· 90
和食の食事作法の基本　　Basic table manners of Washoku ······························ 92
料理の歴史について知ろう　　The history of Japanese food ···························· 94
季節感をたいせつにする和食　　Washoku values seasonality ···························· 96
茶の湯とは　　What is "Cha-no-Yu (Tea ceremony)"? ·································· 98
日本茶について知ろう　　What is Japanese tea? ··· 100
世界遺産になった和食　　Washoku designated UNESCO Intangible Cultural Heritage ··· 102

パート2　つくろう！　食べよう！　Let's make it ! Let's eat it !

煮物わん　カニしんじょうわん　　Simmered food bowl Crab shinjo dumpling soup ······· 106
焼き物　カマスの幽庵焼
　Grilled dish Grilled barracuda marinated with soy sauce, sake, mirin and Yuzu citrus ········· 108
預け鉢　小かぶとアナゴと春菊の炊き合わせ
　Simmered dish Simmered turnip, conger eel and crown daisy ···························· 110
八寸　雷白うり　Hassun (nibbles for sake) Pickled Cucumis melo ················ 112
　　　エビのつや煮　Hassun Simmered shrimp ·· 113

第4章 和食からWASHOKUへ 世界にひろがる和食
chapter 4　From "和食" to "Washoku"　Washoku spreading all over the world

パート1　知ろう！　調べよう！　Let's know it !　Let's research it !

世界じゅうで人気の日本食　Washoku is popular all over the world ……… 116
海外のすしは巻きずしから　Roll Sushi in foreign countries ……… 118
すしが世界で人気のわけ　Why sushi is popular all over the world? ……… 120
そもそも「日本料理」とは？　What is Japanese cuisine? ……… 122
和洋折衷の日本の料理　Washoku mixed with Western style ……… 124
すしのつぎに人気の日本料理は？　What is popular Japanese food next to Sushi? ……… 126
ラーメンも日本の食文化だ！　Ramen is one of Japanese gastronomic cultures ……… 128
日本発の新しい食文化　Newborn culinary culture generated from Japan ……… 130
しょうゆとみそ　Soy sauce and Miso ……… 132
日本のソースとうま味調味料　Japanese sauce and Umami seasonings ……… 134
あらためて考える「和食」　Re-evaluation of Washoku ……… 136
和食の海外普及　The expansion of Washoku throughout the world ……… 138
和食を未来へ引きつぐ　Inheritance of Washoku to the next generation ……… 140

パート2　つくろう！　食べよう！　Let's make it !　Let's eat it !

てんぷら・かき揚げ　Tempura and Kakiage (mixed vegetable and seafood tempura) ……… 142
ドラゴンロール　Dragon Roll Sushi ……… 144
焼きとり　Yakitori (grilled chicken) ……… 146
カツ丼　Katsudon (pork cutlet on a bowl of rice) ……… 148

和食の調理道具・和食の料理用語　Cooking tools and terms of Washoku ……… 152
さくいん　INDEX ……… 154
英語さくいん　INDEX ……… 158

第1章
chapter 1

一汁三菜とは
What is "1 Soup and 3 Dishes"?

和食と日本文化
Washoku and Japanese traditional cultures

一汁三菜とは
和食と日本文化

パート1 知ろう！調べよう！

伝統行事と和食 [01]

和食というと、どういう料理が思いうかぶでしょうか。
はじめに、伝統行事の和食について見てみましょう。

● おせち料理 ● [02]

右の写真は、正月のおせち料理です。めでたい正月にふさわしく、美しく盛りつけられていますね。おせち料理は、代表的な和食といえるでしょう。

もともとおせち（御節）は、一年のはじめである正月（1月1日）や、季節の区切り目とされていた五節句（1月7日、3月3日、5月5日、7月7日、9月9日）に、家内安全と家族の健康、子孫繁栄、豊作・豊漁を願って、えんぎのよい食べ物を神さまにおそなえしたのがはじまりです。それが、いまでは正月の料理だけをおせちというようになったのです。

おせちにつかわれている食材は、魚介や野菜、いも・豆が主で、それぞれに意味がこめられています。調理には、素材のもち味を引きだすため、こんぶやかつおぶしなどからとった「だし（→14ページ）」をつかい、油脂はほとんどつかわれません。

おせち
重箱にさまざまな料理をつめ、みんなで少しずつ取りわけて食べる。重箱は5段重ねが正式だが、現代では3段重ねが一般的。[11]

たけのこの煮しめ ひと晩に数メートルものびるというたけのこにあやかって、運勢が勢いよくのびるようにという願いがこめられている。[12]

節句と食べ物 [04]

正月[05] （1月1日）	七草の節句[06] （1月7日）	桃の節句[07] （3月3日）	端午の節句[08] （5月5日）	七夕の節句[09] （7月7日）	重陽の節句[10] （9月9日）
もち、雑煮、おせち料理	七草がゆ	草もち、ひしもち、あられ、白酒	ちまき、かしわもち	そうめん	菊めし、菊花酒

---

01 Traditional events and Washoku **02 Osechi-Ryori, Special dishes for the New Year** /Osechi is one of the typical traditional Washoku and is beautifully dished up to celebrate the New Year. Origin of Osechi is to offer the gods foods which are believed to bring luck, and people have prayed for well-being and health of family, fertility, rich harvest and big catch. Seafood, vegetables, roots and beans are used for Osechi, and all of these ingredients have meanings. "Dashi"(Japanese soup stock) is used to make the most of the tastes of each ingredient. Fat and oil are almost never used. **03 Mochi is an offering to the gods** /Rice has been a special food for Japanese since early times. Mochi was offered to the gods at every seasonal festival. After the festival, people received offerings to make Zoni soup. Zoni has each local taste. **04** Seasonal festivals and foods **05** New Year's Day (January 1st): Mochi, Zoni soup, Osechi **06** Seven Herbs Festival (January 7th) : Seven herbs porridge **07** Girls' Festival (March 3rd): Mugwort mochi **08** Boys' Festival

黒豆 まめに（健康に）くらせるようにという願いがこめられている。⑬

紅白なます だいこんの白とにんじんの赤で、お祝いの水引をかたどっている。だいこんやにんじんは根菜なので、家の土台がしっかりするようにという願いがこめられている。⑭

ごまめ（田づくり） ごまめはカタクチイワシの幼魚を干したもの。むかし、畑の肥料としてイワシをつかったことから、作物がたくさんとれますようにという願いがこめられている。⑯

かずのこ かずのこはニシンの卵。夫婦のあいだに子どもがたくさん生まれますようにという願いがこめられている。⑮

えび 長いひげ、曲がった腰をお年寄りに見立てて、長生きできるようにという願いをこめている。⑰

● 神さまにそなえるおもち ● ⓷

日本人にとって、昔から米はとても貴重な食べ物でした。節句などには、米をついてつくったおもちが神さまにそなえられました。正月に神さまにおそなえしたのが、鏡もちのはじまりです。そして、おそなえしたおもちを下げて、ほかのそなえ物といっしょに煮て食べたのが、雑煮のはじまりだといわれています。

雑煮の汁や具、おもちの形は地方によってもちがい、それぞれ特徴があります。

こんぶ、干し柿、だいだいを飾った鏡もち。⑱

角もちを焼いて、しょうゆ味の汁に入れた関東風の雑煮。⑲

(May 5th): Rice dumplings wrapped in bamboo leaves ⑨ Star Festival (July 7th): Somen noodles ⑩ Chrysanthemum Festival (September 9th): Chrysanthemum rice and chrysanthemum sake ⑪ Osechi: Foods are packed in 3 or 5 tiered boxes. ⑫ Simmered bamboo shoot: Bamboo shoots symbolize good fortune because of their quick growing. ⑬ Black beans: Beans are symbols of health and longevity. ⑭ Vinegared daikon and carrot: White and red symbolize Mizuhiki cord used for wrapping of festive gifts. Daikon and carrot are both root vegetables and symbolize strengthening the base of the house. ⑮ Herring roe: Numerous eggs symbolize fertility. ⑯ Dried sardine: Sardine was used as a fertilizer in the past and symbolizes rich harvest. ⑰ Shrimp: Long barbs and crooked shape symbolize longevity. ⑱ Round shaped Kagami-mochi offered to the gods. Decorated with kelp, dried persimmon and topped with daidai-citrus. ⑲ Zoni soup from Kanto region. Grilled square mochi and clear soup seasoned with soy sauce.

一汁三菜とは

日本の主食は米です。昔ながらの日本型食生活は、ごはんを中心に、「一汁三菜」を基本とするおかずで組み立てられています。

主菜
いりどり とり肉、にんじん、ごぼう、れんこん、干ししいたけ、こんにゃくなどを、少量の油でいためて甘辛く煮た料理。「筑前煮」とよぶ地域もある。

ごはん
基本は白いごはん。旬のたけのこを入れて炊いた「たけのこごはん」にすれば、より春らしい献立になる。

●ごはんとおかず●

ごはんを中心とした和食は、栄養バランスのとりやすい食事です。それは、淡白な味のごはんには、どんなおかずでもよくあうからです。おかずを「一汁三菜」にすれば、たくさんの食材をつかうので、栄養バランスはさらに高まります。

「一汁三菜」というのは、汁物1品と、おかず3品（主菜が1品、副菜が2品）を組みあわせた食事のことです。ごはんでエネルギー源となる炭水化物を、汁物で水分を、おかずでその他の栄養素をバランスよくとることができるのです。

主菜には、魚や肉、卵、とうふなどのたんぱく質をたくさんふくむ食材がつかわれます。副菜には、

---

01 What is "1 Soup and 3 Dishes"? **02** Rice and Okazu (dishes eaten with rice) /Washoku is good for balancing nutrition. We eat white rice as the staple food, and we can add any kind of dishes because they go well with white rice. Various ingredients can be used for okazu. "1 Soup and 3 Dishes" means 1 soup, 1 main dish and 2 side dishes with rice. Carbohydrates in rice are a source of energy, soup is for water, and other dishes are for other nutrients for balancing the nutrition. Main dish is fish, meat, egg, tofu, etc. which are rich with protein. Side dishes consist of potatoes, taros, beans, mushrooms, seaweed and other vegetables which contain vitamins, minerals and fibers. Washoku consists of seasonal ingredients. This photo is an example of typical 1 Soup and 3 Dishes in spring. Summer and autumn dishes are introduced in part 2 with recipes. Here is an example of typical winter menu: rice, tofu and mushroom miso soup, grilled pork with ginger for main dish, simmered red bream and braised burdock root for side

パート1 知ろう！調べよう！

副菜1 05
厚焼き卵 和食の定番おかずのひとつ。だしと砂糖、塩としょうゆ少々をまぜた卵液を卵焼き器に流し入れ、巻きながら焼き上げる。

副菜2 06
いんげんのごまあえ「ごまあえ」というのは、ごまをいってすり、だし、砂糖、しょうゆで調味して、ゆでた野菜などをあえた料理。いんげんのほか、ほうれんそうでもよくつくられる。

汁物 07
ハマグリの潮汁 春に旬をむかえるハマグリからでるうま味を生かし、塩のみで味つけした汁。

PFCバランスのとれた和食 08

PFCバランスというのは、食生活のなかで、たんぱく質（P）、脂肪（F）、炭水化物（C）がバランスよくとれているかどうかをあらわした指標です。健康的な生活をおくるための理想的なPFCバランスは、たんぱく質が15パーセント、脂質が25パーセント、炭水化物が60パーセントとされています。PFCバランスがよくとれていれば、きれいな三角形になります。

1985年ごろの日本のPFCバランスはきれいな三角形でしたが、食事が洋風化し、肉や油脂類を多くとるようになった結果、最近はPFCバランスがくずれてきています。

そのため、いま、一汁三菜の食事形式のよさが見直されているのです。

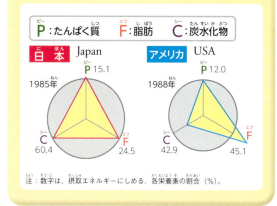

注：数字は、摂取エネルギーにしめる、各栄養素の割合（％）。

野菜、いも、豆、きのこ、海藻など、ビタミンやミネラル、食物せんいをたっぷりとれる食材がつかわれます。

和食の献立は、なるべく旬（→28ページ）の食材を取り入れて組み立てるように、さまざまに工夫されています。上の写真は、春の食材をつかった一汁三菜の献立例です。

夏、秋の一汁三菜の献立例は、パート2でつくり方とともに紹介しています。冬の一汁三菜としては、つぎのような献立が考えられます。

ごはん ごはん　　**汁物** とうふとなめこのみそ汁
主菜 ぶた肉のしょうが焼き
副菜 キンメダイの煮つけ　**副菜** きんぴらごぼう

dishes. 03 Main dish: "Chikuzen-ni": braised chicken, carrot, burdock root, lotus root, dried shiitake mushroom and konnyaku with salty and sweet taste. 04 Rice: unseasoned rice is the basic. Seasonal ingredients can be added, e.g. bamboo shoot rice is a spring delicacy. 05 Side dish 1: "Atsuyaki Tamago": Japanese thick omelet; Mix egg with dashi, sugar, salt and soy sauce, then make an omelet using an omelet pan. 06 Side dish 2: "Goma-Ae" of kidney bean; "Goma-Ae" is a dish dressed with sesame paste, dashi, sugar and soy sauce. Other than kidney beans, spinach is also a popular ingredient. 07 Soup: Clear soup with clam. Hamaguri clam is a spring delicacy. Season with only salt to make the most of umami taste of clam. 08 Washoku is well-balanced with protein[P], fat[F] and carbohydrate[C]. Ideal balance of PFC is 15% P, 25% F and 60% C. But nowadays, the balance of PFC is getting worse. Japanese traditional 1 Soup and 3 Dishes meal is well-balanced in PFC and this dietary habit is reconsidered.

ごはんについて知ろう

日本人は、いまのような白いふっくらごはんを、昔から食べていたわけではありません。ごはんの歴史を見てみましょう。また、なべでふっくらごはんを炊く方法をマスターしましょう。

ごはんの歴史

日本の米づくりの歴史は古く、縄文時代末期から弥生時代にかけておこなわれるようになったといわれています。岡山県で縄文時代末期（いまから2500年ほど前）の水田あとも発見されています。でも、当時の人びとが食べていたのは、玄米（もみがらをとりのぞいただけの米）を煮たり蒸したりした、水気の多いおかゆのようなものでした。いまのようなごはんが食べられるようになったのは、ずっとあとになってからです。

弥生時代
（いまから2000年以上前）
水気の多い玄米のおかゆ。

奈良時代
（いまから1300年ほど前）
水分が少ないかためのおかゆ。

平安時代
（いまから1200年ほど前）
もっと水分が少なくなった、いまのごはんに近いもの。

鎌倉時代
（いまから800年ほど前）
米が水分を吸収してしまうまで炊いたごはん。

江戸時代中ごろ
（いまから300年ほど前）
厚手のふたをつけた羽釜（まわりにつばのついた金属製の釜）で炊いた、ふっくらごはん。

江戸時代中ごろから、いまのようなごはんの炊き方がひろまっていきました。でも、ごはんを食べられたのは、上流階級のわずかな人たちだけでした。

当時の米づくりは気候に大きく左右され、収穫量はいまとはくらべものにならないほど少なかったのです。また、農民は米を年貢（税金）としておさめなくてはならなかったので、手元に残る米はほんのわずかでした。それで、ふだんはアワやヒエなどの雑穀を食べたり、米に雑穀やいもなどをまぜて炊いたものを食べたりしていました。貴重な米は、節句やたいせつな行事のときにしか食べられなかったのです。

なべでごはんを炊く

ごはんは、炊飯器でなくても、なべでおいしく炊くことができます。ふっくらごはんの炊き方を覚えましょう。

1 米を、正確に計量カップ (180mL) ではかって、ボウルに入れる。

2 たっぷりの水を加え、サッとかきまぜて、すぐ水を捨てる。

3 手のひらで、かるくシャッシャッと米をとぎ、水を捨てる。

4 ふたたび水を入れて2〜3回とぎ、米を1時間ほど水につけておく。

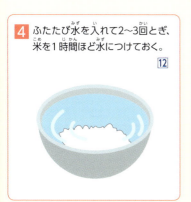

5 ざるにあけて水を切った米をなべに入れ、米の1.2倍の水を入れる。

6 なべにふたをして、強火にかける。ふきこぼれたら、弱火にする。

7 15分くらい弱火のままにし、最後は一瞬だけ強火にして火を止める。

弱火で約15分　　一瞬強火

8 ふたをしたまま、しばらく蒸らしてから、ごはんをさっくりまぜておく。

---

to the present cooked rice and less water than porridge in Nara period. **06** Kamakura period: 800 years ago. Cooked rice with all the water absorbed by the rice. **07** Mid-Edo period: 300 years ago. Soft and plump rice cooked in a metal pot with a thick wooden lid. **08 How to cook rice** /You can cook rice by a pot even if you do not have a rice cooker. **09** 1.Measure rice with 180mL rice cup. Put the rice in a bowl. **10** 2. Rinse the rice with full of water, mix it lightly and drain water immediately. **11** 3. Pour water, rub the rice lightly with the palm and drain water. **12** 4. Repeat (3) 2 or 3 times, then add water and leave the rice for an hour. **13** 5. Transfer the rice to a colander and drain water, then put the rice in a pot and add 1.2 times amount of water to it. **14** 6. Cover the lid of the pot and cook over strong heat. Turn down to low heat when it reaches the boiling point. **15** 7. Keep low heat for 15 min and turn up the heat just for a second before turning off the heat. **16** 8. Keep the lid on and steam the rice for several min, then mix it.

味の決め手は「だし」

和食では、素材のもち味を引きだすために、「だし」をつかって調理します。「だし」のおいしさのひみつは？

●「だし」のうま味●

日本の食事は、昔から淡白な味の穀物類が中心でした。そのため、「だし」やしょうゆ、みそなどをじょうずにつかって、おいしく食べる工夫をしてきました。

「だし」のおいしさのひみつは、うま味成分がたっぷりふくまれていることです。うま味というのは、甘味（あまい）、塩味（しおからい）、苦味（にがい）、酸味（すっぱい）とならぶ基本五味のひとつです。

「だし」のうま味のもとは、こんぶに多くふくまれるグルタミン酸、かつお節や煮干しに多くふくまれるイノシン酸、干ししいたけなどにふくまれるグアニル酸です。これらのうま味成分をあわせると、相乗効果でさらにおいしくなることがわかっています。こんぶとかつお節の合わせだし（一番だし・二番だし）がおいしいのは、そのためです。

●基本のだし●

一番だしと二番だしは、こんぶとかつお節をつかう、和食の基本のだしです。

一番だしは、上品な味のだしです。こんぶを煮立たせないで、サッと引き上げるのが、おいしいだしをとるコツです。一番だしはどんな料理にもあいますが、透明感のあるすまし汁などに最適です。

二番だしは、一番だしをとったあとのこんぶとかつお節を、もう一度つかってとるだしです。みそ汁や煮物などのだしに適しています。

材料のこんぶの表面に白い粉がついていることがありますが、うま味成分が流れてしまうので、水で洗ったりしてはいけません。かたくしぼったぬれぶきんで、軽くふきとるだけでだいじょうぶです。

うま味のもと / umami components

こんぶ Kelp / グルタミン酸 glutamic acid

干ししいたけ dried shiitake mushroom / グアニル酸 guanylic acid

かつお節、煮干し dried bonito / イノシン酸 inosinic acid

---

01 **"Dashi" is the key to Japanese taste** 02 **Umami taste of Dashi** /Washoku is cooked with dashi (Japanese soup stock) to make the most of the flavor of each ingredient. The secret of dashi is "umami" taste. Umami is one of the basic 5 tastes, with sweetness, saltiness, bitterness and sourness. Umami components are glutamic acid richly contained in kelp, inosinic acid in dried bonito and guanylic acid in dried shiitake mushroom. They have a synergistic effect by being combined together. 03 **Basic Dashi** /First and second dashi (soup stocks) made by kelp and dried bonito are the basic dashi of Washoku. A tip to make good dashi is to take out kelp from the soup just before boiling. First dashi is good for any kind of dishes, especially for clear soup. Second dashi is made with re-used kelp and dried bonito, and good for miso soup or simmered dishes. 04 **How to make first dashi** /Ingredients: water 1.5L, kelp 30g, dried bonito 45g /1. Pour water into a pot and soak kelp for 2-3 hours. /2. Heat the water and take out kelp just before boiling

パート1　知ろう！調べよう！

一番だしのとり方 04

【材料】
- 水……1.5L
- こんぶ……30g
- かつお節……45g

1 なべに分量の水を入れて、こんぶをひたし、夏場は2時間ほど、冬場は3時間ほどつけておく。

2 1のなべを火にかけ、煮立つ寸前にこんぶを引き上げる。

3 火を弱め、なべにかつお節を入れて、すぐに火を止める。

4 かつお節がしずんだら、静かにこす。

5 一番だしの完成。

●干ししいたけのだし● 05

干ししいたけは、もどす前に1時間ほど日光に当てると、ビタミンDがふえて栄養価が高まります。干ししいたけのだしは、うま味とともに、しいたけ独特の香りが特徴です。干ししいたけのだしは、色・香り・味が強いので、煮物や麺つゆなどに適しています。

干ししいたけのだしのとり方 06

【材料】
- 干ししいたけ……30g
- 水……1L

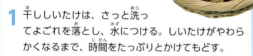

1 干ししいたけは、さっと洗ってよごれを落とし、水につける。しいたけがやわらかくなるまで、時間をたっぷりとかけてもどす。

2 やわらかくもどした干ししいたけは、水気をしぼって取りだし、煮物などにつかう。

3 もどし汁をだしとしてつかう。

●煮干しのだし● 07

カタクチイワシの煮干しが代表的ですが、アジやトビウオなどの煮干しもあります。だしをとる前に、煮干しの頭とはらわたを取りのぞいておくと、だしに魚のくさみが残りません。

煮干しのだしは、味・香りが強いので、みそ汁や煮物など、濃いめの味の料理に適しています。

煮干しのだしのとり方 08

【材料】
- 煮干し（頭とはらわたをとりのぞいたもの）……20〜30g
- 水……1L

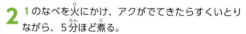

1 なべに水と煮干しを入れ、30分〜半日ほど置く。

2 1のなべを火にかけ、アクがでてきたらすくいとりながら、5分ほど煮る。

3 火を止め、こし器をボウルで受け、だしをこす。

/3. Lower the heat and put the dried bonito, remove it from the heat. /4. Filter out the dried bonito. /5. First soup stock is ready. **05 Dashi made with dried shiitake mushroom** /This dashi has strong color, flavor and taste, so it is good for simmered dishes or noodle soup. **06 How to make** /Ingredients: dried shiitakes 30g, water 1L /1. Rinse dried shiitakes and soak them in water until they get soft. /2. Rehydrated shiitakes can be used for simmered dishes. /3. Liquid is used as dashi. **07 Dashi made with dried sardines** /Typical dried fish used for dashi is small sardines, but dried horse mackerels or flying fish are also good. Remove the head and guts to avoid bad smell of fish. Dried sardine dashi has strong taste and flavor, so it is good for miso soup or simmered dishes. **08 How to make** /Ingredients: dried small sardines without head and guts 20-30g, water 1L /1. Put water and sardines into a pot and leave it for 30 min to half a day. /2. Heat the water about 5 min and remove the scum. /3. Turn off the heat and strain dashi.

乾物について知ろう

乾物というのは、豆類や野菜類、魚介類、きのこ類などの水分を太陽の光と風によってとばして、乾燥させたものです。

こんぶとかつお節

日本の代表的な乾物が、だしの材料であるこんぶとかつお節です。

こんぶは、食用の海藻を乾燥させたものです。日本で食べられているこんぶの約90パーセントが、北海道産です。

こんぶの種類はたくさんありますが、よく知られているのが、下の4種類です。

海から刈り取ったこんぶは、すぐに天日干しされる。

かつお節というのは、カツオの身を煮てから乾燥させたものです。

かつお節をつくるには、まず四つ割りにしたカツオの切り身を熱湯で煮ます。それを冷ましたあと、けむりでいぶしながら乾燥させます。これに独特のカビをつけて、保存性を高めます。でき上がったかつお節は、すっかり水分がぬけ、カチンカチンにかたくなっています。

かつお節の産地として有名なのは、鹿児島県、静岡県、高知県です。

四つ割りにしたカツオの切り身

完成したかつお節

真こんぶ
北海道南部でとれる、幅広で肉厚のこんぶ。だし用こんぶの最高級品といわれる。

利尻こんぶ
北海道北部でとれるこんぶで、幅が細め。真こんぶにつぐだし用こんぶの高級品。

羅臼こんぶ
知床半島の南岸でとれる、幅広のこんぶ。

日高こんぶ
日高地方の沿岸でとれる、細くてやわらかいこんぶ。だし用にもつかわれるが、こんぶ巻きなどの煮物に適している。

かつおだしをとるときは、かつお節をうすくけずった「けずり節」をつかいます。

独特のけずり器でかつお節をけずる。

---

01 What is dried food? 02 Kombu (Kelp) and Katsuo-bushi (Dried Bonito) / Typical Japanese dried foods which are used for dashi are kelp and dried bonito. Kelp is dried seaweed and 90% of Japanese kelp is produced in Hokkaido. There are many kinds of kelps and the following 4 are well known: "Ma-kombu", "Rishiri-kombu", "Rausu-kombu" and "Hidaka-kombu". The processes of making dried bonito is, first cut bonito into 4 fillets and boil them. Next is cooling and smoke-drying process. Preservative quality is improved by putting mold in a special culture. Finished dried bonito is completely dried and is very hard like a rock. Kagoshima, Shizuoka and Kochi prefectures are famous for producing dried bonito. 03 Ma-kombu: produced in southern Hokkaido. Wide and thick. The best brand of kelp to make dashi. 04 Rishiri-kombu: produced in northern Hokkaido. Narrow. The second-best kelp coming after Ma-kombu. 05 Rausu-kombu: wide kelp produced in southern shore of Shiretoko Peninsula. 06 Hidaka-kombu:

かんぴょう 10

乾物は、冷蔵庫に入れなくても保存がきき、一度に食べきれなくても残しておくことができる、とてもべんりな食品です。かんぴょうも、そんな昔の人の知恵がいっぱいつまった乾物です。

かんぴょうは、白くて長いひものよう。11

畑にできたユウガオの実。13

かんぴょうの天日干し。14

は、スイカのように大きくて丸いユウガオの実を、リンゴの皮をむくようにクルクルとまわしながらむき、できた細長いひも状のものを乾燥させたものなのです。かんぴょうの90パーセント以上が、栃木県で生産されています。

かんぴょうをじょうずにもどすには、まず塩をふって、やわらかくなるまでよくもむことです。そのあと、ゆでてから料理につかいます。

甘辛く煮たかんぴょうがおいしい、かんぴょう巻き。12

かんぴょうを塩もみしているところ。15

かんぴょうは、かんぴょう巻きの具としてよく知られていますが、なにを乾燥させたものかは、あまり知られていません。じつは、かんぴょう

produced in Hidaka region in Hokkaido. Very narrow and soft. Suitable for rolled kelp dishes. 07 Bonito fillet cut into 4 blocks. 08 Dried bonito. 09 A special shaver for dried bonito. 10 Kanpyo /Dried food is a useful ingredient which has excellent storage stability and does not need to be kept in a refrigerator; does not need to be used at one time. Kanpyo is a kind of dried food known as kanpyo roll sushi, but it is not well known what the original ingredient of kanpyo is. Kanpyo is the long shaved and dried Yugao gourd. 90% of kanpyo is produced in Tochigi Pref. Kanpyo needs to be rehydrated before cooking it. Rub it with salt until it gets soft. Then boil it. 11 Kanpyo looks like white long tape. 12 Kanpyo roll stuffed with salty-sweet kanpyo. 13 Fruit of a Yugao gourd in the field. 14 Kanpyo exposed to the sun. 15 Rubbing kanpyo with salt: preparation process to cook kanpyo.

汁物のいろいろ

一汁三菜の献立のなかで、汁物はたいせつな1品です。汁物には多くの種類があり、だしとさまざまな具を組みあわせてつくられます。

●汁の種類●

家庭で食べる汁物というと、みそ汁がもっとも一般的ですね。みそ汁というのは、だしで具を煮て、みそで味をつけた汁のことです。

汁物は、なにで味をつけるかによって、みそ仕立て、しょうゆ仕立て、塩仕立てに、大きく分けられます。みそ仕立ての場合は、つかうみその種類（→20ページ）をかえると、味わいの異なるみそ汁ができます。

みそ仕立て — みそ汁
みそで味をつける。

しょうゆ仕立て — すまし汁
しょうゆだけ、または、塩としょうゆで味をつける。

塩仕立て — 潮汁
塩だけで味をつける。

●代表的な汁物●

汁の具には、魚や貝、野菜やきのこ、とうふ、卵など、さまざまな食材がつかわれます。ただ、この具にはしょうゆ仕立てが、あの具にはみそ仕立てがあうというように、それぞれの具にはよくあう味つけがあります。ここで、家庭でよくつくられる汁物の例を紹介しましょう。

みそ汁

具がよく煮えてから、最後にみそをとき入れます。みそのとき方は、みそこしをつかう方法と、おたまにみそをのせて汁でといていく方法があります。

シジミのみそ汁

シジミからはうま味たっぷりのだしがでる。シジミはすまし汁にもつかわれる。

とうふとワカメのみそ汁

たんぱく質いっぱいのとうふと、ミネラルを豊富にふくむワカメのみそ汁は、栄養満点。

---

01 **Various kinds of Japanese Soup** 02 **Variations of Soup** /Miso-shiru (miso soup) is a typical home-cooked soup. Ingredients of Miso-shiru are cooked with dashi before adding miso paste. There are 3 types of soup: miso soup, clear soup with soy sauce, and clear soup with salt. You can enjoy different flavors of Miso-shiru by using different kinds of miso. 03 **Typical Japanese Soup** /Many ingredients are used for soup such as fish, shellfish, vegetables, mushrooms, tofu, eggs and so on. There are good combinations between the ingredients and the taste of the soup. 04 **Miso-shiru (miso soup)** /Add miso after ingredients are well cooked. There are 2 ways to mix miso: using miso strainer or putting miso on a ladle and dissolving it with dashi. 05 **Shijimi Miso-shiru** /Shijimi clam is rich with umami. Shijimi is also used for clear soup. 06 **Tofu and wakame soup** /Tofu is rich with protein and wakame seaweed is rich with minerals. This soup is highly nutritious. 07 **Miso-shiru with daikon and deep-fried tofu** /Cook daikon

パート1　知ろう！調べよう！

すまし汁 08

すまし汁は、だしのうま味がそのままでる汁ですので、だしをしっかりとるようにしましょう。味つけは、まず塩を入れ、そのあと、うま味を足すような感じでしょうゆを入れます。

若竹汁 10
やわらかく煮たたけのことワカメを組みあわせた、シンプルなすまし汁。

かきたま汁 09
水ときかたくり粉を入れて煮立たせた汁に、とき卵を流しこんでかきまぜてつくる、とろみのあるすまし汁。

潮汁 11

潮汁は、具としてつかう魚や貝からでるうま味を利用して、塩だけで味つけをする汁です。貝は、海水ていどの塩水につけて砂ぬきをしてから、汁に入れます。魚は、生ぐささがでないように、サッと湯通ししてからつかいましょう。

ハマグリの潮汁 12
ハマグリとこんぶ、水を入れたなべを火にかけ、こんぶとハマグリからじっくりとうま味を引きだした汁。

だいこんと油揚げのみそ汁 07
たんざくに切ってやわらかく煮ただいこんに、油揚げでコクをつけたみそ汁。

タイのあらの潮汁 13
タイの頭やカマ、腹骨などからとれる、おいしいだしを利用した汁。

---

radish sliced in rectangular soft and add rich flavor by deep-fried tofu. 08 Sumashi-jiru (Clear soup) /Basic taste of clear soup is dashi, so making good dashi is the key. Seasoned with salt and soy sauce. 09 Egg drop soup /Boil water and add starch to thicken the soup. Pour beaten egg and stir it. 10 Bamboo shoot soup /Parboil bamboo shoot soft. Simple clear soup with bamboo shoot and wakame seaweed. 11 Ushio-jiru (Clear soup with clam and fish) /Just seasoned with salt to make the most of umami taste of fish and clam. Remove shell sand by soaking in salted water with same salt concentration of seawater before cooking. Remove bad smell of the fish by parboiling it quickly. 12 Hamaguri clam soup /Put water, hamaguri clam and kelp into a pot and heat it. Rich with umami taste of hamaguri clam and kelp. 13 Sea bream fish head soup /Clear soup made from leftover fish-head and scrapes.

みそとしょうゆについて知ろう

みそとしょうゆは、大豆を発酵させてつくる日本独特の調味料です。発酵によって、大豆のたんぱく質がアミノ酸といううま味のもとに変化するのです。みそ・しょうゆについて、調べてみましょう。

米みそ・麦みそ・豆みそ

みその原料は、大豆に、米または麦と塩です。みそは大豆を発酵させてつくりますが、発酵にはさまざまな微生物が活躍します。そのなかで、いちばん重要な微生物が、麹菌（カビの一種）です。麹菌を米につけて発酵させたものを米麹といい、麦につけて発酵させたものを麦麹といいます。米麹をつかうと米みそに、麦麹をつかうと麦みそになります。麹をつかわず、直接大豆に麹菌を加えて発酵させると、豆みそになります。

日本でもっとも一般的につかわれているのは米みそで、色や味にはさまざまな種類があります。麦みそは、農家の自家用としてつくられたものが多く、味も個性的です。豆みそは、濃厚なうま味としぶ味をもつのが特徴です。

地方によってちがうみそ

みそは「おふくろの味」といわれるほど、地方によって、いろいろな味・色のみそがあります。それは、原料の配分や麹のちがいによって風味のちがうみそができるからです。また、みそのできぐあいは温度や湿度に大きく影響されるので、同じ原料や麹をつかっても、気候・風土のちがいによってできぐあいもちがってくるからです。

味については、甘い順に、甘みそ、甘口みそ、辛口みそに分けられます。麹をたくさんつかうほど、甘いみそができます。

色については、色のうすい順に、白みそ、淡色みそ、赤みそに分けられます。大豆を煮て短期間で熟成させると白みそに、長時間かけて熟成させると赤みそになります。

01 What is Miso and Shoyu (Soy sauce)? 02 Rice Miso, Barley Miso, Bean Miso /Miso is made from soy beans, salt and rice or barley, and many microorganisms take part in fermentation process. The most important microorganism is koji mold. Fermented rice with koji mold is named rice koji, fermented barley with koji is barely koji. Miso made from rice koji is named Rice Miso, and miso made from barely koji is named Barley Miso. Bean Miso is made when soybeans are fermented directly with koji mold. 03 Local tastes of miso /Taste of miso is said as "mother's cooking," and each region has its own miso. Because of the difference of recipe, temperature and humidity, each miso has different taste. Taste of miso can be classified into 3 types, sweet, semi-sweet and salty. The higher the proportion of koji is, the sweeter the taste of miso is. Color varieties can be described as white miso, brown miso and red miso. Compared to red miso, white miso has short fermentation time. 04 Soy sauce, essential for Washoku /Ingredients of

日本の食卓になくてはならないしょうゆ 04

　しょうゆの原料は、大豆と麦と塩で、麹菌をつかうこともみそづくりと同じです。ただ、みそづくりには大麦（はだか麦の場合もある）をつかいますが、しょうゆづくりには小麦がつかわれます。小麦は、しょうゆに香りと甘味をつけるはたらきがあるのです。

　日本でもっとも一般的につかわれているしょうゆは「こいくちしょうゆ」です。たんに「しょうゆ」というと、こいくちしょうゆのことをさします。

　「うすくちしょうゆ」というしょうゆがありますが、これは味がうすいのではなく、色がうすいしょうゆのことです。素材の色を生かして仕上げる料理につかわれます。ほかに「たまりしょうゆ」という、とろみと濃厚なうま味をもつしょうゆもあります。このしょうゆは、おもにさしみやすし用としてつかわれます。

　いまでは、しょうゆは、独特の味わいが肉料理にもよくあうと、海外でも人気があります（→第4章）。

こいくちしょうゆ
dark soy sauce

うすくちしょうゆ
light soy sauce

たまりしょうゆ
tamari soy sauce

しょうゆのルーツ 05

　しょうゆのルーツは、古代に中国から伝わった「醤」であるといわれています。これは、食べ物を保存するために塩漬けにしたことから生まれたものです。穀類を漬けこんだ「穀醤」、野菜を漬けこんだ「草醤」、肉を漬けこんだ「肉醤」、魚をつかった「魚醤」などがありました。日本のしょうゆは、穀醤がもとになっています。

　魚醤は、秋田県のしょっつるや石川県のいしる、タイのナンプラーやベトナムのヌックマムなど、魚を発酵させてつくる魚しょうの原型だといわれています。

秋田県のしょっつるは、ハタハタという魚を発酵させてつくられる。
Shottsuru from Akita is made from fermented Hatahata.

タイの魚しょう、ナンプラー。
Nam pla, fish hishio from Thailand.

soy sauce are almost the same as those of miso: soy bean, salt and koji. The difference is that miso contains barely and soy sauce contains wheat. Wheat adds aroma and sweetness to soy sauce. Most popular soy sauce is "dark soy sauce" and it is called "soy sauce." "Light soy sauce" is the soy sauce with light color. It is used when we want to keep the original color of the ingredients. "Tamari soy sauce" is thick and rich with umami and good for sashimi and sushi. Nowadays, soy sauce is popular in foreign countries because original taste of it goes well with meat, too.

05 Origin of soy sauce /Roots of soy sauce go back to "Hishio" which was introduced from China. Hishio was by-products of salted preservative food. Hishio has varieties: crop hishio, vegetable hishio, meat hishio and fish hishio. Typical fish hishios, fermented fish sauces, are "Shottsuru" from Akita Pref., "Ishiru" from Ishikawa Pref., "Nam pla" from Thailand and "Nuoc mam" from Vietnam.

和食の調理の基本は「切る」こと

和食の調理は、包丁をつかって「切る」ことに重点がおかれています。
料理人は、食材の種類や料理にあった包丁をつかい分けます。

●引いて切る和包丁●

和食の料理人を、とくに「板前」とよぶことがあります。まな板の前で包丁をもって仕事をすることから、そうよばれるのです。日本では昔から、包丁さばきが料理のできぐあいを左右すると考えられてきました。

日本で昔からつかわれている包丁を和包丁といいます。西洋の包丁とくらべて特徴的なのが、片刃の包丁だという点です。片刃とは、刃先の断面の片側だけに食材を切ることのできる刃がついていることです。押したり引いたりして切る両刃の包丁とちがい、片刃の包丁は引いて切るので、食材に余計なきずをつけずに切ることができるのです。

家庭では、用途ごとの包丁をそなえておくことはむずかしいので、牛刀のように、野菜や魚、肉などなんにでもつかえる両刃の万能包丁がよくつかわれています。

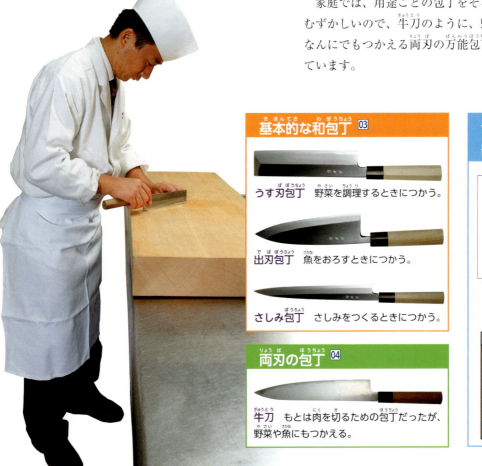

基本的な和包丁
- うす刃包丁　野菜を調理するときにつかう。
- 出刃包丁　魚をおろすときにつかう。
- さしみ包丁　さしみをつくるときにつかう。

両刃の包丁
- 牛刀　もとは肉を切るための包丁だったが、野菜や魚にもつかえる。

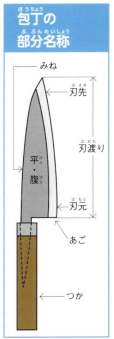

包丁の部分名称: みね／刃先／刃渡り／平・腹／刃元／あご／つか

---

01 "Cutting" is the basic technique of Washoku /There are many varieties of Japanese knives and chefs use knives properly for each ingredient. 02 Japanese knives, cutting ingredient by pulling /Japanese chefs are sometimes called "Itamae." "Ita" means a cutting board and "mae" means front so Itamae indicates a chef stands in front of the cutting board and uses knives. Good chefs are considered to have excellent knife skills. Japanese knives are single-edged blade and Western knives are double-edged. Double-edged knife cut ingredients by repeating pushing and pulling toward them, but single-edged knife is just pulling, so it does less damage to ingredients. Double-edged utility knives are often used at home for multiple purposes such as cutting vegetables, fish or meat. 03 Typical single-edged Japanese knives /Usuba: to cut vegetables /Deba: to cut fish /Sashimi: to slice sashimi 04 Double-edged knife /Gyuto: utility knife for meat, fish and vegetables 05 How to cut vegetables /Hold a handle of the knife with middle, third

パート1 知ろう！調べよう！

●野菜の切り方 05

包丁のにぎり方は、つかに中指、薬指、小指をそえ、親指と人さし指で刃をはさむようにしてもつのが基本です。

野菜の切り方はいろいろありますが、むらなく火が通るようにするためには、ひとつの料理につかう材料は、同じ形・大きさに切ることがたいせつです。基本の切り方のうち、家庭でもよくつかう切り方には、つぎのようなものがあります。

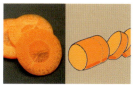

輪切り 断面が丸い。06

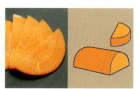

半月切り 断面が半月の形。輪切りの半分。07

いちょう切り 断面がいちょうの葉の形。半月切りの半分。08

たんざく切り 断面がたんざく（長方形）の形。09

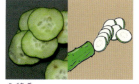

小口切り きゅうりやねぎなどを、うすい輪切りにしたもの。10

乱切り 材料をまわしながら、同じかさになるように切る。11

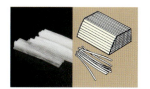

千切り 材料を細く切る。12

くし形切り 放射状に切る。13

●魚のおろし方 14

魚をおろすには、出刃包丁をつかいます。アジを例にして、三枚おろしの方法を説明しましょう。

1 尾のほうから包丁を入れ、ぜいご（とげ状のうろこ）を取る。ひっくり返して、うらも同様にぜいごを取る。

2 頭をおさえて、胸びれの下に包丁を入れて、頭を落とす。

3 腹びれを落とし、親指ではらわたをこそげとり、水でよく洗う。

4 うら身＊の頭のほうから包丁を入れ、骨の上にそわせて尾のほうまで切り下げる。

5 魚をおもてに返し、おもて身＊も同様にする。

6 腹骨をそぎとる。

7 三枚おろしのでき上がり。上から、おもて身、中骨、うら身。

＊魚は、頭を左、腹を手前にして盛りつけるため、その状態のとき、上側にある身をおもて身、下側の身をうら身とよぶ。

---

and fourth fingers and hold blade with thumb and index finger. There are many ways to cut vegetables. It is important to cut in the same shape and size so that vegetables are cooked evenly. 06 **Round thick slice** 07 **Half-moon slice** 08 **Quarter slice** 09 **Rectangular slice** 10 **Thin round slice** 11 **Rolling cut** 12 **Thin strip slice** 13 **Wedge slice** 14 **How to fillet fish** /Use Deba knife to cut fish. Here is an example of how to cut a horse mackerel. /1. Lay the fish on a cutting board with face on the left. Remove thorny scale. /2. Hold the head by the left hand and put the knife under pectoral fin and cut off the head. /3. Cut off ventral fin and remove guts with the thumb. Rinse the fish well with water. /4. Lay fish with tail fin on the left and belly toward you. Cut flesh along the backbone to the tail fin. /5. Turn over the fish and cut the same along the backbone. /6. Remove belly bone. /7. Three fillets slice are ready.

調理の五法

和食には、基本的な調理法が5つあります。
それが、生・焼く・煮る・蒸す・揚げるの五法です。

●「生」という調理法●

和食は、素材にあまり手を加えず、素材のもち味を引き立たせる調理法が重視されます。魚を切るだけで料理になるさしみは、生食の文化がある日本ならではの調理法なのです。

また、和食は、ナイフをつかわずおはしをつかって食べるため、素材はあらかじめ食べやすい大きさに切りそろえられます。切り方も、それぞれの魚の特性にあわせて工夫され、品よく美しく盛りつけられます。

切り方の種類

平づくり
身の右側に包丁を入れ、手前にまっすぐ引いて、切り角をきちんとつけて切る。マグロ、カツオなど、身のやわらかい魚にむいている切り方。

そぎづくり（うすづくり）
包丁を少し右にねかせて入れ、左はしからそぐようにうすく切る。切った身は、左手にとる。
タイやヒラメなど、身のしまった白身魚にむいている切り方。

糸づくり
包丁の先をつかって、細く切る。キス、サヨリなど細身の魚や、身のうすいスルメイカ、ヤリイカなどに適した切り方。

さざ波づくり
包丁をこまかく振動させながら、左はしからそぐように切る。身がしまったゆでダコやアワビなどに適した切り方。切り口が波を打ったようになり、おはしでもち上げやすくなる。

---

01 5 cooking methods /There are 5 basic cooking methods: "raw", "grill", "simmer", "steam" and "deep-fry" for Washoku. **02** "Raw" cooking method /Washoku focuses on cooking methods which make the most of the original tastes of ingredients. Sashimi made by just cutting raw fish is a unique cooking method, peculiar to Japanese habit of eating raw fish. Washoku is eaten not with a knife and fork, but with chopsticks, so each ingredient is cut into bite-sized pieces and dished up beautifully. **03** The way of cutting fish **04** Hirazukuri (thick slice) /Use a knife from right side of the fish and pull it toward yourself. Suitable for soft fish like tuna or bonito. **05** Usuzukuri (thin slice) / Use a knife from left side of the fish. Slice fish thinly at a slant. Suitable for whitefish like sea bream or flatfish. **06** Itozukuri (thin strip slice) /Use the point of the knife to cut the fish into thin strips. Suitable for narrow fish like sillago, halfbeak or squid. **07** Sazanami zukuri (surface wavelet slice) /Make a slice from left side of the fish. Pulling

● 焼く ● 08

　焼き物は、表面を色よく焼き、食材の内部にうま味と栄養をとじこめる調理法です。

　魚の場合、基本は塩焼。魚をざるにのせ、1尾丸ごとの魚なら約30分ぐらい前に、切り身なら15分ぐらい前に塩をふっておきます。あまり早く塩をふると、水分とともにうま味もぬけてしまうからです。

　焼くときは、火加減と焼き加減が重要です。火加減は強火の遠火で、おもてになる面から焼きます。焼き加減は、おもて四分、うら六分に焼くのが基本です。焼く前に、右の写真の魚のように、表面に飾り包丁（→153ページ）を入れることもあります。

　幽庵焼というのは、しょうゆ1・みりん1・酒1の割合であわせた調味液にゆずのうす切りを2～3枚入れたタレ（このタレを「幽庵地」という）に素材を漬けてから焼くというもの。この焼き方をした魚は冷めても味がかわらないので、懐石料理（→第3章）や弁当などによくつかわれます。

タレに漬けた魚を焼く、幽庵焼。
Yuan-yaki, marinated and grilled fish

アユの塩焼　grilled sweetfish with salt

　塩焼のほかに、照焼（つけ焼ともいう）や幽庵焼という焼き方があります。照焼は、素材を七～八分まで素焼きにしたあと、しょうゆとみりんをあわせたタレを2～3回に分けてかけ、照りよく焼き上げる方法です。

串を打つ 09

　素材に串をさすことを、料理用語では「串を打つ」といいます。串を打つのは、魚をすがたよく焼き上げるためです。1尾丸ごとの魚を焼く場合、切り身の魚を焼く場合など、素材や目的にあわせて串の打ち方が工夫されています。

---

knife forward and under to make wavelet. Suitable for firm flesh like boiled octopus or abalone. 08 **Grill** /Grilling is a cooking method to sear the surface of the ingredient and seal in umami and nutrients. Basically fish is grilled with salt. Sprinkle salt and leave for 30 min for whole fish, and 15min for fillets before cooking. Do not leave salted fish so long because umami goes out with water. Appropriate strength of the fire and roasting extent are important factors. Basically grill from the dishing surface with strong fire with some distance. The degree of grilling is that dishing surface is 40% and the back side is 60%. There are other methods of grilling: Teriyaki and Yuan-yaki. Teriyaki is to grill meat or fish with soy sauce and mirin with shiny surface. Yuan-yaki is to grill fish marinated with same amount of soy sauce, mirin and sake. Yuan-yaki keeps good taste even if it gets cold. 09 **Put fish on a skewer** /By using a skewer, fish can be cooked beautifully. There are many ways to use a skewer and it depends on ingredients or eating occasions.

●煮る● 01

「煮る」は、調味料を加えて加熱する調理法です。味をしみこませながら、材料に火を通し、やわらかくします。煮ているあいだに栄養素がとけだしても、煮汁ごと食べることができるという利点があります。

もっともよくつかわれる調理法ですが、材料や味つけなどのちがいによって、さまざまなつくり方があります。下は、代表的な煮物です。

煮魚 02

煮魚は、煮汁を煮立ててから魚を入れます。こうすることで、魚の生ぐささをふせぎます。また、魚の表面のたんぱく質が熱ですぐかたまり、魚のうま味が煮汁にとけだすのもふせぎます。煮汁の量は、魚の表面が汁から少しでるくらいがよく、魚はおもて側を上にしてならべます。

また、魚は煮くずれしやすいので、魚をなべの中でひっくり返さないようにします。味をしみこませるには、落としぶた（→153ページ）をして煮たり、ときどき煮汁をすくって魚にかけたりします。

いため煮（いり煮ともいう） 03

下処理した材料を油でいため、濃いめの味の煮汁で照りよく煮上げます。野菜のいため煮をじょうずにつくるコツは、材料を同じ大きさに切ることと、できるだけ少なめの煮汁で煮ることです。

代表的ないため煮としては、筑前煮やきんぴらごぼうがあります。

煮びたし 04

煮びたしというのは、下処理した野菜や魚をうす味の煮汁でサッと煮て、そのまま冷まして味をふくませる料理です。野菜の煮びたしには、ほうれんそうや小松菜、菜の花、なすなどがよくつかわれます。アユなどの川魚も煮びたしによくします。

---

01 **Simmer** /Simmering is a cooking technique with which foods are cooked in hot liquid with seasonings and is the most popular cooking technique. It allows the seasonings penetrate into ingredients while cooking soft. Even if nutrients liquate out from ingredients, simmered broth is wholly eatable. 02 **Simmered fish** /Put fish into boiling broth to deodorize bloody smell of the fish. Coagulating the protein of the surface of the fish by the heat makes umami sealed inside. The best quantity of the soup is not covering the whole fish, just a little bit of the surface of the fish comes out of the liquid. Lay the dishing surface of the fish upside. Fish meat easily falls apart, so do not turn it upside down in the pot. Use drop-lid to cover fish with the liquid or pour the soup on the fish. 03 **Braised dish** /Fry ingredients with oil, then simmer them with strong taste. Some tips of making good braised vegetables are to cut vegetables into the same size and simmer them with small amount of broth. Typical braised dishes are Chikuzen-ni,

パート1　知ろう！調べよう！

●蒸す● 05

材料に直接火を当てるのではなく、水蒸気の熱で加熱する調理法です。食材の形がくずれにくい、栄養をにがさない、乾燥しない、こげない、といった特徴があります。

蒸し物の代表といえば、茶わん蒸しです。

●揚げる● 06

高温の油の中に材料を入れて加熱する調理法です。高温で調理するため、材料の余分な水分がでていき、うま味が凝縮されます。そのためには、下ごしらえをきっちりとしてから揚げることがたいせつです。

揚げ物には、小麦粉と卵を水でといた衣をつけて揚げる「衣揚げ」と、衣をなにもつけずに揚げる「素揚げ」の2種類があります。衣揚げの代表が、てんぷらです。

さしすせそ 07

「さしすせそ」というのは、煮物をするときの調味料を入れる順番をあらわしたことばです。昔の人の知恵がつまったことばですね。

- **さ** 砂糖：甘味をつけるほか、ほかの調味料の味をしみこませやすくする。
- **し** 塩：材料にすぐしみて、肉や魚などの味を引きしめる作用があるので、かならず砂糖のあとに入れる。
- **す** 酢：材料のくさみをぬいたり、やわらかくする作用がある。
- **せ** しょうゆ（せうゆ）：材料の生ぐさみを取って、うま味を加える。
- **そ** みそ：味つけ・風味づけにつかう。長時間加熱すると風味がとんでしまうので、最後のほうに入れる。

07の英訳は➡P42

---

braised chicken and vegetables, and Kinpira-gobo, braised burdock root and vegetables. 04 Stewed vegetables with a mild broth /This is called "Nibitashi" in Japanese and is a cooking technique to stew vegetables or fish with a mild broth and let it cool so that seasonings penetrate into the ingredients. Spinach, komatsuna (Japanese mustard spinach), rapeseed blossom or eggplant is used for this cooking. River fishes such as Ayu (sweetfish) are also used well as ingredients. 05 Steam /Steaming is a cooking technique using heated steam and not cooking by direct heat. It has an advantage of keeping the shape and nutrients of the ingredients, not getting dried or burned. Typical steamed dish is Chawan-mushi, savory steamed egg custard. 06 Deep-fry /Deep-frying is to cook ingredients in the highly heated oil. Excess water is released and umami is concentrated by deep-frying. Preparation of ingredients should be done before frying. There are 2 types of fried dishes: frying with or without batter. Tempura is a typical fried food with batter.

季節感をたいせつに 01

和食は、旬の食材をつかい、料理に葉や花をあしらい、季節にあった食器をつかうなど、季節感をたいせつにします。

●旬の食材● 02

自然のなかでとれる野菜や魚には、旬があります。旬というのは、その食べ物が一年でもっともたくさんとれて、おいしくて、栄養価も高い季節のことです。

和食では、旬の食材をつかい、調理や味つけは最小限にして素材のもち味を最大限に引きだすようにします。また、料理に葉や花などをそえたり、季節に応じた器をつかうなどして、季節感を演出することをたいせつにしています。

代表的な旬の食材 03

春 04 — ハマグリ、アスパラガス、いちご、そらまめ、たけのこ、ふきのとう

夏 05 — アユ、かぼちゃ、きゅうり、すいか、トマト、なす

秋 06 — サンマ、きのこ、くり、さつまいも、さといも、ぶどう

冬 07 — ブリ、フグ、みかん、だいこん、ほうれんそう、白菜

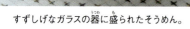

すずしげなガラスの器に盛られたそうめん。

---

01 Emphasis on seasonality of Washoku /We use seasonal ingredients and decorate plates with leaves and flowers which match to the season for Washoku. **02 Seasonal ingredients** /Both vegetables and fish have seasonality. It means that each ingredient has the best season for good harvest, tasting good and rich with nutrients. We use seasonal ingredients, add minimum seasonings and make the most of the tastes of the ingredients for Washoku. **03 Typical seasonal ingredients 04 Spring** /hamaguri clam, asparagus, strawberry, horsebean, bamboo shoot, flower bud of fuki **05 Summer** /sweetfish, pumpkin, cucumber, water melon, tomato, eggplant **06 Autumn** /Pacific saury, mushroom, chestnut, sweet potato, Japanese taro(sato-imo), grape **07 Winter** /amberjack, blowfish, mikan citrus, daikon radish, spinach, Chinese cabbage **08 5 Colors of the food** /"5 Colors" is the basic concept of Washoku: green, yellow, red, white and black. Washoku combines these five colors and make use of each color. By adding many kinds

五色の料理

「五色」というのは、和食の基本をあらわしたことばです。五色の食材を組みあわせて、その色をできるだけ生かすように工夫して調理します。厳密に五色がそろわなくても、意識していろいろな食材をそろえることで、いろどり豊かな料理になるのです。そして、しぜんと味のバラエティーも広がり、栄養のバランスもよくなります。

また、和食でよくつかわれる黒塗り・朱塗りのお盆やおわん、料理にそえられる葉や花などの色彩も、全体として五色のいろどりのひとつとなっているのです。

- 青（緑）：みつば
- 黄：ゆず
- 白：茶わん蒸しの地
- 黒：しいたけ
- 赤：エビ

五色とは

青（緑）　黄　赤　白　黒（紫）

いろどり野菜

しそ、みょうが、木の芽などは、香辛野菜といいます。料理の主役にはなりませんが、料理に色や香りをそえて、料理を引き立てるというだいじな役目をもっています。

木の芽　さんしょうの若芽のこと。独特のよい香りを生かして、吸物や蒸し物につかわれる。

青じそ　一般に大葉とよばれ、香りのよさと美しい緑色を生かして、さしみにそえたり、てんぷらにしたりする。

紫芽・青芽　赤じそ・青じその若い芽のこと。さしみのつまや薬味につかわれる。

みょうが　独特の香りとシャキッとした歯ざわりが特徴。薬味のほか、汁の実やてんぷら、酢の物などにつかわれる。

花穂じそ　花が三分ぐらい開いた状態のしその花穂。うす紫色の色あいが美しく、さしみなどにそえられる。

根わさび　わさびの根茎のこと。すりおろして、本わさびとしてつかわれる。

---

of ingredients, food and table will be decorated colorfully and beautifully even if all the five colors are not applied. These dishes have many varieties of tastes and well-balanced nutrition. Black and red lacquerware, decorated flowers and leaves can be the source of colors and producing harmony among 5 colors. Herb and vegetable garniture / Shiso, myoga ginger, sansho leaves are condiment vegetables to add colors and flavor to foods. /Kinome: A leaf bud of sansho pepper. Add its own unique aroma. For clear soup and steamed dishes. /Green shiso: Add good aroma and green color to sashimi. Fried as tempura. /Murame, Aome: Murame is a leaf bud of red shiso and aome is a leaf bud of green shiso. For sashimi condiments. /Myoga ginger: Add unique aroma and crisp texture. For condiments or ingredients to soup, tempura or vinegared dishes. /Shiso flower: Spike of shiso flower. Add beautiful light purple color to sashimi. /Wasabi: Wasabi is a root. Grated wasabi is used as spice condiment.

和食の食事作法

「作法」というと古めかしくきこえますが、「マナー」のことです。
日本には、美しい食事作法があります。

● いただきます ●

　日本には、「いただきます」という食事のあいさつがあります。このあいさつは、「これから食べはじめます」というけじめのことばでもありますが、魚や肉、野菜など命あるものをありがたくいただきますという、感謝の気持ちをあらわすことばでもあるのです。

　そして、食事が終わったら、食事をつくってくれた人への感謝の気持ちをこめて、「ごちそうさま」とあいさつします。「いただきます」「ごちそうさま」のあいさつは、和食の食事作法の基本です。

● 和食の配膳 ●

　一汁三菜（→10ページ）の基本の配膳は、まず、ごはんが左手前、汁物が右手前です。おはしは、その手前に、はし先を左にして置きます。それは、おはしは右手でもち、左手でごはん茶わんをもち上げるからです。

　和食では、１つの料理を食べつづけるのではなく、ごはんとおかずを交互に食べて、口のなかでかみあわせて調和させる食べ方をします。このため、口に運ぶ回数がもっとも多いごはんを、左手前に置きます。そして、つぎにもち上げるひん度が高く、こぼしやすい汁を右手前に置くのです。

　また、主菜の位置にも意味があります。さしみや焼き魚などの主菜は、食器をもち上げずに食べるのが作法です。そのため、主菜は、おはしをもつ右手をのばしやすい位置に置くのです。もちろん、ごはんと汁物は、食卓に置いたまま食べるのではなく、器をもち上げて食べるのが作法です。

　この基本の配膳の形は、日本の食文化の歴史のなかから生まれてきたのです。

01 **Table manners of Washoku** /Japanese people have beautiful manners to eat Washoku. 02 **"Itadakimasu"** /Japanese people have a habit to say "itadakimasu" at the beginning of the meal to greet each other. It shows eaters' gratitude to the animals or the plants we eat as daily meal. People say "gochisosama" when they finish eating. It shows appreciation for the people who prepared the meal. These 2 words "itadakimasu" and "gochisosama" are very basic manners to eat Washoku. 03 **How to place Washoku dishes on a table** /A basic way to place dishes is the rice bowl on the left hand side, and the soup bowl on the right hand side. Put chopsticks just in front of rice and soup, with the tips on the left hand side. Use right hand for chopsticks and left hand to hold a rice bowl. To keep eating the same dish is not a good manner in Washoku. Instead, we eat rice, eat side dishes and sip soup in turns, and mix them in the mouth. Rice is the most frequent dish to eat, so put rice bowl on your left hand side. Putting soup bowl on the

パート1 知ろう！調べよう！

●ごはん茶わんのもち方 04

ごはん茶わんのもち方は、ふだんはあまり気にとめていないかもしれませんが、和食の食事作法の基本として、ここで確認しておきましょう。

へり 08
胴 09
糸底 10

糸底は、茶わんをつくるとき、ろくろから糸でくくりとったあと。糸底があることで、温かいごはんの入った茶わんをもっても、直接指に熱さが伝わらずにすむ。

渡し方 05

受け方 06

もち方 07

✗ してはいけないもち方 11

茶わんの中にゆびを入れてもつ。

茶わんの胴を指を広げてもつ。

糸底を人さし指と中指ではさんでもつ。

---

right hand side helps us not spill soup. Main dish is placed on the right side in the back so that it is easy to pick up food with chopsticks. In most cases main dish plate is heavy and it is the manner not to hold the plate. Regarding rice and soup bowl, it is the manner to hold up by left hand and eat. These basic manners have developed in the history of Japanese culinary culture. **04 How to hold a rice bowl** /How to hold a rice bowl is a basic manner of eating Washoku. 05 How to pass 06 How to receive 07 How to hold up 08 Edge 09 Body 10 Base section of the rice bowl. This part divides the body and the bottom of the rice bowl, so even if hot rice is served, heat does not transmit to the bottom. 11 What we should not do /Do not hold a rice bowl with your fingers inside. /Do not hold the body of rice bowl with your fingers open. /Do not sandwich the bottom with the first finger and the second finger.

●はしづかいの作法● 01

わたしたち日本人が食事をするときに不可欠なおはしですが、じょうずにおはしがもてない人、まちがったつかい方をしている人もいます。和食のたいせつな食事作法である、正しいおはしのつかい方をマスターしましょう。また、食べるときの姿勢にも気をつけましょう。

食べるときの姿勢 02

- 食卓にむかってまっすぐにすわる。 03
- 背中をまっすぐのばす。 04
- 足はきちんとそろえる。足を広げたり、組んだりしないようにする。 05
- 食卓とのあいだは、にぎりこぶし1つぶんをあけると食べやすい。 06
- 食卓にひじをつかないようにする。 07

正しいおはしのもち方 08

- 親指と中指、人さし指で、上のはしをおさえる。 09
- もつ位置は、まん中より少し上くらい。 10
- 親指のつけねと薬指で、下のはしをささえる。 11
- はし先は、そろえる。バラバラだと、食べ物をうまくはさめない。 12
- 下のはしを軸にして、上のはしだけを動かして、食べ物をはさむ。 13

---

01 **Manners to use chopsticks** / Chopsticks are indispensable for eating Washoku. Some Japanese do not have good manners to use chopsticks. Keep good posture. Using chopsticks in a correct way while eating is very important. 02 **Correct posture while eating** 03 Sit squarely in front of the table. 04 Straighten the back. 05 Put legs and feet together. Do not open or cross legs. 06 Take about 15cm space toward the table. 07 Do not put your elbows on the table. 08 **Correct way to hold chopsticks** 09 Hold upper chopstick with thumb, index finger and middle finger. 10 Adjust your grip about one-third of the way from its head. 11 Hold lower chopstick with the base of thumb and third finger. 12 Align tips of the chopsticks together so that it is easy to pinch the food. 13 Do not move the lower chopstick, just move upper one.

[14] Taboos to avoid when using chopsticks [15] Neburi-bashi: Lick the tips of the chopsticks or hold in the mouth. [16] Komi-bashi: Push plenty of food into the mouth in one time. [17] Saguri-bashi: Find a food by rummaging in the plate. [18] Mogi-bashi: Remove the rice or food adhering to the chopsticks with the mouth. [19] Utsuri-bashi: Touch the food once but not taking it and pick up other one. [20] Mayoi-bashi: Hovering chopsticks from dish to dish when trying to choose which one to take. [21] Yose-bashi: Pull the plate or bowl closer with chopsticks. [22] Sashi-bashi: Spear food with chopsticks.

夏の一汁三菜

一汁三菜とは
和食と日本文化

パート2 つくろう！ 食べよう！

枝豆の緑色がさわやかな枝豆ごはんと、
アジやなすなど季節の食材を組みあわせた一汁三菜です。

ごはん	枝豆ごはん
汁物	アジのつみれ汁
主菜	とり肉の照焼
副菜	タコの酢の物
副菜	焼きなす

01 **1 Soup and 3 Dishes in Summer** 02 Menu: Edamame Rice, Minced Horse Mackerel Ball Soup, Chicken Teriyaki, Vinegared Octopus and Grilled Eggplant
03 Rice /**Edamame Rice**
04 Ingredients for 4 servings
- rice : 2 rice cups (360mL)
- kelp : about 5g
- water : 2 cups
- salt : 2/3 tsp
- edamame beans : 2/3 cup

05 How to make
1. Soak kelp in water for 1-3 hours to make dashi. /2. Wash rice, soak it in water for 30 min to 1 hour and drain the water through a colander. /3. Set (2) rice, (1) kelp, dashi and salt into a rice cooker. Cook the rice. /4. Boil edamame in salted boiling water for 7-8 min. Drain the water and leave them for cooling, then take out beans from seed pods. /5. Add edamame after the rice is cooked. Let the rice steam for about 10 min, then remove the kelp and mix the rice lightly.

ごはん 枝豆ごはん 03

夏が旬の枝豆を
色よくゆで、
こんぶだしと塩だけで
シンプルに味つけしたごはん。

【材料 4人分】 04

米	2合（360mL）
こんぶ	約5g
水	2カップ
塩	小さじ2/3
枝豆	2/3カップ
	（ゆでてさやからだした豆の量）

つくり方 05

1. こんぶを水に1〜3時間つけて、だしをとる。
2. 米をとぎ、30分〜1時間ほど水にひたし、ざるに上げて水気を切る。
3. 炊飯器の釜に2の米、1のこんぶとこんぶだし、塩を入れて炊く。
4. 枝豆は、塩を少々加えた熱湯で7〜8分ゆでる。ざるに上げて冷まして、さやから豆をとりだす。
5. ごはんが炊けたら4の豆を加える。10分ほど蒸らしたあと、こんぶを取りのぞき、サッとまぜあわせる。

汁物 アジのつみれ汁 06

旬の魚アジをこまかく
たたいてつくるつみれと、
だいこんやにんじん、
しいたけなどを入れた
具だくさんの汁です。

【材料 4人分】 07

アジ(120gほどの大きさ)	4尾
A みそ	小さじ2
とき卵	1/2個分
ねぎ(みじん切り)	1/2本分
しょうが(みじん切り)	少々
だし	4カップ
B 塩	小さじ1弱
うすくちしょうゆ	大さじ1
酒	大さじ1
だいこん	1/8本
にんじん	1/4本
生しいたけ	4枚
わけぎ	1本

つくり方 08

1. アジは三枚におろし、小骨と皮をとり、包丁でこまかくたたく。

2. 1をすりばちに入れ、Aのみそ、とき卵を入れてよくまぜあわせてから、Aの残りの材料を加えて軽くまぜ、すり身をつくる。

3. にんじんは半月切りに、だいこんはいちょう切りにし、下ゆでする。

4. 生しいたけ、わけぎは、ひと口大に切る。

5. なべに分量のだしと3を入れて火にかける。汁がふっとうしたら、2のすり身を左手でにぎり、少しずつおしだしながらスプーンですくいとり、汁に入れる。

6. 5の汁にBの調味料を入れて味をととのえる。仕上げに、4の生しいたけとわけぎを入れて、サッと火を通し、器に盛りつける。

06 Soup /**Minced Horse Mackerel Ball Soup**
07 Ingredients for 4 servings
- horse mackerel : 4 fishes
- A: miso : 2 tsps • beaten egg : 1/2 • Welsh onion : 1/2 stalk • ginger : a small amount
- dashi : 4 cups
- B: salt : 1 tsp or less • light soy sauce : 1 tbsp • sake : 1tbsp
- daikon radish : 1/8 • carrot : 1/4
- shiitake mushroom : 4 • scallion : 1 stalk

08 How to make
1. Cut horse mackerels into fillets, remove skin and small bones. Chop the fillets finely. /2. Put the minced fish, miso and beaten egg into a mortar and grind them with a pestle. Add rest of (A) ingredients and mix them lightly. /3. Cut carrot into half-moon, daikon into fan shape and parboil them. /4. Cut shiitake and scallion into bite-sized pieces. /5. Put dashi, (3) carrot and daikon into a pot and heat it. Add (2) fish balls once it boils; hold the fish paste on the left hand and squeeze it by thumb and index finger, then scoop it up with a spoon. /6. Add seasonings into (5) soup and make taste. Put the shiitake and the scallion at the last and dish up the soup.

主菜 とり肉の照焼

低脂肪で良質のたんぱく質をふくむとり肉は、主菜にぴったりの食材。
皮をカリッと焼きつけ、おいしそうな照りをつけて仕上げましょう。

【材料 4人分】
とりもも肉	2枚
油	大さじ2
水	2/3カップ
A 酒	大さじ6
砂糖	小さじ4
みりん	大さじ2
しょうゆ	大さじ2
レタス	適量
トマト	適量

つくり方

1 とり肉は黄色い脂肪を切りとり、身の厚いところに包丁で切りこみを入れて開き、厚さを均一にする。

2 レタスはばらして洗い、トマトは洗って、くし形切りにする。

3 フライパンを熱して油を入れ、とり肉の皮目を下にして中火で焼く。焼き色がついたらうら返す。

4 うらにも焼き色がついたら、分量の水を加え、落としぶたをして蒸し焼きにする。

5 水が半分ぐらいになったら、落としぶたで肉をおさえながら汁を捨てる。

6 ふたたび中火にかけてAの調味料を加え、落としぶたをして中まで火を通す。竹串をさして、すんだ汁がでてきたら肉を取りだし、残った汁を煮つめる。

7 汁にとろみがついてきたら肉をもどし入れ、汁をかけながら照りよく仕上げる。

8 あら熱がとれたら、切り分ける。器に盛りつけて汁をかけ、2のレタス、トマトをそえる。

Main Dish / Chicken Teriyaki

Ingredients for 4 servings
- chicken leg : 2　・oil : 2 tbsps
- water : 2/3 cup
- A: sake : 6 tbsps　・sugar : 4 tsps
- 　 mirin : 2 tbsps
- 　 soy sauce : 2 tbsps
- lettuce to taste
- tomato to taste

How to make

1. Remove yellow fat of chicken, make a small cut on the surface and open the meat to same thickness. /2. Wash lettuce and tomato. Cut the tomato into the wedge shape. /3. Heat a frying pan and pour oil, first grill the chicken skin on a medium fire. Turn it over when the skin gets browned. /4. Add water when the other side is browned, put a drop lid and braise. /5. Drain excess water by holding the chicken with the drop-lid when the water reduced to half. /6. Heat on a medium fire again, add (A) seasonings, put the drop lid and cook. Test the chicken with a skewer to see if it is cooked. The chicken is done if clear liquid comes out, then take out it and thicken the sauce. /7. Put back the chicken into the pan and heat with pouring sauce, make the chicken shiny. /8. Cut the chicken into good size of amount to eat and dish up. Garnish lettuce and tomato.

パート2 つくろう！食べよう！

副菜 タコの酢の物

酢の物というのは、魚や貝、野菜や海藻などに合わせ酢をかけたさっぱりとした味の料理。

【材料 4人分】

ゆでダコ	1本
きゅうり	3本
生ワカメ	40〜60g
うど（うす切り）	少々
おろししょうが	少々

＜土佐酢＞

水	1カップ
酢	1カップ
塩	少々
うすくちしょうゆ	小さじ2
砂糖	大さじ1と1/2
けずり節	少々

つくり方

1. タコは水で洗い、さざ波づくり（→24ページ）にする。

2. きゅうりは小口切りにし、立て塩（→153ページ）に漬ける。

3. 生ワカメは塩を洗い流し、たっぷりの水につけてもどす。かたい部分は切りとり、食べやすい大きさに切って、サッと熱湯に通し冷水で冷ます。

4. 片手なべに土佐酢の材料を入れて火にかける。ふっとうしたら、けずり節を加えて火を止め、1〜2分おいてからこす。

5. 器にタコときゅうり、ワカメを盛り、土佐酢をかける。最後に、松葉の形に切ったうどとおろししょうがをそえる。

副菜 焼きなす

焼きなすは、こげるぐらい強めの直火で焼くのがコツ。ガラスの器に盛り、しょうがをそえると、いかにもすずしげ。

【材料 4人分】

なす	8本
┌ だし	40mL
A うすくちしょうゆ	5mL
└ みりん	5mL
針しょうが	少々

つくり方

1. なすは、がくを切りそろえ、皮にたてに浅い切りこみを4〜6本入れる。

2. 1のなすを焼き網にのせて、さいばしで転がしながら強めの中火で焼く。さいばしでおしてみて、やわらかくなっていたら氷水にとる。

3. 指を氷水で冷やしながら2のなすの皮をむき、食べやすい大きさにさく。

4. Aのだしと調味料をまぜあわせる。3を器に盛ってAをかけ、針しょうがをそえる。

Side Dish / **Grilled Eggplant**

Ingredients for 4 servings
- eggplant : 8

Ⓐ • dashi : 40mL • light soy sauce : 5mL • mirin : 5mL
- thin strips of ginger : a small amount

How to make
1. Cut off the top of eggplants, make 4 to 6 length wide cuts on the surface. /**2**. Grill the eggplants on a grid with strong medium fire. Remove from the heat when they get soft and soak into iced water. /**3**. Peel off skin of the eggplants in iced water, split into good size of amount to eat. /**4**. Mix (Ⓐ) sauce ingredients, dish up eggplants and pour sauce. Put topping with thin strips of ginger.

Side Dish / **Vinegared Octopus**

Ingredients for 4 servings
- boiled octopus leg : 1 • cucumber : 3
- fresh wakame seaweed : 40-60g
- thin slices of udo : a small amount
- grated ginger : a small amount

[Tosazu vinegar]
- water : 1 cup • vinegar : 1 cup • salt : a small amount
- light soy sauce : 2 tsps • sugar : 1.5 tbsps
- dried bonito flake : a small amount

How to make
1. Wash octopus and cut into surface wavelet slice. /**2**. Cut cucumbers into thin round slices, soak into salted water. /**3**. Rinse salt of wakame and rehydrate in water. Cut it into good size of amount to eat, parboil and then, put into iced water. /**4**. Put ingredients of Tosazu vinegar into a pot and heat. Add dried bonito flakes once it boils and remove from the heat, leave it for 1- 2 min. Drain bonito. /**5**. Dish up octopus, cucumbers and wakame, and pour Tosazu vinegar. Put topping with pine needle-shaped udo and grated ginger.

秋の一汁三菜

きのこごはんにとん汁、
サンマの塩焼や肉じゃがなど、
人気のおかずを組みあわせた
秋の献立です。

ごはん	きのこの炊きこみごはん
汁物	とん汁
主菜	サンマの塩焼
副菜	菊花びたし
副菜	肉じゃが

01 1 Soup and 3 Dishes in Autumn **02** Menu: Mushroom Rice, Pork Miso Soup, Grilled Pacific Saury, Boiled Chrysanthemum, Braised Beef and Potato

03 Rice / **Mushroom Rice**

04 Ingredients for 4 servings
- rice : 2 rice cups (360mL)
- fresh shiitake mushroom : 50g
- shimeji mushroom : 50g   • enoki mushroom : 50g
- deep-fried tofu : 1   • dashi : 2 cups
- Ⓐ • mirin : 2 tsps   • soy sauce : 2 tbsps   • sake : 1 tbsp
- salt : 1/3 tsp

05 How to make
1. Wash rice, soak in water for 30 min to 1 hour and drain the water through a colander. /2. Cut deep-fried tofu in half lengthwise then cut into rectangles. /3. Cut off bottom of mushrooms, make thin slice of shiitake. Separate bunch of shimeji and enoki mushrooms into small pieces by hand. /4. Mix dashi and Ⓐ seasonings and pour into a rice cooker. /5. Put the rice, (2) deep-fried tofu and (3) mushrooms into the rice cooker and cook. /6. Mix the rice after cooked, and steam about 5 min. Dish up.

🍚 きのこの炊きこみごはん

生しいたけ、しめじ、えのきだけをたっぷりとつかった、秋の香りをたのしめる炊きこみごはん。

【材料 4人分】

米	2合(360mL)
生しいたけ、しめじ、えのきだけ	各50g
油揚げ	1枚
だし	2カップ
A　みりん	小さじ2
しょうゆ	大さじ2
酒	大さじ1
塩	小さじ1/3

つくり方

1. 米をとぎ、30分〜1時間ほど水にひたし、ざるに上げて水気を切る。

2. 油揚げは、たて半分に切ってから細めのたんざく切りにし、熱湯でサッとゆでて油ぬきをする。

3. 生しいたけは石づきを切りとり、うす切りにする。えのきだけ、しめじは石づきを切りとり、食べやすくほぐしておく。

4. だしとAの調味料をあわせ、炊飯器の釜に入れる。

5. 4に水切りした米を入れ、2の油揚げと3のきのこを加え、ふつうに炊く。

6. 炊き上がったらザッとまぜあわせ、5分ほど蒸らしたあと、器に盛りつける。

🥣 とん汁

たくさんの野菜やぶた肉のうま味がとけこんだ、みそ味の汁物。

【材料 4人分】

ぶたばら肉（うす切り）	150g
だいこん	1/4本
にんじん	1/2本
さといも	6個
油揚げ	1枚
ごぼう	1/4本
わけぎ	2本
だし	6カップ
赤みそ	50g

つくり方

1. ぶたばら肉は食べやすい大きさに切る。

2. だいこん、にんじんは半月切り、または、いちょう切りにする。油揚げは角に切る。

3. さといもは皮をむいて乱切りにする。熱湯でサッとゆでて冷水にとり、ぬめりを洗う。

4. ごぼうは細いささがきにし、水にさらす。

5. なべにだしを入れて強火にかける。ぶた肉を加えて、煮立ってきたら火を弱め、アクをとる。

6. 5に、だいこん、にんじん、さといも、油揚げ、半量の赤みそを加え、弱火で煮こむ。

7. 材料がよく煮えたら、残りのみそで味をととのえる。ここに、ごぼう、わけぎを入れ、ひと煮立ちさせて、器に盛る。

---

06 Soup /**Pork Miso Soup**
07 Ingredients for 4 servings
- pork lib slices : 150g
- daikon radish : 1/4
- carrot : 1/2
- sato-imo (Japanese taro) : 6
- deep-fried tofu : 1
- burdock root : 1/4　• scallion : 2 stalks
- dashi : 6 cups　　• red miso : 50g

08 How to make
1. Cut pork into good size of amount to eat. /2. Cut daikon and carrot into half-moon cut, deep-fried tofu into square. /3. Peel off skin of Japanese taro and cut into chunks by rolling cut. Parboil and soak into iced water, remove stickiness. /4. Shave burdock root as if sharpening pencil and soak into water. /5. Pour dashi into a pot and heat over strong fire. Add the pork, lower the fire and skim off the scum when it comes boiling. /6. Add the daikon, carrot, Japanese taro and half amount of red miso, cook over low fire. /7. After vegetables are well cooked, add rest of miso, the burdock root and scallion. Dish up.

主菜 サンマの塩焼 [01]

秋の旬の魚といえば、サンマ。脂ののったサンマに塩をふり、香ばしく焼き上げましょう。

【材料 4人分】 [02]

サンマ	4尾
塩	適量
だいこん	適量
すだち	2個
しょうゆ	少々

つくり方 [03]

1. サンマのおもて面に飾り包丁を入れ、両面に塩をふり、串を打つ。
2. 焼き網が赤くなるまで充分に熱し、おもて面から焼く。グリルの場合はおもてを上にして焼く。
3. きつね色にきれいに焼けたらうら返し、中まで火を通す。
4. だいこんはすりおろし、すだちは横半分に切る。
5. 器にサンマを盛り、だいこんおろしとすだちをそえ、しょうゆをおろしにたらす。

副菜 菊花びたし [04]

秋の花といえば、菊。黄菊（食用菊）の花びらと春菊をつかったおひたしは、秋の献立にぴったり。

【材料 4人分】 [05]

春菊	1たば
黄菊	10輪
しめじ	1/2パック
<酒塩>	
酒	大さじ2
塩	少々
A ┌ だし	2カップ
｜ うすくちしょうゆ	大さじ3
｜ みりん	小さじ1/2
└ ゆずのしぼり汁	少々
ゆずの皮	少々

つくり方 [06]

1. 春菊は葉をつみ、熱湯でゆでて冷水にとり、水気をしぼる。

2. 黄菊は花びらをとり、熱湯に少量の酢を加えた中でゆで、水にさらして水気をしぼる。

3. しめじは小分けにする。小なべに酒塩としめじを入れ、サッと火を通す。

4. ゆずの皮をうすくむき、白いわたをそぎ落としてから千切りにしておく。

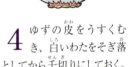

5. Aのだしと調味料をまぜる。これに1・2・3を加え、軽くまぜる。
6. 5を器に盛り、上に4のゆず皮の千切りをのせる。

---

[01] Main Dish / Grilled Pacific Saury
[02] Ingredients for 4 servings
- Pacific saury : 4 • salt to taste • daikon radish to taste
- Sudachi citrus : 2 • soy sauce : a small amount

[03] How to make
1. Make small decorative cuts on the surface of Pacific saury. Sprinkle salt for both sides, put on skewers. /2. Grill the saury on the red-hot grid iron from the dishing up side. /3. Turn over when dishing up side gets browned, and grill until it is cooked. /4. Make grated daikon, cut Sudachi into half crosswise. /5. Dish up the saury with the head on the left, garnish with the grated daikon and Sudachi citrus.

[04] Side Dish / Boiled Chrysanthemum
[05] Ingredients for 4 servings
- crown daisy : 1 bunch
- yellow chrysanthemum : 10 flowers
- shimeji mushroom : 1/2 bunch
- sake : 2 tbsps   • salt : a small amount
- A • dashi : 2 cups   • light soy sauce : 3 tbsps
- mirin : 1/2 tsp   • juice of Yuzu citrus : a small amount
- Yuzu zest : a small amount

[06] How to make
1. Picking leaves of crown daisy, boil and soak into iced water. Squeeze excess water. /2. Picking petals of chrysanthemum, boil with a little bit of vinegar. Soak into water and squeeze. /3. Cut off bottom of shimeji and cook slightly with sake and salt. /4. Peel off Yuzu zest thinly and remove white part of the zest, then cut into thin strips. /5. Mix dashi and seasonings. Add (1) (2) (3) and toss. /6. Dish up and put topping with the Yuzu zest.

副菜 肉じゃが

肉じゃがは、家庭の「おふくろの味」の代表ともいわれる煮こみ料理です。

【材料 4人分】

牛ばら肉（うす切り）	300g
じゃがいも	大4個
にんじん	2/3本
たまねぎ	小2個
しらたき	1玉
きぬさや	12枚
油	大さじ4
〈煮汁〉	
だし	6カップ
酒	大さじ6
砂糖	大さじ6
しょうゆ	大さじ5

つくり方

1 じゃがいもは皮をむき、大きめのひと口大に切り、サッと水洗いして水気を切る。にんじんは皮をむいて乱切りに、たまねぎは大きめのくし形切りにする。

2 牛肉は食べやすい大きさ（4〜5cm）に切る。

3 しらたきは食べやすい長さに切り、熱湯で軽くゆでてざるに上げ、水気を切っておく。

4 きぬさやはすじをとり、塩を少々加えた熱湯で色よくゆで、冷水にとって水気を切る。

5 なべに油と**2**の肉を入れて中火にかけ、サッといためる。

6 肉の色がかわったら、**1**のじゃがいも、にんじん、たまねぎ、**3**のしらたきを加え、だしと酒をそそぐ。

7 落としぶたをし、強火で煮る。

8 煮立ったら中火にし、浮いてきたアクをていねいにすくいとる。

9 砂糖を入れて4〜5分煮たあと、しょうゆを加え、落としぶたをしてさらに4〜5分煮る。

10 味見をして、足りなければしょうゆで味をととのえる。煮汁の量が1/2〜1/3ぐらいになるまで煮つめて、火を止める。

11 器に盛り、きぬさやをちらす。

**Side Dish /
Braised Beef and Potato**

Ingredients for 4 servings
- beef lib slices : 300g
- potato big : 4 • carrot : 2/3
- onion small : 2
- Shirataki (devil's tongue noodles): 1 pack
- sugar pea : 12 • oil : 4 tbsps

[braising stock]
- dashi : 6 cups • sake : 6 tbsps
- sugar : 6 tbsps • soy sauce : 5 tbsps

How to make
1. Peel off skin of potatoes and cut into rather large bite-sized, rinse slightly and drain water. Peel off carrot and cut into chunks. Cut onions into rather large wedges. /2. Cut beef into good size of amount to eat, about 4-5cm. /3. Cut devil's tongue noodles to good length to eat, parboil and drain. /4. Remove fiber of snow peas and boil in salted water to keep bright color, then soak into iced water and drain. /5. Put oil and the beef into a pot and heat on a medium fire. /6. Add the potatoes, carrot, onion and Shirataki after color of the beef changed, then add dashi and sake. /7. Put drop-lid on and braise over strong fire. /8. Bring to the boil then lower the heat and simmer on a medium fire, skim off the scum. /9. Add sugar and braise for 4-5 min, add soy sauce and put drop lid again and braise for another 4-5 min. /10. Add soy sauce if it has weak tastes. Braise till the soup reduced to 1/2 or 1/3 volume. /11. Dish up and garnish with snow peas.

はみだし豆知識

合わせ酢と土佐酢 01
合わせ酢は、酢にしょうゆ、みりんなどの調味料をまぜあわせたものです。基本の合わせ酢に、三杯酢があります。昔、酢、しょうゆ、みりんを杯1杯ずつ調合したため、この名がついたのです。いまは、みりんのかわりに砂糖をつかうことも多く、調合の割合も料理によってさまざまです。土佐酢は、この三杯酢にかつお節を加えた、まろやかな味の合わせ酢です。土佐酢とよばれるのは、土佐（現在の高知県）がかつお節の名産地だったためです。

しらたきとは 02
しらたきというのは、糸のように細長いこんにゃくのこと。糸こんにゃくともよばれます。こんにゃくの原料は「こんにゃくいも」です。こんにゃくいもを乾燥させて粉にし、それを湯でといて石灰水を加え、四角くかためたものが板こんにゃくで、穴のあいた板からおしだしてかためたものが、しらたきです。

こんにゃくいも

背の青い魚 03
サンマやアジ、サバ、イワシなど、背が青っぽい色をしている魚は、健康によいといわれています。それは、これらの魚の脂肪には、DHA（ドコサヘキサエン酸）とIPA（イコサペンタエン酸）という成分がたくさんふくまれているからです。DHAとIPAは、脳の発育やはたらきを活発にするとともに、血液をサラサラにして流れやすくする作用があります。それで、血管がつまったり、心臓のはたらきが悪くなったりする病気を予防すると考えられているのです。

---

01 "Awasezu vinegar" and "Tosazu vinegar"
Awasezu vinegar is a seasoning sauce with vinegar, soy sauce and mirin. Basic Awasezu vinegar is "Sanbaizu vinegar" which means "3 cups vinegar," because it used to be made by same cup of vinegar, soy sauce and mirin. Now the mix proportion of ingredients have a wide variety. Tosazu vinegar is made from Awasezu vinegar and dried bonito. It has soft taste. Why it is called Tosa is because famous production region of dried bonito is Kochi Pref. which used to be called Tosa.

02 What is Shirataki (devil's tongue noodles)?
Origin of devil's tongue noodles is kind of taro called "devil's tongue." Dry devil's tongue and process into powder, add hot water and limewater to congeal. Square-shaped is called "Konnyaku" and noodle-shaped is "Shirataki."

03 Blueback fish
Blueback fish like Pacific saury, mackerel and sardine are said to be good for health. They contain DHA and EPA which have a good effect for brain growth, activate the brain function and make healthy blood. DHA and EPA have an effect to prevent cardiovascular disease.

p27
07 Sa, Shi, Su, Se, So
When simmering the ingredients, we put the seasonings in the order of Sa, Shi, Su, Se and So, so that the seasonings penetrate into them well.
Sa: sugar   **Shi**: salt   **Su**: vinegar   **Se**: soy sauce   **So**: miso

第2章
chapter 2

郷土料理を知ろう
Japanese local foods

日本各地の和食
Washoku in each local region

郷土料理を知ろう
日本各地の和食

パート1　知ろう！　調べよう！

伝統行事と郷土料理

郷土料理というと、どういう料理が思いうかぶでしょうか。
はじめに、お正月に食べる雑煮について見てみましょう。

●郷土の雑煮●

郷土料理は、地域でとれる野菜や魚介類をじょうずにつかってつくられ、人びとのくらしのなかで受けつがれてきました。お正月に食べる雑煮は、代表的な郷土料理といえるでしょう。

雑煮は、地方によってさまざまです。イラスト地図を見てもわかるように、西日本では丸もちをつかう雑煮が多く、東日本では角もちをつかう雑煮が多いですね。汁も、しょうゆ仕立てにする地方もあれば、みそ仕立てにする地方もあります。

福井県
茎つきのかぶとかぶの葉、丸もちの入った赤みそ仕立て。

長崎県
焼いた丸もちに、エビ、ブリ、たけのこ、さといも、かまぼこ、だて巻きなどが入った豪華なすまし汁。

島根県
あずき汁に丸もちを入れた雑煮。

広島県
だいこん、にんじん、さといも、焼き魚、カキ、丸もちを入れたすまし汁。

香川県
だいこん、にんじん、さといもと、丸いあんこもちを入れた白みそ仕立て。

---

01 Traditional Events and Local Foods **02** "Zoni soup" from each local region / Each local region has its local vegetables or seafood produced in each area and had been eaten in daily life. "Zoni soup" is one of the most typical local dishes. There are many recipes of Zoni. Zoni in western Japan contains round mochi and eastern Japan contains square mochi. Soup also has varieties, made with soy sauce or miso. **03** Nagasaki Pref.: Clear soup with grilled mochi, shrimp, yellowtail, bamboo shoot, Japanese taro (sato-imo), kamaboko (steamed fish paste cake), datemaki (rolled omelet with fish paste). **04** Shimane Pref.: Azuki (red bean) soup with round mochi. **05** Hiroshima Pref.: Clear soup with round mochi, daikon radish, carrot, Japanese taro, grilled fish, oyster. **06** Kagawa Pref.: White miso soup with round mochi stuffed with red bean paste, daikon radish, carrot, Japanese taro. **07** Fukui Pref.: Red miso soup with round mochi, turnip with stem and leaves. **08** Kyoto Pref.: White miso soup with round mochi, Japanese taro, taro

北海道の郷土料理
ジンギスカン

広大な大地がひろがる北海道では、牧畜や酪農がさかんです。ジンギスカンは、そんな北海道の代表的な郷土料理です。

ジンギスカンの鉄なべ。

●ジンギスカンとは●

ジンギスカンというのは、羊の肉の焼肉料理。一般の焼肉とちがい、中央が盛り上がった独特の形をした鉄なべで肉を焼きます。北海道では、季節に関係なく、人が集まるときにはジンギスカンがよく食べられます。

ジンギスカンという料理名は、モンゴルの英雄チンギス・ハン（ジンギス・カン）からきています。モンゴルを統一したチンギス・ハンが、戦場となったモンゴルの草原で、羊の肉を焼いて食べたのが、ジンギスカンの始まりだといわれています。

01 **Local food of Hokkaido — Genghis Khan Barbecue** /Hokkaido has vast land and thrives with cattle breeding and dairy industries.
02 **What is Genghis Khan?** /Genghis Khan is mutton and lamb barbecue and is a typical local food of Hokkaido. A unique mountain-shaped iron pan is used for this food. People in Hokkaido often eat Genghis Khan regardless of season when they come together. The name of this dish derives from Mongolian hero Genghis Khan. It is said that Genghis Khan grilled mutton in the green battlefield of Mongolia. It is the origin of Genghis Khan Barbecue.
03 Iron pan for Genghis Khan.
04 **Mutton and lamb** /Hokkaido has started breeding sheep to get wool in Taisho period. After the World War II, Genghis Khan Barbecue has spread as a good way to eat mutton and lamb. It is said that climate in Hokkaido and

パート1　知ろう！調べよう！

羊の肉

北海道では、大正時代に、羊毛をとるために羊がさかんに飼育されるようになりました。第二次世界大戦後、羊から毛をとるだけでなく、肉のおいしい食べ方として、ジンギスカンがひろまっていったのです。北海道の気候や風土がモンゴルと似ていたため、北海道でジンギスカンが受け入れられたともいわれています。

羊の肉は、一般にラム（生後1年未満の羊の肉）やマトン（生後1年以降の羊の肉）という名で流通しています。肉類のなかではコレステロールの含有量が少なく、ヘルシーな食材だといわれています。現在のところ、ほかの肉とくらべると国内の流通量はあまり多くありません。だからこそ北海道の郷土料理となっているのですね。

魚介類の郷土料理

北海道は、まわりを海にかこまれ、大きな川も流れているため、豊かな漁場をもっています。そんな北海道には、魚介類をつかった郷土料理も数多くあります。たとえば、サケをたっぷりとつかった石狩なべ。ぶつ切りのサケの身、キャベツ、じゃがいも、たまねぎなど、北海道特産の食材がたっぷりと入っている、みそ仕立てのなべ料理です。

イカの胴に米をつめ、しょうゆ味のだしで煮た「イカめし」（→70ページ）は、駅弁としても有名です。

昔、サケ漁がさかんだった石狩川の漁師たちが食べたことが始まりという石狩なべ。

Mongolia is similar, so Genghis Khan easily become familiar in Hokkaido. There are two types of meat; lamb is the meat of a sheep less than one year of age. Mutton is the meat from a sheep aged over one year. Lamb and mutton contain low cholesterol and are said as healthy food. Lamb and mutton in Japan have small market compared with other meat. This is why Genghis Khan is local food of Hokkaido.

05 Local food with seafood /Hokkaido is surrounded by the sea and has big rivers so it is a good place for fishing. Hokkaido has many local foods using seafood. Ishikari Nabe is miso-flavored hot pot cuisine with a lot of local ingredients produced in Hokkaido like salmon, cabbage, potato and onion. Ika-meshi, squid stuffed with rice and stewed in soy sauce is a well-known food as Ekiben (a box lunch sold on a train or at stations).

06 Ishikari Nabe originates from the meal of fishermen who were fishing salmon around Ishikari River.

秋田県の郷土料理 きりたんぽ

秋田県は、西部は日本海に面していますが、残りの三方は山でかこまれています。きりたんぽは、県北部の郷土料理です。

いろりのまわりに立てて焼くたんぽと、きりたんぽなべ。

● 「たんぽ」と「きりたんぽ」 ●

たんぽは、つぶしたごはんを串に巻きつけたものです。その形が槍の刃先カバー（たんぽ）に似ていることから、「たんぽ」と名づけられたといわれています。たんぽをいろりのまわりに立てて、みそやしょうゆをつけてこんがり焼くのが、もっとも素朴な食べ方です。

焼けたたんぽを串からぬいて、食べやすい大きさに切ったものが「きりたんぽ」です。これを、とり肉、ねぎ、せり、ごぼう、きのこ類などとともになべに入れて煮ると、「きりたんぽなべ」になります。山の料理なので、基本的に魚介類はつかわず、しょうゆで味つけします。きりたんぽなべは、体の芯からあたたまる雪国ならではの料理です。

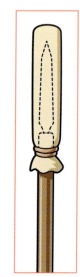

槍のたんぽ。

01 Local food of Akita — Kiritampo /Akita faces the Japan Sea on the west and is surrounded by the mountains. Kiritampo is a specialty of northern Akita. **02 "Tampo" and "Kiritampo"** /Tampo is smashed rice bar on a skewer. Its name originates from spearhead cover "Tampo" because their shapes resemble each other. The simplest way to eat tampo is spreading miso or soy sauce on it and grilling at the irori (Japanese sunken hearth). Kiritampo is the grilled tampo cut into good size of amount to eat. Kiritampo is a hot pot cuisine with Kiritampo, chicken, Welsh onion, water dropwort, burdock root and mushrooms. Kiritampo is the food from mountainous regions, so seafood is not used. It is seasoned with soy sauce. Kiritampo is the local food in snowy districts which warms body. **03** Tampo grilling at Japanese sunken hearth and Kiritampo hot pot. **04** Spearhead cover called Tampo. **05 The origin of Kiritampo** /It is said that woodcutters and hunters carried smashed rice bars when entering into mountains. They grilled the rice

●きりたんぽの由来● 05

昔、きこりや猟師たちは山に入るとき、携帯用の食料として、つぶしたごはんを串に巻きつけてもっていったといいます。それを、山小屋でみそをつけて焼いて食べたり、山中でとった山どりやきじ、山菜といっしょに煮こんで食べたりしたのが、きりたんぽの始まりだといわれています。

しょっつるなべ 08

秋田県西部は日本海に面し、昔からハタハタ漁がさかんです。県の特産品にハタハタを発酵させてつくる魚しょう「しょっつる」（→21ページ）があります。魚と野菜をしょっつるで煮る「しょっつるなべ」は、県を代表する郷土料理のひとつです。

いろりばたで食べるきりたんぽなべ。

ハタハタを入れたしょっつるなべ。

きりたんぽが郷土料理として受けつがれてきたのは、秋田県がおいしい米の産地であることと、比内地どりというおいしい地どりがあることが関係しています。比内地どりは、県北部で昔から飼育されていた比内どり（天然記念物）を品種改良したにわとりです。寒い冬にたえるため、皮の厚さがふつうのにわとりの3倍あるといわれています。そのため、肉は加熱してもかたくならないのです。

また、たんぽを巻きつける串には、秋田杉がつかわれています。秋田杉がごはんの余分な水分をしっかり吸収するので、もちもちしたおいしいきりたんぽができるのです。

比内地どりの肉は、なべ物のほか、焼きとりなどによくつかわれる。06

木曽ヒノキ、青森ヒバとならぶ日本三大美林のひとつ、秋田杉。07

---

bars in the mountain lodge and cooked with mountain birds, pheasants and wild plants. Akita produces good rice and Hinai chicken so that Kiritampo has been inherited in this area. Hinai chicken is a cross between the Hinai-dori bird which is a national treasure and a red chicken. Hinai chickens have three times thicker skin than other chickens so that they can survive harsh winter. Meat does not get hard even if it is cooked. Akita cedar, used for skewers, absorbs excess water of the rice, so firm and sticky Kiritampo can be made. 06 Hinai chickens are often used for hot pot dishes or Yakitori. 07 The forest of Akita cedar is known as one of the most beautiful forests in Japan along with Kiso cypress forest and Aomori cypress forest. 08 Shottsuru Nabe /The western side of Akita faces the Japan Sea and sandfish catching is active. Shottsuru, which is a seasoning made by fermented sandfish, is a specialty of Akita. Shottsuru Nabe is a hot pot with simmered sandfish and vegetables in Shottsuru, and is a typical local food of Akita.

宮城県の郷土料理 [01]
はらこめし

石巻、気仙沼という大きな漁港をもち、北上川、阿武隈川という大河が流れる宮城県。昔から魚介の郷土料理が受けつがれています。

●イクラたっぷり、はらこめし● [02]

「はらこ」というのは、サケの卵、イクラのこと。サケのおなか（腹）に入っていた子どもだから、「はらこ」とよばれるのです。はらこめしは、サケの切り身をしょうゆ・酒をあわせた煮汁でサッと煮て、その煮汁で炊いたごはんに、サケとはらこを盛りつけた丼です。海と川が出合う阿武隈川の河口付近一帯に昔から伝わる郷土料理です。

このあたりは昔からサケ漁がさかんでした。秋から冬にかけて、銀色のうろこを光らせてサケの大群が阿武隈川をさかのぼってきます。そんな光景が伝統の郷土料理、はらこめしを生みだしたのです。いまでは、仙台駅など東北各地で駅弁としても売られています。

---

[01] **Local food of Miyagi — Harako (Salmon roe) rice bowl** /Miyagi has two big fishing ports named Ishinomaki and Kesen-numa, and two big rivers, Kitakami River and Abukuma River. Thanks to geographical environment, local foods using fresh fish and shellfish have been handed down until today. [02] **Rice bowl with plenty of Harako (salmon roe)** /Another name of harako is ikura (salmon roe). "Hara" means belly and "ko" means child. It is why salmon roe is called harako. Salmon roe rice bowl is a dish with salmon roe and salmon fillet cooked lightly with soy sauce and sake, and placed on the top of rice. Rice is cooked with simmered salmon broth. It is a local food around the mouth of Abukuma River area. Salmon fishing has thrived in this area since the old days. From autumn to winter, many salmons having shiny scales travel Abukuma River upstream. [03] **Salmon roe rice bowl eaten by Lord Masamune Date** /Miyagi was called Sendai Domain in the Edo period. The lord of those days, Masamune Date looked over restoration

伊達政宗も食べたはらこめし

宮城県が仙台藩とよばれていた江戸時代、仙台藩の城主となった伊達政宗が阿武隈川の修復工事の視察に訪れました。そのとき地元の漁師がはらこめしを献上したところ、政宗はたいそう気に入りました。それ以降、はらこめしが藩内で知られるようになったといいます。

ひと口にはらこめしといっても、家庭によってその味は少しずつちがいます。はらこを生のままではなく、煮汁でサッと煮てからごはんに盛りつけることもあります。昔は各家庭でつくったはらこめしを、親戚や近所におすそ分けして、いろいろな味を食べくらべていたのです。

伊達政宗騎馬像。伊達政宗（1567～1636年）は、独眼流政宗として知られる戦国時代から江戸時代初期にかけての武将で、仙台藩62万石の基礎をきずいた。

宮城県の海の幸

宮城県のサンマの漁獲量は北海道につぐ2位です。サンマは、さしみで食べたり、塩焼にしたりと、地元ではもっとも身近な魚です。また、沿岸ではカキの養殖もさかんです。酢ガキや焼きガキ、土手なべ（→52ページ）などが、名物料理となっています。沿岸ではハゼという魚がよくとれます。このハゼを炭火でよく焼いてからけむりでいぶした焼きハゼが、昔からだしをとるのにつかわれています。

磯の香りたっぷりの宮城の焼きガキ。
Grilled oyster with rich ocean flavors.

焼きハゼでだしをとり、大きなハゼをのせるのが特徴の宮城県の雑煮。
Typical Zoni soup of Miyagi. Make dashi from grilled goby and top with goby on the Zoni soup.

米どころが生んだずんだもち

宮城県は、仙台平野を中心に米づくりがさかんです。そのため、昔からおいしいおもちがつくられてきました。

なかでも、枝豆をゆでてすりつぶし、砂糖をまぜたあんをもちにまぶしたずんだもちは、宮城県を代表する郷土料理として受けつがれています。

枝豆の旬は夏。ずんだもちは、もとはお盆のおそなえ物として家庭でつくられてきました。さわやかな緑色のずんだは、あずきのあんよりあっさりとしていて食べやすく、食欲の落ちる夏の栄養補給源でもあったのかもしれません。

「ずんだ」の語源は、「豆を打つ」という意味の「豆打」がなまって「ずんだ」になったという説や、伊達政宗が陣中で太刀で枝豆をくだいて食べたことから、「陣太刀」がなまって「ずんだ」になったという説などがあります。

06の英訳は ➡ P78

work of Abukuma River. Local fishermen offered him the salmon roe rice bowl and he liked it very much. After that, salmon roe rice bowl became popular food in Sendai Domain. Each home has its own taste of salmon roe rice bowl. People shared each family's salmon rice and enjoyed the difference of the tastes. 04 Statue of Masamune Date (1567-1636), well-known military commander in the Warring states period to the early Edo period. Date has established the foundation of Sendai Domain as one of the largest domains in northern Japan. 05 **Seafood from Miyagi prefecture** /The saury catch of Miyagi ranks second after Hokkaido. Saury is the most popular fish in Miyagi and eaten as sashimi or salt-grilled. Oyster farming is active along the coastal area. Vinegared or grilled oysters and hot pot cooking are well-known. Many goby fishes caught around the coast have been used as an ingredient of dashi since the old days.

なべ料理について知ろう 01

日本各地には、郷土の産物をふんだんにつかった、独特の味わいをもつなべ料理があります。そのいくつかを紹介しましょう。

北海道（地図①） 02
石狩なべ （→47ページ）

秋田県（地図③） 04
しょっつるなべ （→49ページ）

山梨県（地図⑥） 07

ほうとう

ほうとうは、手打ちの独特の幅広の麺を、にんじんやごぼう、かぼちゃなどといっしょにみそ味で煮こんだなべ料理。ほうとうの麺は、打ったあとねかさずすぐに切って煮こむため、煮くずれしやすい。煮くずれてとろりとした味と舌ざわりが、ほうとうの特徴。

青森県（地図②） 03

じゃっぱ汁

青森県の冬の魚といえばタラ。じゃっぱ汁は、タラのあらとだいこんやねぎなどの野菜をみそ味で煮こんだ、青森県を代表する郷土料理。「じゃっぱ」は、津軽弁で「残飯、いらないもの」という意味。

宮城県（地図④） 05
カキの土手なべ

宮城県の三陸海岸は、広島湾についで養殖カキの名産地。なべの内側に調味したみそを土手のようにぐるりとぬりつけ、少しずつときながらカキを煮て食べる土手なべは、広島県と同じく、宮城県の郷土料理となっている。

茨城県（地図⑤） 06

アンコウなべ

アンコウなべは、茨城県を代表する冬の味覚。アンコウは、グロテスクな姿に似あわず淡白な味の魚で、なべの味つけは、みそ仕立てかしょうゆ仕立てにする。

© Yamaguchi Yoshiaki

「ほうとう」のいわれ 08

戦国時代の甲斐国（いまの山梨県）の武将・武田信玄が、武田家に代々伝わる宝刀で麺を切ったことからその名がついたという説や、麺と野菜をいっしょに煮こむ手間いらずの戦陣食として、信玄が考えだしたという説がある。

The war flag of Takeda family. 武田家の家紋が入った軍旗。

---

01 What is Nabe (hot pot) cuisine? 02 Hokkaido Pref. Map① /Ishikari Nabe 03 Aomori Pref.② /Jappa-jiru soup: Jappa is miso soup with cod, daikon, Welsh onion or other vegetables. Cod is a winter fish in Aomori. Jappa means leftover in Tsugaru dialect. 04 Akita Pref.③ /Shottsuru Nabe 05 Miyagi Pref.④ /Oyster hot pot: Sanriku coast is famous for producing oysters second to Hiroshima. Spread miso around the edge of the pot and cook. 06 Ibaraki Pref.⑤ /Anglerfish hot pot: Typical winter dish in Ibaraki using anglerfish seasoned with miso or soy sauce. 07 Yamanashi Pref.⑥ /Houtou noodle: Handmade noodle cooked with carrot, burdock root and pumpkin in a pot. 08 The origin of Houtou /Military commander Shingen Takeda in Kai Domain in the Warring states era is said to cut the noodle with treasured sword, "houtou" in Japanese. 09 Tokyo Pref.⑦ /Chanko Nabe: Chanko is a meal made by sumo wrestlers. Ryogoku has been thrived as Sumo town. Traditional chanko is to simmer chicken and vegetables

東京都 (地図⑦) 09
ちゃんこなべ

「ちゃんこ」というのは、相撲の力士がつくる料理のこと。東京の両国は、相撲のまちとして昔からにぎわっていた。伝統的なちゃんこなべは、とりがらのだしでとり肉と野菜を煮るしょうゆ味のなべ。4本足の牛やぶたは手（前足）をつくので、「負ける」につながることから、2本足のとりの肉がつかわれたという。

兵庫県 (地図⑨) 11
ぼたんなべ

いのししの肉を、ねぎやごぼう、しいたけ、とうふなどといっしょに煮てみそで味をつける、兵庫県丹波地方の郷土料理。「ぼたん」というのは、いのししの肉のあざやかな赤い色が、ぼたんの花のようだからという説がある。

山口県 (地図⑪) 13
ふくちり

瀬戸内海と日本海の接点にある下関市の南風泊港は、フグの水揚げ港として有名。下関では、えんぎをかついで、フグのことを「ふく（福）」とよぶ。フグのなべ料理「ふくちり」が有名。

愛知県 (地図⑧) 10
ひきずり

愛知県の地どり「名古屋コーチン」の肉をつかったすきなべ。肉の汁がたれないように、なべからひきずるようにして自分の器に取ったことから、この名がついたといわれている。

広島県 (地図⑩) 12
カキの土手なべ

広島県はカキの養殖では日本一。カキの土手なべは、広島県の冬を代表するなべ料理。

福岡県 (地図⑫) 14
水炊き

水炊きは、とりがらでとった白濁したスープに、骨つきのとり肉やとり肉だんごと野菜を入れて、煮えたらポン酢しょうゆで食べるなべ料理。とり肉には博多地どりをつかい、白菜ではなく、キャベツをつかうのも、福岡の水炊きの特徴。

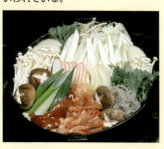

with chicken broth and soy sauce. Four-legged beef or pork is not used because it associates with hands touching the ground and it means losing the sumo match. 10 Aichi Pref.⑧ /Hikizuri (Nagoya Cochin chicken hot pot): Hot pot with Aichi's local chicken, Nagoya Cochin and vegetables. 11 Hyogo Pref.⑨ /Wild boar hot pot: Wild boar meat, Welsh onion, burdock root, shiitake and tofu are seasoned with miso. Local food of Tamba area. Wild boar meat is vivid red and called "botan" which means peony. 12 Hiroshima Pref.⑩ /Oyster hot pot: Hiroshima is the top producer of farmed oysters. 13 Yamaguchi Pref.⑪ /Blowfish hot pot: Shimonoseki faces Seto Inland Sea and the Japan Sea, and is well-known for blowfish. Blowfish in Japanese is "fugu," but in Shimonoseki it is called "fuku," which is a homonym of happiness. 14 Fukuoka Pref.⑫ /Chicken hot pot: Simmered chicken with vegetables in a chicken broth. Eat with ponzu sauce. Its unique point is using cabbage instead of Chinese cabbage.

新潟県の郷土料理

のっぺ

新潟県は日本でもっとも雪の多い地域ですが、
山の幸、海の幸にめぐまれ、
数多くの郷土料理が受けつがれています。

● さといもが主役の郷土料理、のっぺ ●

新潟県内で「新潟の郷土料理は？」とたずねると、真っ先にその名があがるのが、のっぺです。

のっぺというのは、さといもが主役の煮物料理。材料は、とり肉、さといも、ごぼう、にんじん、れんこん、たけのこ、きのこ、こんにゃく、きぬさやなど。だしは貝柱と煮干しでとり、しょうゆ、砂糖、酒、塩などでうすめに味つけして、大なべでコトコトと煮こみます。煮こんでいくにつれ、さといものぬめりが料理全体を包んで、のっぺりした感じになります。それで、のっぺという名前がついたともいわれています。

01 Local food of Niigata — Noppe soup /Niigata is one of the most heavy snowfall areas but rich with food ingredients from the sea and the mountains. Many local foods have been handed down. **02 Main ingredients of Noppe is Japanese taro(sato-imo)** /If you ask a question "What is the local food of Niigata?", the answer would be "Noppe." Noppe is a kind of soup with simmered Japanese taro, chicken, burdock root, carrot, lotus root, bamboo shoot, mushroom, konnyaku, snow peas and others. Dashi is made with shell ligament and dried small sardine, and soup is lightly seasoned with soy sauce, sugar, sake and salt. The ingredients are simmered gently in a big pot. As Japanese taro is cooked, soup gets thick and slimy. Noppe is from Japanese word "nopperi" which means slimy. Each family has its own Noppe recipe and taste. In some areas, salmon is added instead of chicken. Shape of ingredients differs on the occasions. Ingredients are cut into small cubes on festive occasions like weddings, and ginkgo nut, chestnut

のっぺは、家庭によって入れる具もちがえば味もちがいます。とり肉のかわりにサケを入れる地域もあります。また、行事によって材料の切り方をかえ、結婚式などのお祝い事では小さな角切りにし、お葬式などでは大きめの乱切りにすることが多いといいます。お祝い事では、ぎんなんやくり、イクラなどを上にちらしたりもします。

● 新潟県の米とさといも ● 03

新潟県は日本一の米どころ。いちばん人気の銘柄がコシヒカリです。米の産地だけあって、米をついて、もちやだんごがよくつくられてきました。なかでも、米の粉によもぎをまぜてつくっただんごを笹の葉で包んだ笹だんごは、昔から伝わる郷土料理です。よもぎや笹の葉の強い香りが魔よけ・厄払いにつながるということで、端午の節句に食べられています。

また、のっぺにはなくてはならないさといもが、信濃川・阿賀野川流域のよく肥えた水はけのよい地域を中心に生産されています。新潟のさといもは丸形で、独特のぬめりが特徴です。煮くずれせず、白くねっとりした肉質がのっぺに向いているのです。

村上の塩引きザケ 05

新潟県の川には多くのサケがさかのぼってきていて、昔から地域の人たちの貴重な栄養源として食べられていました。こんぶ巻きや煮物など、多くのサケ料理がいまに受けつがれています。サケがたくさんとれたときは、保存するために塩引きサケにされました。内臓を取りのぞいたサケを丸ごと塩漬けにしてから、寒風にさらして熟成させたものを、塩引きザケというのです。

塩引きザケの産地として有名なのは、新潟県北部の村上市です。村上の塩引きザケの特徴は、腹の一部を切らずに残すこと。これは、城下町だった村上で、武士の切腹を思わせる切り方をさけたためといわれています。塩引きザケは、正月や祭りのときに料理につかわれるのです。

新潟名物、笹だんご。 04

村上の塩引きザケ。 06

05以降の英訳は ➡ P78

or salmon roe are placed on the top. Ingredients are cut into rather big chunks at a funeral. 03 **Rice and Japanese taro produced in Niigata** /Niigata is the top producer of rice. The most popular brand of rice is Koshihikari. Mochi and dumpling balls have often been made in this area. "Sasa-dango", rice flour dumpling mixed with mugwort and wrapped with bamboo leaf, is especially a traditional local food of Niigata. It is said that strong flavor of mugwort and bamboo leaf protect people from evil, so it is served at Boy's Festival. Japanese taro which is essential for Noppe is produced in Shinano River and Agano River areas. These areas have rich soil and well-drained land. Japanese taro in Niigata has a round shape and a peculiar slimy texture. It does not fall apart while cooking, a white and sticky texture is suitable for Noppe. 04 A specialty of Niigata, Sasa-dango.

長野県の郷土料理 [01]
おやき

日本アルプスがそびえる長野県は山がちの地形で、冷涼な気候にあう作物を栽培し、多くの郷土料理がつくられてきました。

● 素朴な郷土料理、おやき ● [02]

おやきは、山菜や野菜にみそやしょうゆで味つけした具を、小麦粉とそば粉をこねた生地で包んだ、歯ごたえのあるかたいまんじゅうです。いろりの火でこんがり焼いて食べるので、「おやき」とよばれるようになったのです。中に入れる具やつくり方はさまざまで、昔から各家庭や地域で受けつがれてきました。

米があまりとれない長野県では、米のかわりに、小麦やそばをつかった食べ物が一般的でした。おやきもそのひとつだったのです。

● 昔ながらのおやき ● [03]

長野県では、おやきはお盆のおそなえ物としてよくつくられます。お盆というのは、祖先の霊がこの世に帰ってくるといわれている日です。祖先の霊は、あの世とこの世の境のがんじょうな石の戸を、そなえ物のかたいおやきを投げつけてたたきやぶって帰ってくると信じられていたのです。それほど、昔ながらのおやきは、かたい生地でつくられていたのです。いまでは、生地にふくらし粉などを入れて、蒸してふっくらと仕上げるおやき（→72ページ）も多くなりました。

鉄なべにおやきをのせて、いろりの火で焼いたり、いろりの灰の中におやきをうずめて焼いたりする。[04]

いろりの火のまわりにある渡し（鉄製の網）におやきをのせて、側面もしっかり焼く。[05]

---

[01] Local food of Nagano — Oyaki [02] Rustic local food "Oyaki" /Oyaki is the grilled dumpling stuffed with wild mountain plants and vegetables seasoned with miso or soy sauce. Dough is made from wheat and buckwheat flour, and has a chewy texture. Oyaki means grilling, named because it is grilled at irori (sunken hearth). Each family has its own Oyaki recipe and has handed it down to the next generation. Nagano is not suitable for rice cultivation, so wheat and buckwheat are popular staple food instead of rice. [03] Old-style Oyaki /Oyaki is often made as an offering for Bon festival. Bon is a festival to mourn for the dead and it is said that the spirits of the deceased are coming back from the world after death. It has been believed that ancestral spirits open the stone door between this world and the world after death by throwing hard Oyaki. So, old-style Oyaki has much harder texture than modern one. [04] Grill Oyaki on an iron pot or inside the ash at the sunken hearth. [05] Grill Oyaki on a grid around the fire.

●野沢菜漬けをおやきの具に 06

　おやきの具としてよくつかわれるのが、野沢菜漬けです。野沢菜漬けをこまかく切ってごま油で軽くいため、生地で包むのです。

　野沢菜というのは、背たけが1メートルにもなる長野県特産の野菜。野沢菜を塩で漬けこんだものが、野沢菜漬けです。野沢菜漬けの本場・野沢温泉村では、冬が近づくと、収穫したばかりの野沢菜を温泉の湯で洗う「お菜洗い」の光景が見られます。地元の人たちは、きびしい冬のあいだの保存食として、野沢菜をたくさん漬けるのです。野沢菜漬けは、長野県の長い冬の食卓に欠かせない味となっています。

野沢菜漬け 09

信州そば 10

　長野県あたりを、昔は信州とよんでいました。信州そばは、長野県の代表的な郷土料理です。そばは、寒冷地でも土地がやせていても栽培できるため、信州の人たちのたいせつな主食でもあったのです。

秋にとれたばかりの新そばで打った信州そば。11

共同浴場の温泉で野沢菜を洗う「お菜洗い」。07

白い花が咲く、信州のそば畑。12

野沢菜を大きなたるに漬けこむ。08

---

06 Nozawana pickles as stuffing /Nozawana pickles are popular stuffing for Oyaki. Cut Nozawana pickles into small pieces and saute with sesame oil, then wrap with dough. Nozawana is a local specialty of Nagano Pref. It grows up to 1 meter in height. Nozawana pickles are salt-preserved food. Nozawa-onsen village is the most famous area for producing Nozawana and people wash Nozawana plant with onsen (hot spring) water. Plenty of Nozawana pickles are made as preservative food to survive harsh winter. Nozawana pickles are a symbol of local food in winter in Nagano. **07** Wash Nozawana at communal hot-spring bath. **08** Pickle Nozawana in a big barrel. **09** Nozawana pickles. **10 Shinshu Soba** /Nagano was called Shinshu in the past. Shinshu soba is a typical local food of Nagano. Soba grow up in cold areas or infertile land and used to be a staple food of people in Shinshu. **11** Soba noodles made from freshly harvested buckwheat in autumn. **12** Buckwheat field in Shinshu with white flowers.

千葉県の郷土料理
イワシのごま漬け

千葉県の太平洋側は、暖流の黒潮と寒流の親潮が出合うため、全国有数の漁場となっています。魚介の郷土料理も数多くあります。

● 九十九里地域の郷土料理 ●

太平洋につきでている房総半島の東側には、九十九里浜が長くのびています。ここは、江戸時代のころからイワシ漁がさかんでした。イワシはいたみが早いので、地元の人たちは、たくさんとれたイワシを保存する方法を工夫しました。

イワシの頭と内臓を取ってよく水洗いしたあと、ひと晩塩漬けにします。この塩漬けイワシを水洗いして甘酢に5～6時間ほど漬けたあと、大きなおけに、甘酢に漬けたイワシ、黒ごま、ゆずやしょうがの千切りなどを交互にかさねていき、重石をして漬けこみます。水が上がってきたら、おけを逆さにして水を切れば、でき上がりです。これが、この地方の郷土料理として受けつがれているイワシのごま漬けです。

イワシのごま漬け

見渡す限り果てしなく続く九十九里浜。

01 Local food of Chiba — Salted sardine with sesame /The Pacific side of Chiba is the boundary line between a warm sea current and a cold sea current, so this is one of the richest fishing areas. **02 Local food of Kujukuri area** /Kujukuri beach extends on the east coast of Boso Peninsula to the Pacific Ocean. Sardine fishing has flourished since the Edo period. Sardine is easily spoiled so people thought out a method to preserve the fish. Remove heads and guts of sardine, wash the body and put into salt overnight. Wash the salted sardine and pickle in sweetened vinegar for 5-6 hours. Then pile up the sardine, sesame, thin strips of Yuzu citrus and ginger alternately. Put a lid and stone weight. When water comes out, turn the barrel upside down and drain water. **03** Salted sardine with sesame. **04 Fishing industry thrives in Chiba** /Chiba has many fishing ports; Katakai port in Kujukuri is well known for sardines; Choshi port has one of the largest catches in Japan; Katsuura port is well known for bonitos. Kujukuri Beach has

パート1 知ろう！調べよう！

●水産業がさかんな千葉県

千葉県には、イワシの水揚げで有名な九十九里浜の片貝港や、総水揚げ量が全国トップクラスの銚子港、カツオの水揚げで知られる勝浦港など、多くの漁港があります。

九十九里浜では、江戸時代のころから地引網漁がおこなわれてきました。地引網とは、網を沖合いにおろしたあと、浜で数十人がかりで網を引きよせて魚の群れを捕獲する漁法です。この漁法をおこなう漁師さんは少なくなりましたが、地元の人たちは伝統漁法として残そうと努力しています。

地引網漁を多くの人に知ってもらうためにおこなわれている「観光地引網」。

イワシを煮てから天日に干し、だし用の煮干しをつくる。

千葉の特産、落花生

千葉県は全国一の落花生の産地です。落花生のおもしろいところは、土の中でかたいさやに守られて豆ができること。収穫時期になると、株ごと落花生を土から掘り上げ、天日干しするのです。

落花生には良質なたんぱく質をはじめ、多くの栄養素がふくまれています。いまほど食べ物が豊かでなかった時代に、保存食としてたいせつにされました。この落花生をみそと砂糖で煮た「落花生みそ」は、ごはんにのせて食べたり、お茶受けにしたりと、郷土料理として地元の人たちに食べつがれています。

掘り上げたばかりの落花生。 落花生みそ

八街市の落花生畑。

worked on dragnet fishing since the Edo period. Dragnet fishing is a method to catch fish by putting a net offshore and drag it at the beach with tens of people. Now less fishermen use dragnet fishing, so people in Kujukuri try to inherit this traditional fishing method to the next generation. 05 Showing dragnet fishing to tourists. 06 Make dried sardine for dashi. Boil sardine and dry under the sun. 07 Peanuts are a specialty of Chiba /Chiba is the top producer of peanuts. The unique point of the peanut is peanut pods developing underground. Entire plants are removed from the soil for harvesting and are dried under the sun. Peanuts contain high-quality protein and are rich with nutrients. Peanuts had been cherished as preservative food at the times people did not have so many foods as they have now. Peanuts cooked with miso and sugar is one of the local foods in Chiba and people eat them with rice or as refreshments with tea. 08 Peanuts just after cultivation. 09 Peanuts with miso. 10 Peanut field in Yachimata City.

三重県の郷土料理 ハマグリ料理

三重県では、伊勢湾、志摩半島や熊野灘の沿岸などで漁業がさかんです。新鮮な魚介類をつかった郷土料理が、いまに伝わっています。

●焼きハマグリ●

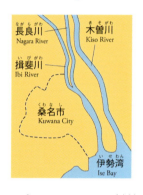

三重県北部の桑名は、木曽川、長良川、揖斐川が伊勢湾に流れこむ河口に位置しています。海水と淡水がまじりあう河口の砂地は貝類の生息に最適で、肉厚で身のやわらかいハマグリがとれるのです。

焼きハマグリは、新鮮なハマグリを網にのせて焼いたもの。焼けて貝が口をあけたところにしょうゆを少したらして、アツアツを食べるのです。「その手は桑名の焼きハマグリ」＊ということばがあるほど、桑名のハマグリは江戸時代から全国に知られた名物でした。江戸時代の桑名は、江戸と京都をむすぶ東海道の宿場町で、街道ぞいの店は旅人にハマグリを焼いて売っていたのです。

＊桑名と「食わない」をかけて、「その手は食わない」（だまされない）という意味のシャレことば。

●おめでたい席の食材●

ハマグリは、焼きハマグリのほかに、酒蒸し、潮汁などによくします。ハマグリの2枚のからは、ほかのハマグリのからとは決してあわないので、夫婦和合の象徴として、結婚の祝いの料理にハマグリはよくつかわれてきました。ひな祭りの食卓にも、ハマグリの吸物がよくだされます。

もうひとつ、おめでたい席に欠かせないものが、伊勢志摩地方の特産、伊勢エビです。その名前の由来は、伊勢の海でとれるエビだからという説や、

01 Local food of Mie — Hamaguri clam dishes /Fishing industry thrives in Ise Bay, Shima Peninsula and Kumano-nada Sea. **02** Grilled Hamaguri clams /Kuwana City stands at the mouth of Kiso River, Nagara River and Ibi River flowing into Ise Bay. Brackish water is the most suitable environment for shellfish. Grilled clam is a simple dish just broiling fresh clams over a charcoal fire and seasoning with soy sauce. Kuwana used to be a post town on the road from Edo to Kyoto in the Edo period and grilled clams were sold to the wayfarers. **03** Foods eaten on festive occasions /Clams are eaten grilled, steamed or as a clear soup. A pair of shells is a symbol of husband and wife because they only match with the original pair. So clams are often used for the wedding ceremony. Clear clam soup is served at Girl's Festival. Another ingredient essential for celebration is Ise-ebi lobster which is a specialty of Ise-Shima region. The name originates from the Ise Bay where lobsters are caught. And Japanese homonym of "being lively and

「威勢がよいエビ」がちぢまったという説などがあります。ピーンと長くのびた触角をもつその姿から、よろいかぶと姿の勇ましい武士を連想させ、曲がった腰をもつことから長寿のシンボルとして、祝いの席の料理につかわれるようになりました。伊勢エビは生でも煮ても焼いてもおいしい、まさにエビの王さまです。

伊勢志摩地方では、とれたての伊勢エビやアワビなどを生きたまま焼く、豪快な食べ方がある。 05

網にかかった伊勢エビ。 04

伊勢志摩地方では、海女たちがいまも伝統の素もぐり漁＊をおこなっている。 06

＊呼吸のための器具をつかわないで水中にもぐって漁をすること。

松阪肉 07

松阪肉は、近江牛、神戸牛とならんで、日本三大和牛とよばれている松阪牛の牛肉です。松阪地方では、松阪牛について、つぎのようなきびしい基準をもうけています。

● 雲出川から宮川のあいだの地域で、500日以上飼育された、子どもをうんだことのないメスの牛であること。

つまり、いくら松阪で育てられた牛でも、上の条件を満たしていない牛は、松阪牛ではないのです。飼育農家は、肉質がよいことで有名な黒毛和牛に、大豆かす、ひき割り麦などの飼料を与え、食欲がないときはビールを飲ませたりマッサージをしたりして、手間ひまかけて育てます。サシが入った(網の目状に脂肪が入った)豊かな味わいの松阪肉はこうして生まれるのです。

08 松阪肉はすき焼きにすることが多い。

energetic" contains "Ise" so Ise has a good meaning. Its long antennae are associated with an armored warrior and crooked shape symbolizes longevity. Ise-ebi is said to be the king of shrimps. 04 Ise-ebi lobster caught in the fishing net. 05 Seafood barbecue in Ise-Shima region. 06 Female skin divers catch seafood by traditional diving fishery in Ise-Shima region. 07 Matsusaka Beef /Matsusaka beef is one of the three major beefs in Japan with Omi beef and Kobe beef. Matsusaka region has strict standards for Matsusaka beef. "● Matsusaka beef has to be a heifer and raised over 500 days around the area between Kumozu River and Miya River." Even if cattles are raised in Matsusaka region and if they do not satisfy the criteria, they can not be named as Matsusaka beef. Breeders feed black-haired "Wagyu, Japanese cattle" with soy beans or oatmeal and spend a lot of time. When cattle have no appetite, they are fed beer to stimulate their eating, and receive massages. 08 Sukiyaki is a popular way to eat Matsusaka beef.

山口県の郷土料理　岩国ずし 01

山口県は日本海や瀬戸内海に面し、海産物をつかった郷土料理も豊富です。岩国や萩には、城下町のおもむきが残されています。

● 岩国ずしは殿さまずし ● 02

　岩国ずしは、3段から5段もかさねてつくる、はなやかな押しずしです。別名「殿さまずし」ともよばれています。江戸時代、この地を治めていた岩国藩主が、山の上の城に運び上げるのに便利な食べ物をつくるように命じたことから生まれたすしのため、その名がついたといわれています。

　岩国ずしをつくるには、大きなもので60センチ四方もあるすし枠をつかいます。まず、すし枠の底にちしゃ*の葉を敷き、アジなどの新鮮な魚をまぜた酢めしをつめます。その上に、錦糸卵、しいたけ、でんぶ、れんこんの酢漬けなどをのせ、またちしゃの葉を敷いて、同じように段をかさねていきます。最後に木のふたをのせて、重石をかけます。

　1段に1升（10合）もの米をつめるため、何段もかさねたすしの枠をぬくのはたいへんです。白たび姿の料理人がふたの上に片足をかけてふんばって、一気に枠を引きぬき、四角く切り分けるのです。まさに殿さまずしという名がよく似合う、豪快な押しずしです。

何段もかさねてつくられた岩国ずしを、豪快に切る。03

*山口県特産の野菜。レタスの一種。

岩国市の象徴でもある錦帯橋。江戸時代に岩国藩主の命で、日本の伝統技法を駆使して創建された。山の上に見えるのが岩国城。04

---

01 **Local food of Yamaguchi — Iwakuni-zushi** /Yamaguchi Pref. faces the Japan Sea and Seto Inland Sea and has many local foods using seafood. Iwakuni region and Hagi region still keep the atmosphere as a castle town. 02 **Iwakuni-zushi is "Sushi of the lord"**/Iwakuni-zushi is pressed and three to five layered sushi with many ingredients. Another name is "Sushi of the lord." Lord of Iwakuni who ruled this area in the Edo period had a castle on the top of the mountain and ordered sushi which was easy to carry up. This is the reason why this sushi is called Sushi of the lord. A sushi mold, the biggest is about 60×60cm, is required to make Iwakuni-zushi. Spread Chisha lettuce at the bottom of the mold, put sushi rice with fresh fish like horse mackerel, then put thin strips of egg, shiitake mushroom, denbu (mashed and seasoned fish), vinegared lotus root, spread Chisha lettuce again and make the same layers. Put a wooden lid at the last and put a weight. Each layer contains 10 cups of rice, so it is a hard work to take off the

パート1 知ろう！調べよう！

● れんこんをたくさん入れるのが特徴

江戸時代、岩国の沿岸地域はさかんに干拓がおこなわれ、低湿地には広大なれんこん畑がつくられていました。岩国藩主の家紋が九曜紋*で、岩国れんこんの穴が同じく9つあるということで、藩主を喜ばせたといわれています。そのため、殿さまずしには、この岩国れんこんがたくさんつかわれたのです。

*九曜紋

いまでも、岩国れんこんはシャキシャキとした歯ざわりと味のよさで、岩国の特産品となっています。れんこんの酢漬けも、岩国ずしとともに祝い事には欠かせない郷土料理です。

ふくさし

ふくさしというのは、下関地方の名物、フグのさしみのこと。フグは、ほかの魚のさしみとちがい、向こうがすけるぐらいうすくそぎ切りにされます。盛られた皿のもようがすけて見えるぐらいです。これは、フグの身は弾力があって、うすく切らないとかみ切れないからです。

下関にはフグの水揚げ港があるので、最高級のトラフグ以外にも、マフグ、シマフグなど比較的安価なフグが手に入ります。そのため、フグが日常的によく食べられています。

ふくさしは、ポン酢とわけぎ、もみじおろし（だいこんととうがらしをいっしょにすりおろしたもの）で食べるのが基本。

06以降の英訳は → P78

岩国れんこん

岩国のれんこん畑。

mold. A sushi chef wearing white tabi socks braces his foot against the lid and pulls out sushi from the mold at one time, then cut into square. According to this process, this dynamic pressed sushi become worthy to be called as Sushi of the lord. 03 Sushi chef dynamically cuts layered Iwakuni-zushi. 04 "Kintaikyo Bridge", the symbol of Iwakuni City was built in the Edo period by the order of the lord of Iwakuni, utilizing traditional construction techniques at that time. Iwakuni Castle is on the top of the mountain. 05 Iwakuni-zushi is characterized by plenty of lotus roots / Reclamation of coastal area of Iwakuni was conducted in the Edo period, and a lotus field expanded in wetlands. The symbol of the lord of Iwakuni was nine-planet crest, which was similar to holes in lotus roots, so lotus farming was recommended to please the lord. Lotus roots produced in Iwakuni have a crunchy texture and taste good. Vinegared lotus roots are festive dishes of Iwakuni region.

すしについて知ろう 01

もともとすしは、魚を保存するために生まれたものです。
すしは、どのようにうつりかわってきたのでしょうか。
また、日本各地に根づいている特色あるすしを見てみましょう。

すしのうつりかわり 02

なれずし 03
生の魚を塩とごはんで漬けこみ、1年くらいかけて発酵させた、魚の漬物のようなもの。ドロドロになったごはんはすてて、魚だけを食べる。

なれずしの原型だといわれている、滋賀県の郷土料理フナずし。

↓

生なれずし 04
1か月ほど魚を漬けこみ、ごはんごと食べられるすし。

↓

早ずし 05
箱などに酢めしをつめ、その上に酢でしめた魚をならべて、重石をして1～2日おいたもの。押しずしがこれにあたる。

↓

にぎりずし 06
おいしいすしを早く食べられるように、酢めしを手でにぎって、その上に酢漬けや味をつけて煮た魚(後には生の魚)をのせたもの。

郷土料理として根づいているいろいろなすし 07

青森県 (地図①) 08
イカのすし
イカの漁獲量が日本一の青森県ならではの郷土料理。内臓を取りのぞいてゆでたイカの胴に、にんじんやキャベツの千切りと小さく切ったイカの足をつめ、半日ほど酢に漬けこんだもの。あわいピンク色をしているので、祝い事などでよくつくられる。

千葉県 (地図②) 09
太巻きずし
祭りや祝い事などのときにかならずつくられる、千葉県独特の巻きずし。のりやうす焼き卵で、酢めしと甘辛く煮たかんぴょうやにんじん、しいたけと、さくらでんぶなどの具を巻いてつくる。切り口にいろいろな絵柄がでるはなやかなすし。

---

01 What is Sushi? /The origin of sushi used to be the way to preserve fish. 02 Generational changes of Sushi 03 Nare-zushi /Nare-zushi is like fish pickles. Pickle fish with salt and rice then undergo fermentation for about 1 year. Remove thick paste of rice and eat fish only. 04 Namanare-zushi /Pickle fish with salt and rice then undergo fermentation for 1 month. Eat fermented fish and rice. 05 Haya-zushi /Press vinegared rice and vinegared fish in a mold, and put a weight for 1 or 2 days. It is pressed sushi. 06 Nigiri-zushi /Make an oblong mound of sushi rice by hand topped with vinegared fish or seasoned and cooked fish. Later on fresh raw fish became topping ingredients. 07 Sushi as local food in each region 08 Aomori Pref. Map① /Squid sushi: Aomori has the largest catch of squid. Remove guts and then boil. Stuff with thin strips of carrot and cabbage, chopped tentacles, then pickle with vinegar for half a day. It is served as a festive food because of its pink color. 09 Chiba Pref.② /Futomaki-zushi: Rolled sushi

東京都（地図③） 10
江戸前ずし
江戸前ずしは、型に入れたり、重石で押したりしてつくるのではなく、酢めしを手でにぎってつくるにぎりずし。当時の江戸の目の前にひろがる海（東京湾）でとれる新鮮な魚介類をすしネタとしてつかったため、江戸前ずしとよばれるようになったという。

三重県（地図⑤） 12
手こねずし
もともとは、漁師がとれたてのカツオを手で小さくちぎってしょうゆをまぶし、酢めしに手でこねるようにまぜたのが始まりとされる。海女（→61ページ）のまちである伊勢志摩地方で、いそがしい海女に負担をかけないようにという思いやりから生まれた料理ともいわれている。

大阪府（地図⑧） 14
バッテラ
三枚におろして酢でしめたサバを酢めしにのせ、重石をかけてつくるサバずし。上に半透明のこんぶをのせるのが、バッテラの特徴。明治時代に大阪湾でたくさんとれたコノシロという魚で押しずしがつくられた。そのすしの形がボートに似ていたので、ポルトガル語でボートを意味する「バッテラ」と名づけられたという。その後、コノシロにかわってサバがつかわれるようになった。

富山県（地図④） 11
マスずし
丸い木のおけに笹の葉を敷き、酢めしと、塩と酢にひたしたマスのうす切りをかさねてつくる押しずし。駅弁としても有名。江戸時代には、神通川をマスが群れをなしてさかのぼってきていたという。当時の富山藩士が、そのサクラマスをつかってつくったのが、マスずしの始まり。

奈良県（地図⑥）・和歌山県（地図⑦） 13
柿の葉ずし
ひと口大の酢めしにサバやサケなどの切り身をのせ、柿の葉で包んで重石をかけた押しずし。江戸時代の中ごろ、紀州（現在の和歌山県）の漁師が熊野灘のサバを塩でしめ、吉野川ぞいの村むらに売ったのが始まりとされている。この地域では夏祭りのごちそうとして食べつがれている。

岡山県（地図⑨） 15
ばらずし
瀬戸内海に面している岡山は、新鮮な魚をつかった郷土料理が多い。ばらずしもそのひとつ。この料理が生まれたのは江戸時代。藩主が「食事は一汁一菜とする」という質素倹約令をだした。それで、人びとは知恵をはたらかせて、上から見えないように、すしめしの中に十種類もの具を入れて食べたという。いまでは、具は堂どうと表面に飾られている。

笹の葉と柿の葉 16
すしに笹の葉や柿の葉がつかわれるのは、なぜでしょうか。それは、食べ物をくさりにくくする効果があるからです。昔の人たちはそのことを経験から知っていて、生活の知恵として伝えていったのです。

13以降の英訳は→P78

---

served at a festival or a celebration. Roll vinegared rice and sweetened ingredients with nori or paper-thin omelet and make a pattern. 10 Tokyo Pref.③ /Edomae-zushi: A hand-shaped oblong mound of sushi topped with fresh and raw fish caught in Tokyo Bay. "Edo" is the old name of Tokyo, "mae" means front. That is why sushi in Tokyo is called Edomae-zushi. 11 Toyama Pref.④ /Trout sushi: Spread bamboo leaves on a round tub. Put vinegared rice, slices of vinegared and salted trout (Japanese name: masu) and press. Trout sushi is well-known as a station bento. In the Edo period many trout traveled Jinzu River upstream. Feudal retainers of Toyama started making trout sushi. 12 Mie Pref. ⑤ /Tekone-zushi: The origin is considered as fishermen tore fresh bonito into small pieces, seasoned with soy sauce and mixed with vinegared rice by hand. Tekone means hand-mixing. Another episode is that female skin divers in Ise-Shima region were very busy, so the people made this dish to treat them.

愛媛県の郷土料理 タイそうめん

愛媛県

北は瀬戸内海に、西は宇和海に面した愛媛県は、漁業がさかんな県です。温暖な気候にめぐまれて、みかん栽培も有名です。

● 鉢盛料理のひとつ、タイそうめん ●

愛媛県では、お祝いや祭りのときによく鉢盛料理がだされます。鉢盛料理というのは、大皿に海の幸や山の幸を豪華に盛りつけた料理全般のことをいいます。代表的な鉢盛料理が「タイそうめん」です。「タイめん」とよぶ地域もあります。

これは、大皿に波に見立てて盛られたそうめんの上に、タイの姿煮をのせ、錦糸卵や細切りのしいたけのうま煮などを盛りつけた料理です。小皿に取りわけ、タイの煮汁にだしを加えたつゆと薬味（ねぎやしょうが）とともに食べるのです。

● 宇和海のタイ ●

リアス式海岸が天然の湾をつくっている宇和海は、魚の宝庫だといわれています。また、マダイやハマチの養殖もおこなわれています。それは、宇和海には、南から暖流の黒潮の一部が流れこんでいて、冬でも水温がそれほど低くならないおだやかな海だからです。愛媛県の養殖マダイの生産量は全国1位です。そのため、この地域ではタイをつかった料理が発展したのです。

宇和島地方のタイそうめん。つゆはつけて食べるのではなく、全体にかけてよくまぜてから食べるのが、この地域独特の食べ方。

マダイの養殖がおこなわれている宇和海。

---

01 Local food of Ehime — Somen noodles with sea bream /Ehime faces Seto Inland Sea on the north and Uwakai Sea on the west. Fishing industry thrives in this region. **02 Somen noodles with sea bream served on a large plate** /"Hachimori cuisine" is the food served on large plates and is often served at festive occasions in Ehime. Typical Hachimori cuisine is somen noodles with sea bream. Somen dished up on a big plate symbolize the wave in the sea. Put simmered sea bream on the top of somen and decorate with thin strips of eggs and simmered thin slices of shiitake mushrooms. Serve into small plates and eat with soup with sea bream broth and soy sauce with condiments like scallion and ginger. **03 Sea bream from Uwakai Sea** /Uwakai Sea has a rias coastline and is a rich repository of fish. Madai (red sea bream) and Hamachi (young amberjack) are cultured in this sea. Warm Kuroshio current flows into Uwakai Sea so its water temperature does not become so low. Ehime is the largest producer of red sea bream farming.

おもてなし料理 06

　鉢盛料理は、たくさんのお客を一度にもてなすために考えだされた料理です。祝い事に欠かせない料理に、タイそうめんのほかに「ふくめん」と「フカの湯ざらし」という郷土料理があります。

　「ふくめん」というのは、甘辛く煮た千切りのこんにゃく（または糸こんにゃく）を、エソ（白身魚）でつくった紅白のそぼろと、黄色い陳皮（みかんの皮）、緑のねぎの葉のみじん切りでおおった、いろどりの美しい料理です。これらをまぜあわせて食べることで、海と山の味がひとつになって、なんともいえないよい味が生まれます。白身魚から動物性たんぱく質を、ミカンの皮と葉ねぎからはビタミンCなどをとることができる、栄養バランスのよい料理です。「ふくめん」というおもしろい名前の由来は、覆面をしたように中身が見えないからだという説のほか、いくつかあります。

愛媛のみかん 08

　愛媛県は、日本一のみかんの産地です。そのまま食べたり、ジュースにしたりするほか、郷土料理にもいろいろな形でつかわれています。たとえば、ふくめんの陳皮。これは、みかんの皮を干したものですが、みかんの皮には、せきをしずめたり胃の調子をととのえたりするはたらきがあり、昔から薬用につかわれていました。それだけでなく、みかんの皮はとてもよい香りがするので、料理につかわれるようになったのです。

海に面した段だん畑で色づくみかん。09　　08以降の英訳は➡P78

ふくめん

　「フカの湯ざらし」のフカとは、小型のサメのこと。湯通しし、水にさらしたフカの身を、からしをきかせた酢みそで食べます。やわらかな口当たりと、あっさりした味わいが特徴の郷土料理です。結びこんにゃく、とうふ、季節の野菜などをそえるのが一般的です。

中央に盛られているのがフカの湯ざらし。07

That is why somen noodles with sea bream have developed in this area. 04 Sea bream somen noodles. Do not dip somen in soup, but pour soup on the dished up plate and mix well, then eat. 05 Uwakai Sea where the red sea breams are farmed. 06 **Festive foods** /Hachimori cuisine was created to serve many guests in one time. There are two famous local foods, "Fukumen" and "Boiled small shark." Fukumen is a dish with salted and sweetened thin strips of konnyaku, and is covered beautifully with white and pink colored fish powder, mikan zest and chopped scallion. Mix all ingredients before eating so that tastes of the foods from mountains and the sea make a synergistic effect. Fukumen means a mask. Konnyaku is hidden with topping ingredients so this is one of the reasons why this dish is named Fukumen. "Boiled small shark" is a dish which serves parboiled shark with vinegared miso and Japanese mustard. It is usually served with string konnyaku, tofu and seasonal vegetables. 07 Boiled shark dished up on the center of the plate.

長崎県の郷土料理 卓袱料理

長崎県

長崎は、日本が鎖国をしていた江戸時代に、外国との貿易がゆるされていた唯一の場所。そのために、特色ある郷土料理が発展しました。

● テーブルをかこんで食べる卓袱料理 ●

卓袱の「卓」は丸いテーブル、「袱」はテーブルクロスの意味です。卓袱料理は、江戸時代に貿易のために長崎に住んでいた中国人やオランダ人の料理をもとにしてできた、長崎ならではのもてなし料理です。

丸いテーブルに、大皿に盛られたたくさんの料理がならべられます。それを、各自のおはしとトンスイとよばれる陶器のスプーンで小皿に取って食べるのです。このような大皿の料理を取りわけて食べるというのは、当時の日本にはなかった食事の形でした。それまでは、料理は一人ひとりお膳にのせてだされていたのです。

また、丸いテーブルは、身分の上下に関係なく席に着くことができます。身分がはっきり決められていた江戸時代では、だれもが平等に料理を取りわけて食べる卓袱料理は、先進的な食事形式でした。

● おひれから食事が始まる ●

卓袱料理の宴会は、客をもてなす側の主人の「おひれをどうぞ」というあいさつで、食事が始まります。「おひれ」というのは、タイやエビ、とり肉、みつばなどが入った吸物のこと。もともとはタイの尾ひれを入れて、「ひとりのお客さまに魚1尾をつかって歓迎している」という意味をあらわしたといわれています。

01 **Local food of Nagasaki — Shippoku cuisine** /Nagasaki was the only place allowed to open a port for trading during the period of national isolation. 02 **Shippoku cuisine** /Shippoku means a round table and tablecloth. Shippoku cuisine is a mixture of Japanese, Chinese and Western cuisine served in large dishes on a round table. This style of eating and entertaining guests developed in Nagasaki during the Edo period with being affected by Chinese and Dutch. The round table is adorned with many large dishes; everybody is allowed to help themselves to serve in small plates. This style of sharing foods by all diners was something new in those days in Japan. Foods were served in trays for each beforehand. Persons in any class could sit anyplace they want. In the Edo period the class system was firmly established, however, shippoku cuisine could be enjoyed evenly regardless of their social status. 03 **Meal starts from "Ohire"** /Meal starts with a soup called "Ohire (a fin)," which contains sea bream or shrimp, chicken and

このはじめのおひれと最後の梅わん以外は食べる順番は決まっておらず、好きなように食べていいのです。コースで食べる卓袱料理は、おもにつぎのような料理がだされます。

小菜 04
冷めても味のかわらない料理。たとえば、さしみ、南蛮漬け、豆の蜜煮など。

中鉢 05
食事の中ほどでだされる、あたたかい料理。とくに、ぶたの角煮（→76ページ）はかならずだされる。

大鉢 06
長崎てんぷら、卵どうふ、かぼちゃ、かぶなど、海と山の幸が、季節ごとの組みあわせで盛られる。

スープやごはん 07
中華風とも和風ともいえるスープがだされる。スープをごはんにかけて食べることもある。

水菓子 08
季節の果物がだされる。

梅わん 09
紅白の梅に見立てた白玉が入っているおしるこ。

新しい調理法 10

長崎では、それまで日本にはなかった調理法も取り入れられました。油をつかう料理がそうです。いまでは代表的な和食となっているてんぷらも、ポルトガルの料理がもととなってつくられたのです。とくに「長崎てんぷら」は、味のついた衣をつかうのが特徴です。また、油で揚げた魚などをとうがらしの入った酢に漬ける料理「南蛮漬け」も、ポルトガルから伝わった料理がもとになっています。長崎てんぷらも南蛮漬けも、卓袱料理によくだされます。

卓袱料理の最後にだされる梅わんには、当時は貴重だった砂糖がつかわれています。このことからも、当時の卓袱料理が豪華で先進的な食事だったことがうかがえます。

エビや野菜の長崎てんぷら。
Shrimp and vegetable tempura in Nagasaki.

長崎ちゃんぽん 11

いまでは全国的に知られている麺類に、長崎ちゃんぽんがあります。これは、明治時代の中華料理店主が、日本にきていた中国人留学生に、安くて栄養価の高い食事を食べさせるためにつくったのが始まりだといわれています。

11の英訳は ➡ P78

---

mitsuba parsley. A tail fin of sea bream was served for each and it showed hospitality of the host. There is an order to eat; Ohire soup is a starter and the last is sweet red bean soup, but you can eat other dishes as you like. Here is an example of a menu. 04 Cold dish: Sashimi, Namban-zuke (deep fried fish or meat seasoned with sweetened vinegar sauce), sweetened beans and so on. 05 Hot dish: Simmered pork is essential. 06 Foods from the mountains and the sea dished up on a big plate: Nagasaki tempura, tamago-dofu (steamed egg custard with dashi) and seasonal ingredients. 07 Soup and rice: Chinese-Japanese fusion style soup. 08 Fruit: Seasonal fruits 09 Sweet red bean soup : Red bean soup with white and pink colored dumplings which resemble Ume flower. 10 New cooking methods /New cooking methods were introduced to Nagasaki. Tempura using frying oil and Namban-zuke originate from Portugal. Sugar which was expensive in those days is used for red bean soup. Shippoku cuisine used to be a feast and advanced meal.

郷土料理を知ろう
日本各地の和食

パート2 つくろう！食べよう！

北海道の郷土料理 01

イカめし

風味豊かなイカをまるごと味わえる一品。
イカの胴に具材をつめるのがたのしい！

ヤリイカ 04
北海道でイカの水揚げ量が多いのは、函館港です。イカめしも、もともと函館地方の郷土料理です。
イカには多くの種類がありますが、ヤリイカは身がやわらかくて味もよく、さしみによくされます。また、煮てもかたくならないので、イカめしによくつかわれるのです。

ヤリイカ

---

01 Local food of Hokkaido **Squid Stuffed with Rice**
02 Ingredients for 4 servings
- spear squid : 4
- glutinous rice : 1 cup
- A ⎰
  - sake : 2 tbsps
  - soy sauce : 2 tbsps
  - mirin : 2 tbsps

[simmering broth]
- water : 4 cups
- sake : 1/2 cup
- soy sauce : 4 tbsps
- mirin : 4 tbsps
- sugar : 4 tbsps

03 How to make
1. Wash glutinous rice on the previous day and soak in plenty of water overnight.
2. Put fingers into the body of squid and pull out tentacles.
3. Cut off guts and eyes from the tentacles, cut into good size of amount and parboil in the hot water. Wash the body of squid.
4. Drain water of the rice, put into a bowl and add (A) seasonings and the tentacles. Soak for 30 min.

【材料 4人分】

<具材>
- ヤリイカ …… 4杯
- もち米 …… 1カップ
- 酒 …… 大さじ2
- しょうゆ …… 大さじ2
- みりん …… 大さじ2

<煮汁>
- 水 …… 4カップ
- 酒 …… 1/2カップ
- しょうゆ …… 大さじ4
- みりん …… 大さじ4
- 砂糖 …… 大さじ4

つくり方

1. もち米は前日にといで、たっぷりの水にひと晩つけておく。

2. ヤリイカの胴に指を入れて、胴と足がくっついているところをはがし、足を引っぱってぬきとる。

3. 足からはらわたや目を切りとる。足はぶつ切りにしてサッと湯通しする。胴は中まできれいに洗う。

4. もち米の水気を切ってボウルに入れ、具材の調味料と3のイカの足を加えてまぜあわせ、約30分漬けておく。

5. 4をざるにあけて、汁気を切る。イカの胴の水気をふきんでふきとる。

6. 汁気を切った具材や、イカの胴に八分目までつめる。つめ口は、ようじでぬうように止める。

7. 6をなべにならべて煮汁を加え、落としぶたをして強火にかける。

8. 煮立ったら弱火にして、アクをとりのぞく。イカをひっくり返して、煮汁がなくなるまで煮る。

9. 8をきれいに切り分けて、器にならべる。

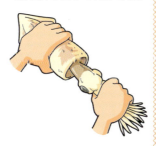

5. Drain liquid of (4) rice and tentacles. Wipe out liquid of the squid and dry.
6. Stuff the rice into the squid to eight-tenths of the body. Stick a toothpick at the end to seal.
7. Put the squid into a pot, pour simmering broth and put a drop-lid on. Simmer over strong fire.
8. Turn down the heat to low flame when it boils. Skim off the scum. Turn over the squid and simmer until the broth is almost evaporated.
9. Cut and dish up.

Spear squid /Hakodate has the biggest squid catch in Hokkaido. Originally, squid stuffed with rice used to be the local food of Hakodate. There are many species of squid and spear squid has soft flesh and tastes good, often served as sashimi. As the spear squid keeps a soft texture even if it is cooked, it is often used for stuffing rice, too.

長野県の郷土料理

おやき

イーストを加えた生地でつくる、ちょっとふっくらしたおやきです。
野沢菜漬けとあずきあんの2種類をつくりましょう。

【材料 12個分】

〈皮〉
- 中力粉 …………………… 300g
- そば粉 …………………… 20g
- 砂糖 ……………………… 10g
- ドライイースト …………… 3g
- ぬるま湯 ………………… 20mL
- サラダ油 ………………… 小さじ1
- 中力粉(打粉として) ……… 適量
- サラダ油(フライパン用) …… 少々

〈具〉
- ●あずきあん 6個分
- 市販のつぶあん ………… 300g

- ●野沢菜漬け 6個分
- 野沢菜漬け ……………… 230g
- いりごま ………………… 大さじ1
- だし ……………………… 80mL
- 酒 ………………………… 大さじ1
- みりん …………………… 小さじ2
- 信州みそ ………………… 大さじ1
- 砂糖 ……………………… 小さじ1
- ごま油(フライパン用) …… 少々

Local food of Nagano **Oyaki (Japanese stuffed dumpling)**

Ingredients for 12 pieces

[dough]
- wheat flour : 300g
- buckwheat flour : 20g
- sugar : 10g
- dry yeast : 3g
- warm water : 20mL
- salad oil : 1 tsp
- wheat flour for dusting : adequate amount
- salad oil (for frying pan) : a small amount

[stuffing]
sweet red bean jam for 6 pieces
- sweet red bean jam with whole beans : 300g

Nozawana pickles for 6 pieces
- Nozawana pickles : 230g
- roasted sesame : 1 tbsp
- dashi : 80mL
- Sake : 1 tbsp
- mirin : 2 tsps
- Shinshu miso : 1tbsp
- sugar : 1tsp
- sesame oil (for frying pan) : a small amount

パート2 つくろう！食べよう！

つくり方 03

1 ぬるま湯にドライイーストを入れ、よくとかしておく。

2 ボウルに中力粉、そば粉、砂糖を入れてよくまぜ、1とサラダ油を加えてよくこねる。

3 2にラップをかけて、30分ほどねかせる。生地をねかせているあいだに、具の準備をする。

4 野沢菜漬けを長さ3cmに切り、水にさらして塩気をぬいたあと、ぎゅっと水気をしぼる。

5 フライパンにごま油をひいて4を軽くいためる。だし、いりごま、そのほかの調味料を加え、汁気がなくなるまでいため、冷ましておく。

6 3を12等分し、手に打粉を少しつけて、丸く広げる。

7 6に具をのせて包み、口をとじる。あずきあんと野沢菜漬けを、それぞれ6個ずつつくる。

8 フライパンにサラダ油をなじませ、弱火で7をこんがり焼く。

9 8を湯気のあがった蒸し器にならべ、中火で10分ほど蒸す。

03 How to make
1. Dissolve dry yeast with warm water.
2. Put wheat flour, buckwheat flour and sugar in a bowl and mix well. Add (1) and oil, and knead well.
3. Cover with cling-film and leave it for 30 min.
4. Cut Nozawana pickles into 3cm length, soak into water and remove excess salt. Squeeze water.
5. Saute (4) with sesame oil. Add dashi, roasted sesame and seasonings. Cook until liquid evaporates. Let it cool down.
6. Divide dough into 12 equal parts. Coat hand with wheat flour, flatten dough into a circular shape.
7. Put stuffing on the dough and wrap.
8. Pour salad oil to the frying pan and grill stuffed dumplings over low flame until golden brown.
9. Transfer the dumplings to a steamer and steam for 10 min over medium fire.

岡山県の郷土料理

ばらずし

岡山県では「祭りずし」ともよばれる、にぎやかなおすし。魚介や野菜を色あざやかに飾りましょう。

【材料 4人分】

- 米 ……… 3合
- <合わせ酢>
  - 酢 ……… 60mL
  - 砂糖 ……… 25g
  - 塩 ……… 5g
- 干ししいたけ ……… 6枚
- <煮汁>
  - だし ……… 3カップ
  - 砂糖 ……… 大さじ5
  - A みりん ……… 大さじ4
  - うすくちしょうゆ ……… 大さじ3
  - 塩 ……… 小さじ1/2
- れんこん ……… 1/2節
- <甘酢>
  - だし ……… 大さじ6
  - B 酢 ……… 大さじ6
  - 砂糖 ……… 大さじ4
  - 塩 ……… 少々
- 卵 ……… 2個
  - 砂糖 ……… 小さじ2
  - C 塩 ……… 少々
  - 水どきかたくり粉 … 小さじ2
- 油 ……… 少々
- エビ ……… 8尾
- ウナギのかば焼 ……… 1串
- きぬさや ……… 16枚
- 焼きのり ……… 2枚
- イクラ ……… 適量
- おぼろ ……… 適量

飯台は水でぬらし、かたくしぼったふきんでふいておく。

つくり方

1 米はふだんより少なめの水で、ややかために炊く。小さな容器に合わせ酢の材料を入れ、よくまぜておく。

2 炊き上がったごはんを飯台にあけ、合わせ酢をしゃもじに伝わらせてまわしかける。手早くまぜ、うちわであおいで冷ます。

3 前日にもどしておいた干ししいたけの石づきをとって、Aの煮汁で、汁の量が1/4になるまで煮る。

4 3が冷めたら、ざるにあけて汁気を切る。1枚は飾り用に1/4に切っておく。残りは千切りにして、2の酢めしにまぜる。

5 れんこんは皮をむき、厚さ3mmのいちょう切りにし、熱湯でサッとゆで、熱いうちにBの甘酢に漬ける。

6 ボウルに卵をときほぐし、Cを加えてよくかきまぜる。油をひいた卵焼き器にうすく流して焼く。できたうす焼き卵を折りかさね、千切りにして錦糸卵をつくる。

7 エビは頭を取り、背わたをぬいて、塩ゆでする。氷水で冷やし、からをむく。

8 ウナギのかば焼は電子レンジであたため、串をぬいて3cm幅に切る。きぬさやはすじを取ってサッと塩ゆでにし、冷水にとる。水気を切って、半分に切る。焼きのりは手でもんでおく。

9 器に酢めしを盛りつけ、のりを全体にちらす。その上におぼろ、錦糸卵、甘酢に漬けたれんこんをちらし、きぬさや、しいたけ、エビ、ウナギ、イクラをいろどりよく盛りつける。

---

01 Local food of Okayama
Bara-zushi (Sushi topped with a variety of colorful ingredients and dished up in a bowl)
/It is called as "Festival sushi" in Okayama Pref. It is decorated beautifully with seafood and vegetables.

02 Ingredients for 4 servings
- rice : 3 rice cups (540mL)

[blended vinegar for rice]
- rice vinegar : 60mL
- sugar : 25g　• salt : 5g
- dried shiitake mushroom : 6

[simmering broth for shiitake]
- dashi : 3 cups　• sugar : 5 tbsps
- A mirin : 4 tbsps　• salt : 1/2 tsp
- light soy sauce : 3 tbsps

- lotus root : 1/2 node

[sweetened vinegar for lotus root]
- B dashi : 6 tbsps　• rice vinegar : 6 tbsps
- sugar : 4 tbsps　• salt : a small amount
- egg : 2

[seasoning for egg]
- C sugar : 2 tsps　• salt : a small amount
- starch with water : 2 tsps

How to make

1. Cook rice with less water than the usual amount. Mix ingredients of blended vinegar for rice. /2. Put cooked rice into a wooden container; pour the blended vinegar by using a rice scoop. Mix quickly and cool the rice by waving a fan. /3. Soak dried shiitake mushrooms into water on the previous day and rehydrate them. Simmer with broth (A) until liquid is reduced to one-fourth. Let it cool down. /4. Drain liquid of shiitakes through a colander. Cut 1 shiitake into quarters like a fan shape. Cut remaining 5 shiitakes into thin slices, then mix with the rice. /5. Peel off skin of the lotus root and slice into 3mm thickness. Cut each slices into quarters like a fan. Parboil and pickle into vinegared sauce (B) while it is still hot. /6. Beat eggs in the bowl, add (C) and mix well. Put oil in the pan, make paper-thin omelets and cut into strips. /7. Remove the head and sand vein of the shrimp, and boil in salted water. Put into iced water and peel off the shell. /8. Warm up grilled eel in the microwave and remove the stick, cut into 3cm width. Remove fiber string of snow peas and boil in salted water, then soak into iced water. Wipe off water and cut into halves. Tear nori into small pieces. /9. Dish up rice and top with nori. Decorate beautifully with sakura-denbu, thin strips of egg, vinegared lotus root, snow peas, shiitake, shrimp, eel and salmon roe.

- oil : a little amount
- shrimp : 8
- grilled eel : 1 stick
- snow peas : 16
- nori (toasted laver) : 2 sheets
- salmon roe to taste
- sakura-denbu (mashed and seasoned fish colored pink) to taste

長崎県の郷土料理 01

ぶたの角煮

卓袱料理には欠かせない一品です。
じっくりと火を通して、
おはしがスッと入るぐらい
やわらかく煮ましょう。

01 Local food of Nagasaki　**Simmered pork cubes**
02 Ingredients for 4 servings
- pork ribs block : 800g

[pre-seasoning sauce]
A
- soy sauce : 4 tbsps
- sake : 4 tbsps
- oil : adequate amount

[simmering broth]
B
- dashi : 8 cups
- soy sauce : 5 tbsps
- sake : 3 tbsps
- sugar : 4 tbsps
- Welsh onion : 10cm × 2
- thin slices of ginger with skin : 1 thumb-size
- string beans to taste
- Japanese mustard to taste

パート2 つくろう！食べよう！

【材料 4人分】

ぶたばら肉（ブロック肉）		800g
A	しょうゆ	大さじ4
	酒	大さじ4
油		適量

＜煮汁＞

B	だし	8カップ
	しょうゆ	大さじ5
	酒	大さじ3
	砂糖	大さじ4
	長ねぎ	10cm×2
	しょうがのうす切り（皮つき）	1かけ分
さやいんげん		適量
ときがらし		少々

つくり方

1 ぶた肉はなべに入る大きさに切り、Aのしょうゆ、酒をもみこんで下味をつける。

2 フライパンに油大さじ1を熱し、1のぶた肉を入れて表面を焼きつける。

3 肉からでた脂はボウルなどにあける。ペーパータオルでふきとってもよい。このひと手間が、おいしい角煮をつくるコツ！

4 肉に写真のように焼き色がついたら、なべにうつしてBの材料を加える。

5 4のなべを強火で煮立てる。煮立ったら弱火にし、厚手のキッチンペーパーでふたをして約1時間煮る。

6 さやいんげんはすじを取り、塩を入れた熱湯でサッとゆでて、氷水にとる。ざるに上げて水気を切り、半分の長さに切っておく。

7 5の肉を厚めに切って器に盛りつけ、煮汁をかける。6のさやいんげんと、好みでときがらしをそえる。

ばら肉とは

ばら肉は、牛肉、ぶた肉などの肉の部位で、あばら骨の周囲の肉をさします。写真のように、赤身と脂身が交互に3層になっているので、三枚肉ともよばれます。全体として肉質がやわらかく、角煮に適しているのです。

How to make
1. Cut pork into good size to simmer in the pot. Season with (Ⓐ) and rub by the hand. /2. Heat a frying pan and oil, sear the pork and brown the surface. /3. Remove excess oil. This is the tip to make good simmered pork. /4. Put simmering broth (Ⓑ) and the pork into the pot. /5. Cook over strong fire and bring to boiling. Turn down the fire to low, put a paper lid and simmer for 1 hour. /6. Remove fiber of string beans and parboil in salted water. Soak into iced water and drain. Cut into halves. /7. Cut the pork into big cubes, dish up and pour thickened simmering sauce. Top with string beans and Japanese mustard to taste.

Ribs /Ribs are a section of pork or beef around rib bones. Red meat and fat meat are piled up in three layers so it is also called "three layers meat." Ribs have a soft texture and are good for simmered pork.

はみだし 英訳

P51

06 Zunda mochi, rice cake covered with sweetened mashed green soybeans /Plenty of rice is produced in Sendai plains. Delicious mochi(rice cake) is also produced here. Zunda mochi, rice cake covered with sweetened mashed green soybeans, is a local specialty. The best season of edamame (green soybeans) is summer. Zunda mochi used to be made as offered food for Bon festival. Fresh green soybean paste has lighter taste than red bean paste, so it is easy to eat in summer when people lose appetite. It is said that the word "zunda" came from "zuda," which meant mashing beans. The following is another episode; the lord Masamune Date ate green soybeans smashed by the sword in the camp, it can be expressed in the word "Jin tachi" and this word corrupted into zunda.

P55

05 Salted and aged salmon in Murakami region / Salmons travel rivers upstream in Niigata and people have eaten salmons as valuable nutrient sources. Many salmon recipes have been handed down: rolled kelp with salmon, simmered dishes and so on. When they had a big catch of salmons, they made salted and aged salmon as the preservative food. Remove guts of salmon and pickle whole salmon in the salt, then expose to cold wind to accelerate aging. Murakami City in the north of Niigata is famous for salted and aged salmon. Characteristic of salted salmon in Murakami is that some part of the salmon belly is kept. Because Murakami used to be a castle town, cutting and removing all the belly part, which resembles a suicide of samurai, has been avoided. Salted salmon is a food served at the New Year or festive occasions. **06** Salted and aged salmon in Murakami region.

P63

06 Blowfish sashimi /Blowfish sashimi is a specialty of Shimonoseki region. As blowfish can be sliced very thin, the pattern of the plate can be seen through. This is because flesh of blowfish is hard and elastic. Shimonoseki has a landing port of blowfish, so not only expensive Torafugu blowfish but also Mafugu and Shimafugu blowfish which are not so expensive are available. People in Shimonoseki often eat blowfish because it is not so expensive in this area.
07 A typical way to eat blowfish sashimi is dipping into ponzu with chopped scallion, grated daikon and red chili.

P65

13 Nara⑥ and Wakayama Pref.⑦ /Sushi wrapped with persimmon leaves : One-bite sized vinegared sushi topped with mackerel or salmon fillet, wrapped with persimmon leaves and pressed. It is said that in the middle of the Edo period fishermen in Kishu, which is the old name of Wakayama, started selling salted mackerel at the villages along Yoshino River. It is the delicacy of summer festivals in this region. **14** Osaka Pref.⑧ /Battera: Cut mackerel into three fillets and pickle in vinegar. Top sushi with vinegared mackerel and thin semi-transparent kelp slice, then put a weight. Konoshiro, gizzard shad fish caught in Osaka Bay was often used for this pressed sushi. In the Meiji period the shape of this sushi resembles the boat, which is "Battera" in Portuguese. This is the origin of the name. Afterwards mackerels began to be used instead of konoshiro fish. **15** Okayama Pref.⑨ /Bara-zushi: Okayama faces Seto Inland Sea and uses a lot of fresh fishes for its food. Bara-zushi is one of the local foods appeared in the Edo period. The lord promulgated the law of simplicity and frugality that meal should be "one soup and one dish." So people mixed varieties of ingredients inside the rice so that the meal did not look extravagant. Nowadays ingredients are decorated on the top of the rice. **16** Bamboo leaves and persimmon leaves /Bamboo leaves and persimmon leaves are used for sushi. This is because they prevent food from decay. People in the old days learned from experience and inherited this knowledge as wisdom for everyday life.

P67

08 Mikan citrus from Ehime /Ehime Pref. is the top producer of mikan citrus. It is eaten as fresh fruit, processed to juice and used in local foods. One example is dried zest powder used in Fukumen dish. Mikan zest has been used as medicinal plant because it suppresses a cough or regulates stomachic activities. In addition to these medicinal effects, it is also used for cooking for its good smell. **09** Mikan changes to orange color at terraced fields which face the sea.

P69

11 Nagasaki champon noodles /Nagasaki champon is a well-known noodle dish throughout Japan. It is said that it originates from a Chinese restaurant where the chef served nutritious and cheap Chinese-style noodles for Chinese students studying in Japan.

懐石料理を知ろう
What is "Kaiseki cuisine"?

和食とおもてなし
Washoku and Japanese hospitality

懐石料理を知ろう
和食とおもてなし

パート1　知ろう！　調べよう！

懐石料理とは

懐石料理というと、どういう料理を思いうかべるでしょうか。
懐石料理は、日本の伝統的食文化のひとつの形です。

● 懐石料理と会席料理 ●

下の写真は、和食の料理屋さんでだされるコース料理の例です。さしみや煮物、焼き物など、たくさんの品数の料理がならんでいますね。それぞれの料理は、旬の食材をつかい、和食の基本である「五法・五色」＊を用いて調理され、美しく盛りつけられています。この写真では、すべての料理が一堂に集められていますが、実際は、料理は一品ずつ順に給仕されます。

このような和食のコース料理をさして、懐石料理とよぶこともあれば、会席料理とよぶこともあります。一般に、もてなしの中心がお茶を飲むことにある場合は懐石料理とよび、もてなしの中心が酒を飲むことにある場合は会席料理とよぶことが多いようです。

また、「京懐石」ということばがあることから、懐石料理というのは、京都の料亭の、日本庭園に面した座敷でいただく上品な料理のことだと思っている人もいるかもしれませんね。

一方、「松花堂弁当」といって、十字の仕切りがある箱形の器に何品かの料理が美しく盛りこまれている弁当形式の和食があります。これは、懐石料理や会席料理を手軽に食べられるようにしたものといえるでしょう。

＊五法は、基本的な和食の調理法である「生・焼く・煮る・蒸す・揚げる」のこと。五色は、「青（緑）、黄、赤、白、黒（紫）」のこと。くわしくは、第1章を参照。

たくさんの料理がならぶ和食のコース料理。

ちらしずし、さしみ、煮物などをつめた松花堂弁当。

---

01 What is "Kaiseki cuisine"? **02** 2 types of Kaiseki cuisine /Kaiseki cuisine is one of the styles of traditional Japanese cuisine. There are 2 types of Kaiseki cuisine written as 懐石料理 and 会席料理. 懐石料理 is a meal for tea ceremony, and 会席料理 is a meal for a banquet to enjoy sake. **04** is an example of the traditional Japanese course meal with sashimi, simmered dish, grilled dish and so on. Each dish is made with seasonal ingredients and cooked with Japanese fundamental cooking "5 Methods and 5 Colors," and dished up beautifully. Each dish is served one by one in a determined order. "Shokado Bento" is a bento-style meal box. This is the simplified way of eating Kaiseki cuisine. **03** *5 Methods: fundamental cooking methods: raw, grilled, simmered, steamed and deep-fried. 5 Colors: green, yellow, red, white and black. **04** Washoku course meal with many dishes. **05** Shokado meal box with chirashi-zushi, sashimi and simmered food. **06** Tea ceremony room. **07** Original Kaiseki cuisine for tea ceremony /Kaiseki cuisine is

お茶を味わうためにつくられたこぢんまりした和室を、茶室という。06

●本来の懐石料理● 07

懐石料理というのは、もともとは、茶の湯（→98ページ）の席に招いたお客さまに、お茶を飲む前に食べていただく質素な料理のことです。おなかをすかせたままではお茶をおいしく味わえないため、お茶を飲むのにさしつかえのない程度の食事を準備するのです。質素な料理といっても、旬のおいしい食材を選び、素材のもち味を引き立たせるように工夫してつくられます。つまり、懐石料理は、食べる人のことを思いやる、おもてなしの心がつまった料理なのです。

茶の湯の席での食事が「懐石」とよばれるようになったのは、つぎのような話に由来するといわれています。

昔、きびしい修行をしていた禅宗＊のお坊さんが、懐にあたためた石を入れて、空腹や寒さをしのぎました。「懐石」は、「懐に石をだく」という意味です。そこから、「懐石」ということばは、「空腹を満たし、体をあたためる質素な食べ物」を意味するようになったのです。

この本来の懐石料理（茶懐石）は、一般的には、ごはん・汁・向付→煮物わん→焼き物→預け鉢の順でだされます。つぎのページから、それぞれの料理についてくわしく見ていきましょう。

＊禅宗とは仏教の一派で、座禅を重んじることに特徴がある。08

ここでいう「お茶」というのは、こまかい粉末になっている抹茶のこと。湯をそそいで、茶せんであわ立てたり練ったりして飲む。09

originally served the guests of tea ceremony before serving Matcha tea. Guests can not enjoy Matcha tea with hunger, so the meal is served beforehand. It is a simple and humble meal, but seasonal ingredients are used and cooked in a way to make the most of their tastes. The host shows hospitality to the guests through this meal. In the old days, one monk of Zen sect who was training very hard kept heated stone in his bosom (懐石) to get over the cold and the hunger. The meaning was transformed into "humble meal to give relief from the hunger and warm the body." Basic Kaiseki cuisine for tea ceremony has an order to serve dishes. Typical order is rice, soup and Mukozuke (sashimi) → simmered food bowl → grilled dish → Azukebachi (simmered dish). 08 ＊One of the Buddhism sects which gives importance on Zen meditation. 09 Tea used for tea ceremony is the powdered Matcha tea. Pour hot water and mix with a whisk.

懐石料理の基本は一汁三菜

一汁三菜とは、ごはんに汁物1品と3品の菜(おかず)を組みあわせた食事のこと。懐石料理の基本は一汁三菜にあります。

● 懐石料理の形式 ● 02

懐石料理は、まず、折敷とよばれるお膳を、亭主(茶の湯の主催者のこと)みずから運び入れ、お客さまに手渡すことから始まります。折敷には、なにがのっているでしょうか。

折敷 03
脚のついていない、漆塗りのお膳。

めしわん 04
ふたつきの漆塗りのおわん。客側から見て、折敷の手前左に置かれる。

---

01 **The basics of Kaiseki cuisine is "1 Soup and 3 Dishes"** /"1 Soup and 3 Dishes" is a meal with rice,1 soup and 3 side dishes. This is the basics of Kaiseki cuisine.
02 **The form of Kaiseki cuisine** /Kaiseki cuisine starts with bringing and handing down the food tray (Oshiki tray) by the host to the guest. What are served on the tray?
03 **Oshiki tray** /Lacquered tray with no legs. 04 **Rice bowl** /Lacquered bowl with a lid. Placed on the left side on the tray. 05 **Mukozuke** /Ceramic plate. "Muko" means over there or opposite side. Mukozuke dish is placed back over rice and soup, so it is called "Mukozuke." 06 **Soup bowl** /Lacquered bowl with a lid. Placed on the right side on the tray. 07 **Rikyu chopsticks** /Cedar chopsticks with both edges tapered. Put the right ends of the chopsticks on the right edge of the tray instead of using a chopstick-rest.

パート1　知ろう！　調べよう！

●ごはん ●08

　和食の基本形式は一汁三菜ですが、ごはんが数に入っていませんね。それは、和食にはごはんはかならずついてくるものなので、かぞえる必要がないからです。懐石料理においても、ごはんが重要な位置をしめていることにかわりはありません。

　折敷の上のめしわんには、炊きたてのまだよく蒸れていないごはんがよそわれます。このごはんには、「お客さまのために炊いたごはんが、いま炊き上がりました。まず、一口どうぞ」という、おもてなしの心がこめられているのです。懐石料理はおなかをいっぱいにするのが目的ではないので、ごはんは、二口から三口ぐらいで食べきれる量が盛りつけられます。

　食事が進んでいくなかで、おかわり用のごはんの入ったおひつがでてきます。このおひつには、最初のごはんとはちがい、よく蒸れたごはんが盛りこまれます。

ごはんの盛りつけ方は、小さな丸型（上）や横一文字型（下）など、茶の湯の流派によりちがう。09

おかわり用のごはんを入れる、漆塗りのおひつ。10

> **向付** 05
> 陶磁器がつかわれる。客側から見て、めしわんと汁わんの向こうに置かれるので、向付という。

> **汁わん** 06
> ふたつきの漆塗りのおわん。客側から見て、折敷の手前右に置かれる。

> **利休ばし** 07
> 両端が細い杉のおはし。はし置きは用いず、折敷の右ふちにのせかけてある。

08 Rice /Basic form of Washoku is "1 Soup and 3 Dishes," however, rice is not included in the number. Because rice is essential for Washoku and served at every meal, so it does not need to be included.
Rice serving on the tray is dished up just after it is cooked and not well-steamed. The host shows the spirit of hospitality with this freshly-cooked rice for the guests. The purpose of Kaiseki cuisine is not to eat full, so rice is dished up in an amount to eat in 2 or 3 bites. As the meal goes on, rice refill in a wooden lacquered container is served. This rice is well-steamed comparing to the rice served at the beginning of the meal.
09 The way how to dish up rice differs depending on the school of the tea ceremony. Usually rice is dished up in a shape of a small ball or rectangular rounds.
10 Wooden lacquered rice container for refilling.

一汁三菜の一汁

折敷で最初にだされる汁は、みそ仕立ての汁です。冬場は白みそ仕立て、夏場は赤みそ仕立て、そのあいだの季節は合わせみそ仕立てにするなど、季節にあわせてつくります。汁の具には、季節の野菜やきのこ、とうふなどがつかわれます。

汁の量は、ごはんにあわせて、二口から三口で飲みきれる量にします。でき上がったばかりのアツアツの汁をだすのが、お客さまへのおもてなしになります。

春の汁（例）

合わせみそ仕立て。具は、たけのこと菜の花。

夏の汁（例）

赤みそ仕立て。具は、白ずいき*とオクラ。

秋の汁（例）

合わせみそ仕立て。具は、栗としめじ。

冬の汁（例）

白みそ仕立て。具は、揚げどうふとせり。

*ずいきは、さといもの葉へいのことで、いもがらともよばれる。皮をむき、ゆでてから酢水にさらしてアクをぬいてつかう。

---

01 Soup of "1 Soup and 3 Dishes" /Soup served on a tray is miso soup. Miso soup has varieties according to the season. Miso soup in winter is made from white miso; in summer it is made from red miso; in spring and autumn it is made from white and red mixed miso. Seasonal vegetables, mushrooms and tofu are used for the soup. The quantity of soup should be consumed in 2 or 3 sips. Freshly cooked hot soup should be served. **02 Spring soup** /e.g. White and red mixed miso soup with bamboo shoot and rape blossom. **03 Summer soup** /e.g. Red miso soup with the stem of Japanese taro and okura. / *Stem of Japanese taro is called Zuiki in Japanese. Peel off the skin of the stem and boil. Soak it into vinegared water to remove harshness. **04 Autumn soup** /e.g. White and red mixed miso soup with chestnut and shimeji mushroom. **05 Winter soup** /e.g. White miso soup with deep-fried tofu and water dropwort. **06 What is Mukozuke?** /Mukozuke is the first dish of 1 Soup and 3 Dishes. Trays, rice bowls and soup

タイのこぶじめの向付。09

向付とは 06

　向付は、一汁三菜の1菜めにあたる料理です。折敷、めしわん、汁わんが塗物であるのに対して、向付には、さまざまな形やもようの焼物がつかわれます。

　料理は、おもにさしみやなますです。なますというのは、魚介類や野菜を細く切ったものを、酢を基本にした調味料であえた料理のことです。正月のおせちに入っている「紅白なます」もそのひとつ。上の写真の向付には、魚介類のなますである「タイのこぶじめ」が盛られています。

扇を開いた形の器。07

タイのこぶじめをつくる 10

　こんぶは、酢をしめらせたふきんでふきます。さしみ用のタイの切り身を細切りにして、こんぶの上に置きます。その上にまたこんぶをかさねて、ラップでピッチリと包みます。冷蔵庫で5時間ほど置けば、食べごろになります。

　冷蔵庫から取りだして、こんぶをはずし、器にこんもりと盛りつけます。そして、酢、しょうゆ、だしと少量のみりんをあわせた酢じょうゆを、器の底にそっとそそぎ入れます。

　こぶじめは、魚の身が引きしまるうえに、こんぶのうま味が加わって、さしみとはまたちがう味わいになります。

おせち用の紅白なます。08

bowls are lacquered but Mukozuke plates are ceramics. Sashimi or Namasu are served as Mukozuke. Namasu is vinegared and thinly cut seafood or vegetables. 09 is one example of Namasu dish as Mukozuke. It is called "Kobujime" in Japanese. 07 Fan-shaped plate. 08 Red and white colored Namasu for the New Year. 09 Mukozuke dish of sea bream seasoned with kelp and vinegar. 10 How to make sea bream Kobujime? /Wipe the kelp with a kitchen cloth moistened with vinegar. Cut sea bream thinly and put it on the kelp. Cover it with kelp and wrap tightly with cling film, then rest in a fridge for about 5 hours until it becomes good for eating. Put out from the fridge, remove kelp, and dish it up in a round shape. Pour sauce made from vinegar, soy sauce, dashi and a little amount of mirin. By wrapping with kelp, the flesh of the fish nicely hardened and umami of the kelp is added. It tastes different with sashimi.

煮物わんから焼き物へ

煮物わんは一汁三菜の2菜め、焼き物は3菜めにあたります。それぞれの特徴を見ていきましょう。

● 煮物わんは、懐石のメイン料理 ●

懐石の煮物わんというのは、ふつうの煮物でも汁物でもありません。おわんに具と汁がたっぷり入った料理で、懐石のなかのいちばんのごちそうです。おわんも、めしわんや汁わんよりひとまわり大きめの、はなやかなものが選ばれます。

煮物わんの汁は基本的にすまし汁で、一番だし*に塩、うすくちしょうゆで味つけします。この汁のことを吸地といいます。

煮物わんの具には、おもに魚や貝、とり肉、しんじょう、ごまどうふなどがつかわれます。

料理に香りをそえ、季節感をだすために、吸口として、木の芽やゆずがよくつかわれます。なぜ吸口とよぶかというと、木の芽やゆずは、おわんの汁を吸い上げる口元近くにおはしでおさえて、汁を吸うからです。

*こんぶとかつお節でとる上品な味のだし。くわしくは14ページ参照。

ごまどうふの煮物わん。吸口として、松葉ゆず（→97ページ）がつかわれている。

「しんじょう」とは

「しんじょう」というのは、エビやカニ、白身魚、とり肉などのすり身に、すりおろした山いもを入れ、味をつけて形づくり、蒸したりゆでたりしたもののことです。山いもをつなぎとしてつかうのが、しんじょうの特徴です。カニをつかったものをカニしんじょう、エビをつかったものをエビしんじょうなどとよびます。おでんなどに入っている「はんぺん」も、しんじょうのひとつです。

ふわっとしたやさしい口あたりのしんじょうは、わさびじょうゆでさしみのように食べたり、吸物やわん物の具にしたりします。

エビしんじょうの吸物。吸口として、木の芽がつかわれている。

はんぺん

04 05 06 の英訳は ➡ P114

---

01 Simmered food bowl and Grilled dish /Nimonowan (simmered food bowl) is the second dish of the "1 Soup and 3 Dishes" and grilled dish is the third. **02 Simmered food bowl is the main dish of Kaiseki cuisine** /Simmered food bowl is to include clear soup and simmered or steamed food that are dished up in a same soup bowl. The bowl, larger and more decorative than rice bowl or soup bowl, is used. Basically the soup is clear and the first soup stock is seasoned with salt and light soy sauce. Fish, shellfish, chicken, shinjo (simmered or steamed fish or meat paste), goma-dofu (sesame paste and starch chilled like tofu) are used as main ingredients. Kinome (sansho leaf) or Yuzu zest are used as the topping to add flavor which reflect the seasons. *First soup stock is the dashi made with kelp and dried bonito, and tastes elegant. **03** Simmered bowl of goma-dofu (sesame paste and starch chilled like tofu). Topped with pine needle shaped Yuzu citrus. **07 Grilled dish** /Simmered food bowl is served individually but grilled dish is

パート1　知ろう！調べよう！

●焼き物　07

　煮物わんがひとり分ずつ器に盛られるのに対し、焼き物は大きめの鉢に人数分が盛られます。亭主から鉢を受け取った客は順に、自分の食べる分を取りばしで取っていきます。このとき、受け皿として、向付の器か煮物わんのふたがつかわれます。

　焼き物には、おもに旬の魚がつかわれ、焼き方もいろいろ工夫されます。一般的な塩焼やつけ焼のほかに、みそ漬け焼や幽庵焼（→108ページ）などがあります。焼き物のひと切れひと切れは、取り皿となる向付の器にむりなく入る大きさでつくられます。また、会の目的や季節に応じて、野菜を焼いたもの、肉をつかったもの、揚げ物などが用いられることもあります。

取りわけやすいよう、ひとり分がはっきりわかるように盛りつけられている。09

盛りつけがくずれないように取る気づかいがたいせつ。10

手つきの器はぶら下げてもっていいの？ 08

　手つきの器というのは、下の写真や108ページのような器のことです。もち手は、器をもつためにつけてあるというより、器のデザインのひとつであることが多いのです。ものによっては取れてしまう場合があるので、ぶら下げてもってはいけません。両手で器の底をしっかりもつようにします。

両手でつぎの人に渡す。11

served on a big plate for the amount of people. The guest who receives the plate from the host dishes out the food for one person. Mukozuke plate or the lid of simmered food bowl is used as the each serving plate. Seasonal fish is the main ingredient of grilled dish. There are many ways to grill fish. Typical way is to grill with salt or to grill after dipping into soy sauce. Dipping into miso or Yuan sauce are well-known grilling ways. Yuan sauce is made with soy sauce, sake, mirin and Yuzu. Each piece of the fish is cut into good size to dish up on a Mukozuke plate. Vegetables, meat or deep-fried foods as well as fish are served as grilled dish. It depends on the season or the purpose of the party. 08 How to hold grip tableware /In many cases, grips are fitted up as the design and not as the functional grips. Hold the bottom of the tableware by both hands. 09 Individual servings are dished up on a big plate. 10 Use serving chopsticks and be aware not to break down food when dishing out. 11 Pass the plate by both hands to the next guest.

預け鉢とは

懐石の基本である一汁三菜のあと、もう1品だす料理を預け鉢といいます。進め鉢、強肴とよぶこともあります。

●炊き合わせ●

預け鉢とよぶのは、焼き物と同じように、料理を盛りこんだ鉢を客に預け、順に取りわけてもらうからです。預け鉢の料理は、とくにきまりはありませんが、炊き合わせや酢の物、おひたしがよく用いられます。

炊き合わせというのは、複数の食材をべつべつのなべでうす味で煮て、ひとつの器に盛りあわせた料理のことです。家庭でよくつくる煮物とのちがいは、このべつべつに煮る点です。複数の食材をべつべつに煮ることで、それぞれのもち味や色を生かして仕上げることができるのです。炊き合わせの食材として、かぶ・さといも・れんこん・たけのこ・しいたけなどの野菜や、エビ・アナゴなどの魚介類、とり肉、しんじょう、高野どうふなどがよくつかわれます。

おひたしとは

おひたしは、おもに葉もの野菜をサッとゆでて、よく水気をしぼり、だしにひたして味をつけた料理のことです。ほうれんそう、小松菜、菜の花、春菊などが代表的な材料です。だしにひたさず、しょうゆをかけるだけの場合もあります。

材料をゆでずに、油で揚げてだしにひたす「揚げびたし」や、だしで煮て味をふくませる「煮びたし」などもあります。

きれいな色に仕上がっている、なすの揚げびたし。

04 05の英訳は ➡ P114

01 **What is "Azukebachi"?** /Azukebachi is additional dish which is served after basic Kaiseki cuisine "1 Soup and 3 Dishes." 02 **Takiawase (simmered food cooked separately and dished up together)** /Azukebachi is served on a big plate as well as the grilled dish. Guests receive the plate from the host and dish out the food to each serving plate. Simmered food, vinegared food or boiled vegetables are served as Azukebachi. Takiawase is the simmered food cooked separately with light taste and dished up together. The different point with home-cooked dishes is that the different ingredients are simmered separately. By simmering each ingredient in a different way, original tastes and colors of them can be drawn out. Turnip, Japanese taro, lotus root, bamboo shoot, shiitake mushroom, shrimp, conger eel, chicken, shinjo and freeze-dried tofu are popular ingredients used for Takiawase dish. 03 Eggplant, pumpkin, chicken meat ball and kidney bean are simmered separately. Purple of eggplant, yellow of pumpkin, green

パート1　知ろう！調べよう！

懐石料理でつかうおはし 06

おはしには、個人が食べるためにつかう「食ばし」と、各自が取りわけるためにつかう「取りばし」があります。

杉の食ばし 07

杉の両細のおはしです。中央がふくらみ、両端が細くなっています。長さは約26cm。杉のはしは、特有の香りがあり、古くからつかわれてきました。

利休ばし　Rikyu chopsticks

竹の取りばし 08

竹のおはしは、じょうぶで、しなりがあり、こまかいものを取りやすいという特徴があります。青竹のものと白竹のものがあります。節の位置によって、中節、元節などとよばれます。これらは、焼き物や預け鉢などの取りばしとしてつかわれますが、懐石の流派によりつかいわけられています。

青竹両細　green bamboo, both tapered edges

青竹中節　green bamboo, nakabushi (a joint in the middle)

青竹元節　green bamboo, motobushi (a joint at the edge)

青竹の取りばし
Green bamboo chopsticks for serving

なす・かぼちゃ・とり肉のつくね・いんげんの炊き合わせ。なすの紫、かぼちゃの黄色、いんげんの緑、つくねの白と、色がきれいにでている。03

なぜ、両細なの？ 09

利休ばしの両端が細くなっているのは、片方を神がつかい、もう片方を人がつかうとされているからです。神と人とが同じおはしをつかい、食事を共にすることで、福を招き、災いを打ちはらうという願いがこめられているのです。そのため、両細のおはしは、祭りや祝いなど特別な日につかわれます。正月につかう柳の木の祝いばしは、その代表的な例です。柳の木がつかわれるのは、春になるとまっ先に芽吹く縁起のよい木であると同時に、じょうぶで折れにくいからです。

正月の祝いばし 10

09 10の英訳は ➡ P114

---

of kidney bean and white of chicken are beautifully kept. 06 Chopsticks for Kaiseki cuisine /There are 2 types of chopsticks. One is chopsticks for each person to eat and the other is chopsticks used to move food from a big serving plate to one's own. 07 Cedar chopsticks for eating /Both edges are tapered, and about 26cm length. Cedar chopsticks have the specific scent and have been used since a long time ago. 08 Bamboo chopsticks for serving /Bamboo chopsticks have some characteristics; they last long and are supple and easy to take small foods. There are 2 colors of the bamboo, green bamboo and white bamboo. It is named Nakabushi (a joint in the middle) chopsticks or Motobushi (a joint at the edge) chopsticks according to the position of joints. These chopsticks are used for the grilled dish or Azukebachi dish and used properly by each school of tea ceremony.

八寸とは [01]

八寸とは、八寸（約24cm）四方の杉のへぎ盆のこと。
転じて、この器に盛る料理のこともさすようになりました。

● 八寸は酒の肴 ● [02]

懐石料理では、ひと通り料理をだしおわったあと、亭主は客と同席して酒を飲みかわすことができます。このとき、酒の肴となるのが、八寸です。肴は、ごはんの菜（おかず）ではなく、酒を飲むときの菜（酒菜）という意味です。

八寸には、海のもの（動物性のもの）と山のもの（植物性のもの）を1品ずつ、客の人数分に亭主の分をあわせて盛りあわせます。盛りあわせる2品は、色・形や味が同じようなものにならないように選ばれます。盛りつけ方は懐石の流派によってちがい、右上に海のもの、左下に山のものを盛る流派と、その逆の流派があります。海のものは、生のものよりもくん製や南蛮漬けのようなものがよく用いられます。

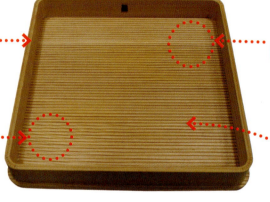

へぎ盆 [03]
へぎ盆とは、杉の木地をうすくけずってつくる、白木の盆のこと。

海のもの [05]
（例）かずのこ

山のもの [04]
（例）こごみ

木目を横にして置く。[06]

へぎ盆は神さまへのおそなえ物を盛る器 [07]

へぎ盆をはじめて知った人もいるかもしれませんが、じつはよく目にするものでもあるのです。たとえば、神社で神さまにそなえものをするときの台がそうです。また、お月見だんごを盛ったり、お正月の鏡もちをのせたりする台を三方といいますが、このだんごや鏡もちをのせる部分が、まさにへぎ盆なのです。

わたしたち日本人は、収穫の喜びと感謝の気持ちをこめて、神さまに鏡もちをおそなえします。おそなえ物を下げていっしょに煮たものが、雑煮の始まりだといわれています。昔から日本人は、神さまと同じものを食べることを大事にしてきたのです。

だんごや鏡もちを盛る台を三方という。

---

01 What is "Hassun"? /Hassun is 24cm square cedar "Hegi" tray and foods dished up on this tray is also called by the same name. Originally Hassun means "8 suns." "Sun" is a Japanese measurement unit and 8 suns is about 24cm.
02 Hassun is nibbles for sake /After tea ceremony dishes are served, the host drink sake with the guests. Foods served with sake are Hassun and they go well with sake. Nibbles for sake are called "Sakana" in Japanese. The word "Sakana" comes from "sake" combined with "na" which means food. Hassun is made with one mountain ingredient (vegetable) and one sea ingredient (animal), and they are dished up in the same number of dishes of the guests with the host. They are chosen carefully to have some different shapes and colors. The ways to dish up depend on tea ceremony schools; one school dishes up sea ingredients at the upper-right corner and mountain ingredients at the bottom-left corner, while the other school dishes up oppositely. Sea ingredients are often smoked or vinegared rather than

和食に欠かせない日本酒 08

稲作を中心に文化をはぐくんできた日本では、米は貴重な食べ物でした。その米からつくられる日本酒もまた、日本の食文化のなかで重要なものとされてきました。

酒づくりは、まず米を蒸すことから始まります。蒸し上がった米に麹と水をまぜて発酵させ、酒のもとになるもろみをつくります。それをしぼったものが酒です。米を発酵させるのに重要なはたらきをするのが酵母で、日本各地の酒蔵はそれぞれ昔から受けついできた酵母をつかって地域独特の酒をつくっているのです。

酒は、神さまに近づくための手段として古くから用いられてきました。地域の祭りでは、かならず神さまに酒がそなえられました。その後、神さまにそなえた酒（お神酒）をみんなで分けあって飲んだのです。こうした酒盛りでは、ひとつの杯を順にまわして飲みました。杯が全員にひとまわりすることを一献といい、一献飲むたびに肴を食べたのです。そのならわしが「献立」ということばを生んだといわれています。

日本酒の原料は米。地域ごとに酒づくりに適した米（酒米）がつかわれる。09

蒸した酒米を広げて、麹菌が繁殖しやすい温度まで冷ます作業。10

鈴木酒造店　長井蔵

神社に奉納された酒だる。11

08以降の英訳は ➡ P114

cooked raw.　03 Hegi tray /White wooden tray made by cedar.　04 Mountain ingredient /e.g. Kogomi (ostrich fern) 05 Sea ingredient /e.g. Herring roe　06 Put wood grain horizontally.　07 Wooden Hegi tray is a dish of offerings to the gods /Hegi tray is often seen at the shrines or other places. The tray dished up offering foods is one example. "Sampo" is a hegi tray-type stand to dish up Tsukimi-dangos (moon-viewing dumplings) or round rice cakes for the New Year. Japanese offer round rice cakes to the gods to show joy and appreciation of the good harvest. Zoni originates from using offering foods to the gods after they are removed from an altar. Japanese have cherished to eat same foods with the gods from ancient times.

和食の食事作法の基本

和食の食事作法といっても、むずかしいことではありません。
美しく食べるための作法は、ふだんの生活にも役に立ちます。

●おはしとおわん●

食事作法の基本は、つくる人・食べる人ともに、たがいのことを思いやる気持ちをもつことです。つくる人は、あたたかいものはあたたかいうちに、冷たいものは冷たいうちに食べてもらえるよう、調理の手順を工夫します。食べる人もつくり手の気持ちを無にしないよう、料理がもっともおいしい状態のときにいただくようにします。

では、おはしのあつかい方や、ごはんと汁のいただき方を、イラストで説明しましょう。おわんをもち上げるときは、両手をつかうことをわすれないようにしましょう。

おはしのあつかい方（和食の正式な作法）

1 2本のおはしを、右手で上からそっともち上げる。

2 左手を、下からささえるようにそえる。

3 右手を右はしへずらし、下側にまわしてもちかえる。

4 そえていた左手をはずす。

5 おはしをつかうときは、下のはしは動かさずに、上のはしだけを動かす。

6 食事がすんだら、おはしは、はし置きにはし先をかけて置く。

折敷の場合、食事がすんだら、折敷の手前におはしをそろえて置く。

---

01 Basic table manners of Washoku **02** Chopsticks and bowls /Essential point of table manners are to care for each other, both who cooks and who eats. Person who cooks serves a hot dish while it is hot and serves a cold dish while it is cold. Person who eats tastes dishes while foods are at the best timing. **03** How to use chopsticks /1. Hold up chopsticks with your right hand gently. /2. Place your left hand under chopsticks. /3. Move your right hand to the right side of chopsticks; put your right thumb on chopsticks and other fingers on the other side. /4. Remove your left hand /5. Move only upper chopstick and do not move lower one. /6. After finishing meal, put chopsticks on a chopstick rest. Or put chopsticks directly nearer side on a tray. **04** How to eat soup bowl dishes /1. Place left hand on the left side of the soup bowl and take off the lid with right hand. /2. Turn over the lid and put it to the right side of the bowl with your both hands. /3. Hold up bowl with your both hands. /4. Put your left thumb on the edge of

パート1　知ろう！調べよう！

おわんのあつかい方（和食の正式な作法） 04

1 左手でおわんをささえ、右手でふたを取る。

2 ふたはうら返して、おわんの右側に、左手をそえて置く。

3 両手でおわんをもち上げる。

4 左手の親指をおわんのふちにかけ、残りの4本の指はそろえて、底をささえる。

5 左ページの1のように、右手でおはしをもち上げ、はし先を左手の人さし指と中指のあいだにはさむ。

6 右手を右のほうへすべらせ、下にまわしてもちかえる。

7 はし先を左手からはずす。汁を飲むときは、おはしで具を軽くおさえる。

8 汁わんを下に置いて、めしわんをもち上げたいときは、まず、おはしをはし置きにもどす。

9 汁わんを両手でもって、下に置く。

10 両手でめしわんをもち上げる。このあと、おはしのあつかい方は5～6と同じ。

茶懐石の汁わんとめしわんのふたの置き方 05

茶懐石の作法では、汁わんとめしわんのふたは、両手で同時にあけることになっています。ふたつのふたはバラバラに置くと見苦しいので、めしわんのふたの上に汁わんのふたを、右のイラストのようにかさねて、折敷の右側に置くのです。

ふたをあけて
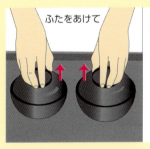

かさねて置く

the bowl and hold the bottom with other 4 fingers. /5. Hold up chopsticks with right hand in a same way with the left page, sandwich the tapered side of chopsticks with left forefinger and middle finger. /6. Move your right hand to the right side of chopsticks and put your right thumb on chopsticks and other fingers on the other side. /7. Remove your left hand from chopsticks. Put chopsticks inside the bowl and hold ingredients with the top of chopsticks to sip the soup. /8. Keep the soup bowl close to the table surface and put chopsticks on the rest. /9. Hold the bowl with your both hands and put on the table. /10. Hold up rice bowl with your both hands. Use chopsticks same as 5-6 directions. 05 How to put lids of soup bowl and rice bowl /In the table manners of Kaiseki cuisine of tea ceremony, it is correct to take both lids of soup and rice bowl at the same time. It does not look good to put two lids on the table separately, so put the lid of the soup bowl over the lid of the rice bowl at the right side of the tray.

料理の歴史について知ろう

日本の料理はどのように発展してきたでしょうか。
代表的な料理形式の流れを見ていきましょう。

大饗料理から精進料理

奈良時代・平安時代の貴族たちは、正月や祝い事のたびに宴会をもよおし、中国の様式をまねて料理をところせましとならべました。この儀式料理を「大饗料理」といいます。料理は生のものや干物などを切ってならべただけのものが多く、めいめいが酢や塩・醤*などで味をつけて食べていたといわれています。

鎌倉時代になると、中国の禅宗の寺院でおこなわれていた料理の技術や作法が日本に伝わり、「精進料理」がつくられるようになりました。「精進」というのは仏教の修行に励むことをいいます。動物性のものを食べないことも、修行のひとつでした。そのため、精進料理は、肉や魚を用いず、野菜を中心に、とうふやゆば、海藻などをつかい、油で揚げる料理も工夫されました。だしも、動物性の煮干しやかつお節はつかわず、こんぶや干ししいたけからとりました。

*穀類などを塩漬けにしたことから生まれた、しょうゆのルーツといわれるもの。

脚つきのお膳でだされる精進料理。

The history of Japanese food **Daikyo cuisine and Shojin cuisine** /Daikyo cuisine is a festive meal for aristocrats in the Nara and Heian periods. They hold banquets in every auspicious occasion and followed Chinese style to place many foods on the table. Most of the dishes were simple raw or dried food, and each guest made a taste with vinegar, salt, hishio and so on. The introduction of Chinese Zen sect cooking methods and manners in the Kamakura period has contributed to the development of Shojin cuisine. "Shojin" means practicing hard in Buddhism discipline. Shojin cuisine does not contain animal or fish, but use vegetables, tofu or yuba (tofu skin layers) and seaweeds. Dashi made from kelp or dried shiitake mushroom is adopted. Dried sardine or bonito were not used. **Shojin cuisine served on a legged table.** **Honzen cuisine** /Samurai in the Muromachi period had a luxurious life and Honzen cuisine was established as a ceremonial cuisine. Honzen cuisine is served at once on individual legged table.

本膳料理 04

室町時代になると、武家の生活がぜいたくになり、儀式のときの食事として「本膳料理」という料理形式ができました。本膳料理は、ひとり分の料理をいくつもの脚つきのお膳にのせて一度にだす「もてなし料理」です。基本は一汁三菜で、豪華になると、汁物が2つ、3つになったり、おかずが5つ、7つになったりします。これらは、二汁五菜、二汁七菜、三汁五菜などとよばれます。

本膳料理の様式例（二汁七菜）
One example of Honzen cuisine: 2 soups and 7 dishes

三の膳 Sannozen: The third tray　　本膳 Honzen: The first tray　　二の膳 Ninozen: The second tray

懐石料理・会席料理・卓袱料理 05

安土桃山時代には、茶の湯の発達にともなって「懐石料理」がつくられました。この料理の特徴は、皿の数を少なくして、一皿食べ終わるとつぎの料理をだすようにしたことです。数多くの料理を一度にだす形式の本膳料理は、すべての料理を前もってつくっておかなければならないため、冷えた料理が多かったのです。その点、懐石料理は一皿ずつだすため、あたたかいものはあたたかいうちに、冷たいものは冷たいうちに食べてもらうというおもてなしがたいせつにされました。

江戸時代に発展した料理屋では、本膳料理の膳の数を減らしてぜいたくさを省いた料理が、酒をともなう宴会の席の料理として用いられていきました。これが「会席料理」（「宴会の席」を略して「会席」）です。

いっぽう長崎では、オランダや中国の料理がそれまでの日本の料理と融合して「卓袱料理」が生まれました。これは、円卓をかこんで、取りばしなどつかわずめいめいのはしで料理を取って食べるおもてなし料理です。

現在の和食は、これらの料理の伝統を受けついだものなのです。

円卓をかこんで食べる卓袱料理。06

Basically it is 1 Soup and 3 Dishes, but a couple more bowls of soup are added and five or seven side dishes are added on more formal occasion. 05 2 types of Kaiseki cuisine and Shippoku cuisine /Kaiseki (懐石) cuisine was established in Azuchi-Momoyama period with the development of tea ceremony. The characteristic of Kaiseki cuisine is serving dishes one by one. Because all the dishes of Honzen cuisine have to be served at the same time, most of the dishes are cold. But Kaiseki cuisine values that the guests eat the hot dish while it is hot and eat the cold dish while it is cold. Restaurants in the Edo period served humbler meal than Honzen cuisine for banquets with enjoying sake. This is another Kaiseki (会席) for the cuisine with sake. Shippoku cuisine was established in Nagasaki. It is a mixture of Japanese, Dutch and Chinese cuisines. At the round table adorned with many large dishes, everybody helps his/herself to serve his/her own plates. These traditions have integrated into modern Washoku. 06 Shippoku cuisine.

季節感をたいせつにする和食

季節ごとの山の幸・海の幸が豊富な日本では、料理に旬の食材を取り入れます。食材の切り方や器のつかい方にも工夫が見られます。

● 季節の料理 ● 02

旬の食材を取り入れた料理は、それだけでごちそうになります。四季それぞれの代表的な料理を見てみましょう。

03 春　若竹煮　春が旬のたけのこと生ワカメを、だしとうすくちしょうゆで煮た料理。たけのこの香りと歯ざわり、ワカメのさわやかな緑色が、春らしい料理。

05 秋　まつたけの土びん蒸し　秋の味覚のまつたけ・白身魚・エビ・とり肉・みつば・ぎんなんなどの具とだしを土びんに入れて軽く蒸したもの。すだちの果汁を器にしぼり入れ、土びんから汁をそそいで吸物風に味わいながら、具も味わう。

04 夏　アユの塩焼　アユは初夏の川魚。塩焼にして、たで酢で食べる。たで酢というのは、たでという植物の葉をすりつぶして、酢とだしをまぜたもの。さわやかな香りがするので、アユの塩焼によくつかわれる。

06 冬　ふろふきだいこん　菊の花の形に飾り包丁を入れただいこんを、こんぶだしでやわらかく炊き、ゆずみそをつけて食べる。アツアツがおいしい冬の料理。

01 **Washoku values seasonality** /Japan is a rich country with seasonal ingredients from the mountains and the sea, and the dishes reflect the season. 02 **Seasonal food** /Seasonal ingredients are delicacies. 03 **Spring** /Simmered bamboo shoot with wakame seaweed /Simmer bamboo shoot and fresh wakame seaweed with dashi and light soy sauce. The flavor and the crunchy texture of bamboo shoot and fresh green of wakame represent this springlike food. 04 **Summer** /Grilled sweetfish /Sweetfish (Ayu) is a seasonal river fish in summer. Broil sweetfish with salt, and eat it with Tadesu vinegar. Tadesu vinegar, the mixture of ground water pepper leaves and dashi, has a fresh flavor, and is often used for the broiled sweetfish. 05 **Autumn** /Matsutake mushroom cooked in a pipkin /Matsutake is an autumn ingredient. Cook matsutake, white fish, shrimp, chicken, Japanese hornwort, ginkgo nut with dashi in a pipkin, and steam them lightly. Squeeze juice of Sudachi citrus into the soup and enjoy both soup and ingredients. 06 **Winter** /

美しく切る

和食の調理の基本は「切る」ことです。料理人にとって、包丁づかいの基本は「かつらむき」だといわれています。いろいろな飾り切り（飾り包丁）をつかうことで、料理がよりいっそう引き立ちます。

さしみの皿などにそえるけんは、かつらむきしただいこんを細切りにしてつくる。

かつらむきは、だいこんなど円筒形の野菜を、ごくうすく帯状にむく切り方。

いろいろな飾り切り（飾り包丁）

菊だいこん
1. 16等分に切りこみを入れる。
2. 切りこみにそって、飾り包丁を入れる。
3. 側面にも飾り包丁を入れる。

ねじり梅

松葉ゆず

花ばす
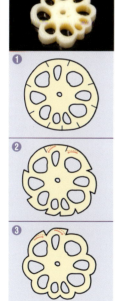

手綱こんにゃく

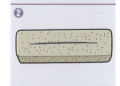

花切りしいたけ

六方むき

※②で八角形をつくってむいていくと「八方むき」になる。

Simmered daikon radish with miso /Cut daikon radish in a chrysanthemum shape and simmer it softly with kelp dashi. Eat the daikon while it is hot with Yuzu flavored miso. **Cut beautifully** /Cutting is the basic technique of Washoku. "Katsura-muki", considered as the standard technique, is a cutting technique to slice the ingredients thinly into a long strip. Decorative cuts make foods more attractive. Vegetable garnish for sashimi is thin strips of daikon radish. Cut daikon into Katsura-muki slice before cutting into strips. Katsura-muki cutting is to slice columnar vegetables like daikon into thin and narrow sheets. Decorative cuttings Chrysanthemum shaped daikon /1.Cut the surface into 16 equal parts. /2.Cut each part into a flower-petal shape. /3.Cut the surface of the side. Japanese apricot shaped carrot Pine needle shaped Yuzu citrus Flower shaped lotus Rope shaped konnyaku Shiitake mushroom with flower cuts Hexagonal cut ※It becomes "octagonal cut" if cut into 8 faces.

茶の湯とは

茶の湯は、日本を代表する伝統文化のひとつです。懐石料理が生まれた背景にある茶の湯の世界をちょっとのぞいてみましょう。

●お茶の伝来●

日本にお茶を飲む習慣をもちこんだのは、鎌倉時代のはじめ（13世紀）に、中国から禅宗の修行を終えて帰国した栄西という僧でした。栄西が中国からもちかえったお茶が「抹茶」です。抹茶は、乾燥させた茶の葉を石臼でひいて粉にしたもので、湯をそそいで茶せんでかきまぜて飲みます。

江戸時代（17世紀）になると、お茶の葉に湯をそそぐだけで飲める煎茶が、中国僧の隠元によってもたらされました。煎茶は庶民のあいだにもひろまっていきました。

●茶の湯の心は「おもてなし」●

抹茶を飲む習慣は貴族や武家にもひろがり、室町時代になると、客を招いて茶をたてる茶会がさかんにおこなわれるようになりました。室町時代末期には、茶会はぜいたくな遊びのひとつとして、にぎやかにおこなわれていました。そうした状況に対して、村田珠光という人が、お茶は心をこめて客をもてなすためにあると考え、静かにお茶を味わうために質素な茶室で茶会をしました。

珠光の精神は、16世紀末に千利休によって茶の湯として完成されたのです。

茶室　Tea ceremony room

千利休の出身地である堺市（大阪府）にある千利休像。
The statue of Sennorikyu.

01 What is "Cha-no-yu (Tea ceremony)"? /Tea ceremony is one of the Japanese traditional cultures. Kaiseki cuisine has been developed from tea ceremony. **02 Introduction of green tea** /It is said that Buddhist priest Eisai introduced Matcha tea to Japan when he came back to his homeland after finishing the training of Zen in China. Matcha is the powdered tea leaves ground by stone mortar. It needs to pour hot water and mix with tea whisk when drinking. In the Edo period (17th century), Sencha was introduced by Chinese monk Ingen. As Sencha could be drunk by just pouring hot water onto tea leaves, it spread among ordinary people. **03 Omotenashi(Hospitality)～The spirit of Tea ceremony** /The habit to drink Matcha spread among the aristocrats and the samurais. Tea parties served Mactha were held frequently in the Muromachi period, and they become luxury gatherings. Jyuko Murata was against this trend, and hosted tea parties at humble tea houses. Jyuko's spirit that tea ceremony is to welcome guests with host's whole heart

パート1　知ろう！調べよう！

茶の湯がさかんになると、茶の湯の席にふさわしい作法がととのえられていきました。お茶にあわせて、お菓子もいろいろなものがつくられていきます。また、茶の湯の作法は、日本人の礼儀作法にも影響をあたえました。

茶の湯では、「一期一会」の精神がたいせつにされます。つまり、その茶会の一時をたいせつにするために、懐石料理は旬の素材をつかい、食器にも心を配ります。茶室へと続く石畳は、はき清めて打ち水がされ、「つくばい」もしつらえられています。部屋には掛け軸がかけられ、季節の花も活けられます。こうしたことすべてが、客へのおもてなしだと考えられているのです。

茶室をのぞいてみよう 04

- **ひしゃく** これで釜から湯をくんで、茶わんにそそぐ。05
- **茶せん** 抹茶をかきまぜるためのもの。06
- **炉** 湯をわかすために火をたくところ。07
- **釜** 湯をわかすためのもの。08

 お茶をたてる。09
 お茶を飲む。10
 お菓子も、季節を感じさせるものがつかわれる。11

茶室に入る前に手を洗うためにもうけられている「つくばい」。
Tsukubai (a wash-basin in Japanese gardens).

美しいしぐさでおじぎをする 12

手のつき方 13

 軽いおじぎ 14
両手の指先をそろえて、ひざの前につく。

 ふつうのおじぎ 15
一度、相手の目を見て、ゆっくり頭を下げる。

 ていねいなおじぎ 16
腰を深く曲げ、手のひらまで畳につける。

12 以降の英訳は → P114

---

was inherited to Sennorikyu who has completed the spirit as tea ceremony at the end of 16th century. The form and manner of tea ceremony have been established along with its popularity. Many kinds of confectioneries has been made that go well with Matcha. The manner of tea ceremony influenced Japanese etiquette and manners. Tea ceremony attach importance on the spirit of "meeting only once in a lifetime," which means that an encounter today can never be experienced again. The host pays attention to every single matter; use seasonal ingredients for Kaiseki cuisine with serving on proper plates; clean and water the pavement to the tea house; set a wash-basin in a Japanese garden; decorate a seasonal tapestry and flowers in the tea room. These attitude and deep consideration to the guests are all considered as the hospitality. 04 In the tea ceremony room 05 Ladle: transfer hot water from the iron pot to the tea bowl 06 Whisk: mix Matcha and hot water 07 Hearth 08 Iron pot 09 make a tea 10 drink a tea 11 seasonal confectionery

日本茶について知ろう

世界で飲まれているお茶のほとんどは紅茶ですが、
日本のお茶は緑茶です。
和食に欠かせない緑茶についてくわしく見ていきましょう。

緑茶と紅茶は同じお茶

緑茶と紅茶は、もととなるお茶の木は同じで、ツバキ科の常緑樹「チャの木」の葉からつくられます。加工法がちがうだけなのです。緑茶は葉を発酵させないでつくりますが、紅茶は完全に発酵させてつくります。その中間にあるのがウーロン茶で、ある程度発酵させてからつくります。緑茶は、発酵を止めるために葉を蒸したり、釜でいったりするのです。

湯のみ茶わんで飲む緑茶。

ティーカップで飲む紅茶。

いろいろな緑茶

緑茶は、木の育て方やつかう葉の部分、製茶法などによっていろいろな種類があります。日本でもっともよく飲まれているのが煎茶で、さわやかな香りとほどよい渋みが特徴です。やわらかい若葉をつみ、蒸したあと、手でよくもみながら乾燥させてつくります。いまは、この工程は機械でおこなうことが多くなっています。立春（2月4日ごろ）から88日めの八十八夜のころにつむ一番茶が、もっともおいしいといわれています。

---

[01] **What is Japanese tea?** /The most popular tea in the world is black tea. Green tea is the most popular tea in Japan and it is essential for Washoku. [02] Green tea and black tea are made from same ingredient /Both green tea and black tea are made from same Camellia sinensis leaves, but the process is different. The process of making green tea does not need fermentation, but black tea needs fermentation process. Oolong tea is half-fermented tea and is the middle of green tea and black tea. [03] Green tea drinking with "Yunomi," a Japanese cup with no handles. [04] Black tea drinking with a teacup. [05] Various types of green tea /There are many types of green tea. It depends on how to raise tea trees, which part of leaves to use, or the difference of manufacturing process. Sencha green tea is the most popular tea in Japan and it has characteristics of fresh flavor and moderate astringency. The process of making Sencha is starting from picking up

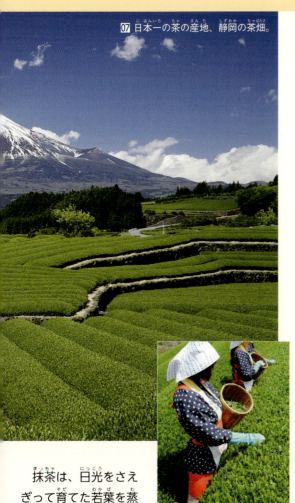

07 日本一の茶の産地、静岡の茶畑。

06 茶つみのようす。

抹茶は、日光をさえぎって育てた若葉を蒸して、もまずにそのまま乾燥させ、石臼で粉にひいてつくります。

茶つみの時期のおそい、かたくなった葉や茎などを原料にしたお茶は、品質がおとるため、番外の茶という意味で「番茶」とよばれます。

ほうじ茶は、煎茶や番茶を強火でいった茶で、香ばしい香りが特徴です。

茶の種類 Type of green tea

抹茶 Matcha

煎茶 Sencha

番茶 Bancha

ほうじ茶 Hojicha

お茶を美しく飲みましょう 08

お茶をそそぐときは、片方の手で急須のふたをおさえましょう。09

湯のみ茶わんの底を左手でささえ、右手を茶わんの側面にそえるようにして、飲みましょう。10

soft leaves, then, steam, rub them with hands, and dry. Nowadays most of the tea producers control all the process by machines. It is said that the leaves picked during February 4th (the first day of spring according to the traditional calendar) to eighty-eighth day from the beginning of spring are the highest quality. Matcha tea is made by young leaves of tea trees which rose up without exposing to the sun. Steam the leaves, then dry them without rubbing with hands and grind them to powder by a stone mill. Bancha tea is made from hard leaves or stems which are not used for green tea. The name implies that it is apart from major green tea. Hojicha is made from roasted Sencha or Bancha and has good roasted scent. 06 Tea leaves picking 07 Tea plantation in Shizuoka, the top producer of tea in Japan 08 Drink tea in an elegant manner 09 Hold the lid of Kyusu with fingers. Kyusu is a pot for serving Japanese tea. 10 Hold the bottom of the Yunomi on the left hand and place right hand on the side.

世界遺産になった和食

2013年12月、和食がユネスコの無形文化遺産に登録されました。登録名は「和食,日本人の伝統的な食文化」です。

*英語では「Washoku, traditional dietary cultures of the Japanese」

登録の理由

和食が無形文化遺産に登録されたおもな理由として、世代から世代に受けつがれるなかで、和食が社会の連帯に大きな役割を果たしていることがあげられました。「無形文化遺産」とは、芸能や伝統工芸技術など形のない文化であって、土地の歴史や生活風習などと密接にかかわっているものが対象になります。文化の多様性を反映していることや、適切な保護措置がはかられているかどうかなども、登録の要件となっています。日本の無形文化遺産は、歌舞伎や能楽、人形浄瑠璃文楽など21件が登録されています。食と関係する無形文化遺産としては、これまでに「フランスの美食術」と「メキシコの伝統料理」「地中海料理」が2010年に、「トルコのケシケキの伝統」が2011年に登録されています。2013年に日本の「和食」のほかに、韓国の「キムジャン」、グルジアの「ワインづくり」、トルコの「コーヒー」が登録され、合計8件となりました。

日本のアピールポイント

日本政府(農林水産省)は、「日本食文化の世界無形遺産登録に向けた検討会」を2011年7月5日より4回に渡り実施し、2012年3月に和食の登録をユネスコに提案しました。「四季や地理的多様性による新鮮な山海の幸」「自然の美しさをあらわした盛りつけ」「正月や田植えなどとの密接な関係」「食育」などをアピールしてきました。その結果、2013年12月4日にユネスコの無形文化遺産に登録されました。

登録決定を受けて、安倍晋三首相は、「心からうれしい。日本人のたいせつな食文化を末永く後世に引きつぎたい。海外の方がたにも和食のよさを理解いただけるよう、さらに発信していきたい」と述べました。林芳正農林水産大臣や下村博文文部科学大臣も「和食が次世代に着実に継承されるよう食育を推進したい」「和食を食べる機会をつくりたい」と語りました。

*2010年に登録されたギリシャ・イタリア・スペイン・モロッコの4か国に加え、2013年にキプロス・クロアチア・ポルトガルの3か国が追加登録された。

和食の無形文化遺産登録決定を報じる新聞記事。

[01] **Washoku designated UNESCO Intangible Cultural Heritage** [02] **Why Washoku is designated World Heritage?** / Major reason is because Washoku has made a big role on social solidarity through inherited from generation to generation. "Intangible cultural heritage" is something like performing arts or techniques to make traditional crafts which have deep relationship with the local history or customs. It also needs to reflect diversity of culture. 21 items such as Kabuki, Noh, Japanese puppet drama and so on have been registered as the intangible heritage. Regarding the gastronomic heritage, "Gastronomic meal of the French", "Traditional Mexican cuisine" and "Mediterranean diet" were registered in 2010, and "Ceremonial Keşkek tradition in Turkey" in 2011. "Kimjan, making and sharing kimchi in the Republic of Korea", "Ancient Georgian traditional Qvevri wine-making method" and "Turkish coffee culture and tradition" has been inscribed in 2013. [03] **Advantage of Washoku** /Japanese Ministry of Agriculture, Forestry and

和食がユネスコの無形文化遺産に正式決定し、京都ではお祝いのちょうちんがかかげられた。04

04以降の英訳は➡P114

登録までの紆余曲折 05

　和食が無形文化遺産に登録されるにいたった経緯はつぎのとおりです。

　近年、日本人が和食を食べなくなるなか、京都の料理人がつくった「日本料理アカデミー」という団体が、近年の和食ばなれを食い止めようとして、無形文化遺産登録を提案しました。しかし、当初は、文部科学省も農林水産省も反応がにぶく、たいした運動にはなりませんでした。ところが、東日本大震災によって傷ついた日本食品のイメージアップのために登録が役立つという考えや、政府が進めているクールジャパン戦略＊の一環として和食を海外へ売りだそうとする考えが政府のなかにでてきました。こうして政府も、和食の登録にしだいに力を入れるようになりました。

＊マンガやアニメ、ファッション、工芸品など、すぐれた日本文化を積極的に世界に発信していこうという取り組み。

「会席料理」から「和食（WASHOKU）」へ変更 06

　日本は「会席料理こそ日本料理の代表」としてアピールしようとしましたが、「一部の人だけのもの」だという意見がだされ、日本と同様に登録をめざしていた韓国の「宮廷料理」が、やはり「一部の人だけのもの」という理由で落選したことから、方針が見直されました。結果、会席を中心とした料理ではなく、「和食」で登録をめざしていくことになりました。

季節を取りこんだ盛りつけが美しい会席料理。07

Fisheries (MAFF) had held four meetings in 2011 of "investigative committee to register Washoku as world heritage," and made a proposal to UNESCO in 2012. "Seasonality and geographical diversity, fresh ingredients from mountain and the sea", "attractive presentation which depicts beautiful natures", "close rink to traditional and annual events" and "food education" had been high appealing effects for Washoku, and it has finally been inscribed as UNESCO Intangible Cultural Heritage in 2013 December 4th. Prime Minister Shinzo Abe of Japan said, "We are truly happy. We would like to pass on Japanese food culture to the future generation and work harder to let foreign people appreciate charms of Washoku." Yoshimasa Hayashi, Minister of MAFF then and Hakubun Shimomura, Minister of Education, Culture, Sports, Science and Technology then said, "We would like to promote food education so that Washoku could be inherited to the next generation," and, "We would like to make more occasions to eat Washoku."

「和食（WASHOKU）」とは？ 01

「なにをもって日本の食とするのか」「どのようにすれば審査に通るのか」という2つの大きな問題が議論されるなか、日本文化や食文化研究で知られる熊倉功夫氏（国立民族学博物館名誉教授、静岡文化芸術大学学長などを歴任）により、「和食（WASHOKU）」とは「洋食に対する概念」であり、「一汁三菜」を基本的な献立としたものと定義づけされました。熊倉氏は、こうすることで、「トンカツ、コロッケ、すき焼きといった近代の家庭料理も入る」と考えたといいます。つまり、登録の成功の理由は、料亭などで提供されている本格的な日本料理だけを取り上げるのではなく、一般家庭で食べられている日本の家庭料理をふくめて「和食」としたからなのです。

それでも保護が必要？ 02

登録されるのが料亭の料理ではなく、一般的な日本の家庭料理であるにもかかわらず、どうして、和食を無形文化遺産として保護しなければならないのでしょうか。

2013年11月6日にNHKの「クローズアップ現代」という番組で、「日本の"心"を守りたい 〜 和食 無形文化遺産へ〜」が放送され、15年前と比較すると、「日本人に和食ばなれが起きている」「日本の食文化を失いつつある」「無形文化遺産への登録が、それを見直すきっかけになればよい」などと話題になりました。

なお、今回の登録は、和食を通して「日本の心」を守るという意味がふくまれているといわれています。

01 **What is Washoku?** /Definition of Washoku is "basically consisting of 1 Soup and 3 Dishes with rice." It was proposed by Isao Kumakura, well-known scholar of Japanese culture and food cultural research, and former emeritus professor of National Museum of Ethnology and former president of Shizuoka University of Art and Culture. Mr.Kumakura says that with this definition modern homemade meals like Tonkatsu (breaded pork cutlet), Japanese croquette and Sukiyaki can be included in Washoku. Why Washoku was designated world heritage is because its definition applies to not only Japanese cuisine served at first-class restaurants but also ordinary homemade dishes.

02 **Why Washoku needs to be protected?** /Why ordinary homemade meals have to be registered as the cultural heritage and need to be protected? One of Japanese TV stations has broadcasted a program regarding the crisis of Japanese food in 2013. The program reported that compared with the situation of 15 years before, Japanese eat less Washoku and Japanese food culture has been disappearing. So the designation as the cultural heritage could be a good opportunity to review the value of Japanese food. Also it has important meaning to protect "Japanese spirit" through Washoku. 03 **People eating less Washoku is a serious problem** /The news that Washoku had been designated as the cultural heritage was widely reported. On the other hand, it was pointed out that less people eat Washoku. Now sushi and sake became the global boom, while the consumption of Washoku in Japan decreases. Annual rice consumption over the last 15 years in Japan has fallen from 9.44 million tons to 7.79 million tons, from 66.7kg to 56.3kg per person

和食ばなれの深刻さ 03

今回の和食の登録のニュースは、大きく報道される一方、和食ばなれについても指摘されました。

すしや日本酒などが世界的にもブームとなっているにもかかわらず、肝心の日本国内では和食の影がどんどんうすくなっているといわれています。

1997年から2012年までの15年間で、米の消費量は年間944万トンから779万トンに減少。ひとりあたりでは、66.7キログラムから56.3キログラム（約16パーセント減）となりました。また、しょうゆの消費量も8.7リットルから6.3リットルと減少しています。

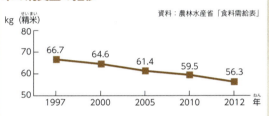

米の消費量の推移（ひとり1年あたり）
資料：農林水産省「食料需給表」

和食ばなれとともに、日本人特有の季節の感覚や作法、さらには家族のきずなが失われるのではないかと危ぶまれています。また、正月やひな祭りなどの年中行事や家庭の祝い事などの際に、和食をつくることがなくなりつつあるともいわれています。

「こ食」を見直す 04

海外では日本食がブームですが、反対に日本では、米やしょうゆ、みその消費が減る現象が生じています。家庭料理からは、かつての日本の一汁三菜の形式はどんどんうすれてしまっています。それにともなって、和食の作法や「いただきます」「ごちそうさま」といって、家族みんなで食卓をかこんで同じ料理を食べるといった習慣もなくなりつつあります。

また、個食（家族がそれぞれ好きなものを食べる）・孤食（家族が不在の食卓でひとりで食べる）・粉食（パンやピザ、パスタなどの小麦粉をつかった料理を好んで食べる）などがふえ、日本人の家族団らんの文化は消えていきつつあります。

こうした「こ食」がふえるなかだからこそ、無形文化遺産への登録が意味をもち、現状を見直すチャンスとなるといわれています。

個食

孤食

粉食

---

that is equivalent to 16% decrease, according to the data from MAFF. Annual consumption of soy sauce has fallen from 8.7L to 6.3L. Less people cook Washoku at the New Year's celebration or at some annual festivals like Girl's Festival. Loss of Japanese specific senses of seasonality, table manners and family bonds are concerned. **04 Reconsideration of "Koshoku"** /Japanese foods are now a big trend worldwide but consumption of rice, soy sauce and miso is decreasing. Less people eat traditional homemade meal of "1 Soup and 3 Dishes." And the habit that a family sitting around the dining table to eat same meal at the same time with studying good table manners are getting disappeared. There are 3 types of Koshoku; 1. each member of the family eats what they want; 2. eating alone; 3. eating meal made with wheat flour. ("Ko" has 3 meanings: "each individual", "lonely" and "flour.") These koshokus are not good habit, so the registration of Washoku as the cultural heritage is said to be a good chance to review our eating habits.

懐石料理を知ろう
和食とおもてなし

パート2 つくろう！食べよう！

煮物わん 01

カニしんじょうわん

漆塗りのおわんに、しんじょうやしいたけなど五色の食材を盛りこんだ料理です。

アツアツのうちにいただきます。

【材料 5人分】 02
- カニのむき身 …………… 20本
- 市販の白身魚のすり身 … 150g
- 塩 ……………………… 少々
- こんぶだし …………… 適量
- 卵白 …………………… 1/2個分
- 山いも（大和いも、長いもなど）… 5g
- かたくり粉（打粉用）……… 適量
- 生しいたけ …………… 5枚
- ほうれんそうの茎 ……… 5本
- ゆず …………………… 適量
- <吸地>
  - だし ……………… 4カップ
  - 塩 ………………… 小さじ1弱
  - うすくちしょうゆ ……… 少々

01 Simmered food bowl　**Crab shinjo dumpling soup**
02 Ingredients for 5 servings
- crab leg meat : 20
- ground white fish paste : 150g
- salt : a little
- kelp dashi : adequate amount
- egg white : 1/2
- yam : 5g
- starch : adequate amount
- shiitake mushroom : 5
- stem of spinach : 5
- Yuzu citrus : adequate amount

[soup]
- dashi : 4 cups
- salt : less than 1 tsp
- light soy sauce : a little

つくり方 03

1. カニのむき身を5本ほぐしておく。

2. すりばちに、すり身と塩を入れ、よくすりあわせる。すりおろした山いも、卵白を加えてまぜ、こんぶだしで、耳たぶより少しやわらかめのかたさに調整する。最後に、1のほぐしたカニの身を入れてまぜる。

3. 器にラップをかけて、カニのむき身を3本きれいにならべる。

4. 3のカニのむき身に打粉をふり、その上に2のすり身の1/5量をのせる。

5. 4をラップごともち上げ、写真のようにして茶巾にしぼる。これを5個つくる。

6. 湯気の上がった蒸し器に5をならべ、7〜8分ほど蒸す。

7. ほうれんそうの茎は、サッとゆでて冷水にとる。おわんの大きさにあわせて長さをそろえておく。

8. なべにだしを入れてあたため、塩で味をととのえる。香りをだすために、うすくちしょうゆを少々入れて、吸地を仕上げる。

9. 生しいたけは、石づきを切りとって飾り包丁（→97、153ページ）を入れ、吸地であたためる。

10. 蒸し上がった6のしんじょうをおわんに入れ、9のしいたけと7をのせて、熱い吸地をはる。最後に松葉ゆず（→97ページ）をあしらう。

---

03 How to make

1. Make crab meat flake from five of the legs. /2. Put ground white fish and salt into grinding bowl and grind well. Add grated yam and egg white; adjust the texture by adding kelp dashi to be comparatively softer than earlobe. Add crab meat flake and mix. 3. Spread plastic cling film onto a small bowl and put 3 crab meats on it. /4. Sprinkle some starch on (3) crab meats, then put 1/5 of (2) fish paste. /5. Wrap crab and fish paste like a ball. Make 5 pieces of the same crab ball. /6. Steam (5) for 7-8 min. /7. Parboil stems of spinach and put them into iced water. Cut them into good length to dish up in a bowl. /8. Heat dashi in a pot and season with salt. Add small amount of soy sauce to add flavor. /9. Cut off bottom of shiitake mushrooms and make decorative cuttings on the surface of them. Put them into (8) soup and cook. /10. Dish up steamed (6) and put shiitakes and spinach stems, then pour hot soup. Put topping with pine needle shaped Yuzu.

焼き物 01

カマスの幽庵焼(ゆうあんやき)

カマスを幽庵地(ゆうあんじ)にしばらく漬(つ)けこんだあと、色(いろ)よく焼(や)き上(あ)げたもの。ゆずの香(かお)りがすがすがしい焼(や)き物(もの)です。

01 Grilled dish

Grilled barracuda marinated with soy sauce, sake, mirin and Yuzu citrus

Yuan-yaki is the grilled fish or meat on the direct fire, marinated with soy sauce, sake, mirin and yuzu citrus. It has fresh flavor of yuzu citrus.

02 Ingredients for 5 servings
- barracuda : 2 and half
- Yuzu citrus : adequate amount

[Yuan sauce]
- light soy sauce : 50mL
- sake : 50mL
- mirin : 50mL

パート2 つくろう！食べよう！

【材料 5人分】

カマス............2尾半
ゆず............適量
〈幽庵地〉
うすくちしょうゆ
............50mL
酒............50mL
みりん............50mL

つくり方

1. 深めのバットに、うすくちしょうゆ、酒、みりんを1:1:1の割合であわせる。ここに、ゆずの輪切りを加えて、漬けダレ（幽庵地）をつくる。

2. カマスは三枚におろして、腹骨をそぎとる。

3. 1の幽庵地に2のカマスを漬けて、20分ほどおく。

4. 3のカマスの汁気を切って、写真のように串を打つ。この串の打ち方を、両づま折という。

5. 盛りつけるときにおもてになる面に、飾り包丁を入れる。

6. まず、おもてになる面から焼き、色よく焼けたら、うらを焼く。

7. カマスが焼き上がったら、串をまわしながらぬき、器に5人分のカマスを盛りつける。

三枚におろす

1尾丸ごとの魚は、流水で洗ってから、うろこやえら、はらわたを取り、水できれいに洗ったあと、料理にあわせて二枚や三枚に切りわけます。これを「おろす」といいます。
中骨のついている身と中骨のついていない身に切りわけることを、二枚おろしといいます。おもて身、中骨、うら身の三枚に切りわけることを、三枚おろしといいます。

二枚おろし

三枚おろし

How to make

1. Pour same amount of light soy sauce, sake and mirin into a deep bat. Put thin slices of Yuzu. /2. Cut barracuda into 3 fillets, remove abdominal bones. /3. Marinate barracuda with (1) Yuan sauce for 20 min. /4. Drain excess sauce of barracuda and put on skewers. Fold both sides of fish inward. /5. Make decorative cuts on the dishing surface. /6. Broil from the surface, turn over and broil the opposite side. /7. Put off skewers.

Cut fish into three fillets slice /Wash whole fish with running water, remove the scales, gills and guts. Rinse with water again and cut into two fillets or three fillets. Two fillets cut is to make fillets with backbone and without backbone. Three fillets cut is to make two fillets without backbone and one very thin fillet with backbone.

預け鉢 01

小かぶとアナゴと春菊の炊き合わせ

小かぶとアナゴと春菊を、それぞれに適した下処理をしたあと、
うす味でべつべつに煮て、ひとつの器に盛りつけます。

【材料 5人分】02
- 小かぶ……………5個
- 米……………ひとにぎり
- アナゴ（開いたもの）
  ……………2尾半
- 春菊……………適量
- ゆず……………適量

＜かぶの煮汁＞
A ┌ だし…………2.5カップ
  │ うすくちしょうゆ…30mL
  └ みりん…………30mL

＜アナゴの煮汁＞
B ┌ だし…………1.5カップ
  │ うすくちしょうゆ…100mL
  └ みりん…………100mL

＜春菊の煮汁＞
C ┌ だし…………2カップ
  │ うすくちしょうゆ…大さじ3
  └ みりん…………小さじ1/2

つくり方 04

1 小かぶは天地を落として八方むき（→97ページ）にし、米ひとにぎりを入れた湯でゆがく。竹串がスッとささるぐらいになったら、水にさらす。

2 1の小かぶの水気を切り、底の広いなべにならべる。Aのだしと調味料を入れて、やわらかくなりすぎないように煮る。

3 アナゴをまな板にのせて、霜降り（→153ページ）する。霜降りは、まな板を立てて熱湯をかけるとよい。

アナゴは細長い姿をした魚。03

4 3のアナゴを氷水で冷やしたあと、皮面のぬめりを包丁の背でこそげとる。そのあと、食べやすい大きさに切っておく。

5 Bのだしと調味料をなべに入れて火にかけ、ふっとうさせる。その中に4のアナゴを入れて、30分蒸し煮にし、そのまま冷ます。

6 春菊は葉をつみ、熱湯でゆでて冷水にとる。

7 6の春菊は、かたくしぼって食べやすい長さに切り、Cのだしと調味料を入れたなべで炊く。

8 ゆずの皮をうすくむき、白いわたをそぎ落としてから千切りにし、水にさらす。

9 器に2、5、7を盛りつけ、8のゆずの皮の千切りをのせる。

---

01 Simmered dish
Simmered turnip, conger eel and crown daisy
Each ingredient is separately cooked and dished up in the same bowl.
02 Ingredients for 5 servings
- turnip : 5
- rice : 1 handful
- conger eel : 2 and a half
- crown daisy : adequate amount
- Yuzu citrus : adequate amount

[simmering broth for turnip]
A ┤
- dashi : 2.5 cups
- light soy sauce : 30mL
- mirin : 30mL

[simmering broth for conger eel]
B ┤
- dashi : 1.5 cups
- light soy sauce : 100mL
- mirin : 100mL

[simmering broth for crown daisy]
C ┤
- dashi : 2 cups
- light soy sauce : 3 tbsps
- mirin : 1/2 tsp

03 Conger eel has an elongated body.

パート2 つくろう！食べよう！

アナゴのぬめり取り 05
アナゴには独特なくさみがあります。そのくさみの元は、アナゴの体表のぬめりです。そこで、アナゴを調理するときには、ぬめり取りをします。

ぬめりを取る方法はいくつかありますが、もっとも一般的な方法が、熱湯をかける方法です。ぬめりの正体はたんぱく質のため、熱湯をかけると、ぬめりが白くかたまって浮いてきます。それを包丁の背でこそげとるのです。

白く浮いてきたアナゴのぬめり。06

05 Removal of sliminess of conger eel /Conger eel has slimy surface and it has bad smell. The effective way to remove sliminess is to pour hot water. The cause of this sliminess is the protein and it coagulates by hot water and changes to white. Remove the sliminess with backside of the knife. 06 The sliminess of conger eel.

04 How to make
1. Cut off the top and the bottom of turnips and peel off skin into 8 faces cut. Boil them with rice until it gets soft enough to easily be stuck by a bamboo skewer. Soak them into water. /2. Drain water of turnips. Pour (Ⓐ) dashi and seasonings into a wide pot; simmer them until turnips get soft. Do not to cook too much. /3. Put fillets of conger eel on a cutting board and pour boiling water. /4. Chill conger eel with iced water; remove sliminess of skin by the backside of a knife. Cut them into good size of amount to eat. /5. Pour (Ⓑ) dashi and seasonings into a pot and boil, and put in conger eel, simmer and steam for 30 min, remove from the heat and let it cool. /6. Pick off leaves of crown daisy and boil the stems, then rinse with water. /7. Squeeze water of crown daisy and cut them into good amount of size to eat. Simmer with (Ⓒ) dashi and seasonings. /8. Peel off the skin of Yuzu very thin; remove white part of the zest. Cut Yuzu into thin strips and soak them into water. /9. Dish up turnips, conger eel and crown daisy, put topping with Yuzu zest.

八寸 01

雷白うり

らせん状に切った白うりを干しているようすが、雷のいなずまに似ていますね。こうして干すことで、バリバリと歯ごたえのよい酢の物ができます。

【材料 6人分】02

- 白うり ………… 1本
- 〈土佐酢〉
  - かつおだし ………… 300mL
  - 酢 ………… 100mL
  - 塩 ………… 少々
- 砂糖 ………… 大さじ2
- うすくちしょうゆ ………… 大さじ1
- いりごま ………… 大さじ3
- おろししょうが ………… 少々

白うりは、きゅうりやすいかと同じ、うり科の野菜。03

03 Cucumis melo belongs to gourd family same with cucumbers and water melons.

つくり方 04

1. 白うりを半分に切り、中心の種の部分をくりぬき器でくりぬく。

2. 筒状になった白うりに、5〜6mm間隔でななめに切り目を入れる。このとき、中心の空洞より下の部分を切りはなさないように、気をつける。

3. 2の切りのこした部分をななめに切っていき、らせん状にする。

赤線のところを切る。

4. 3を立て塩（→153ページ）に1時間ほど漬けたあと、水気を切る。

5. 4をハンガーなどにかけて、日かげの風通しのよいところに干し、水分をぬく。

6. ボウルに土佐酢の材料を入れて、まぜあわせる。5の雷白うりを食べやすい長さに切って、いりごま、おろししょうがのしぼり汁とともにボウルに入れてあえる。

01 Hassun (nibbles for sake) **Pickled Cucumis melo**
Spiral shaped Cucumis melo resembles a thunder lightening. Crunchy texture can be made by the drying process.

02 Ingredients for 6 servings
- Cucumis melo : 1
- [Tosazu vinegar]
  - dried bonito dashi : 300mL
  - salt : a little amount
  - light soy sauce : 1 tbsp
  - roasted sesame seeds : 3 tbsps
  - vinegar : 100mL
  - sugar : 2 tbsps
  - grated ginger : a little

04 How to make
1. Cut a Cucumis melo into halves; remove the core by a hollowing tool. /2. Make a diagonal cuts at 5-6mm intervals on a tubular Cucumis melo. Leave the bottom uncut. /3. Turn over Cucumis melo and cut the red line parts and make spiral-shaped Cucumis melo. /4. Soak (3) into salted water for one hour and drain water. /5. Dry at the shady and airy place. /6. Mix Tosazu vinegar ingredients in a bowl. Cut dried Cucumis melo into good size of amount to eat. Mix Cucumis melo with sesame seeds and juice of grated ginger.

パート2 つくろう！食べよう！

エビのつや煮

車エビをからつきのままうす味で煮て、照りよく仕上げます。

【材料 6人分】

車エビ	6尾	塩	小さじ1
〈つや煮の地〉		砂糖	大さじ2
だし	大さじ4	うすくちしょうゆ	大さじ1
酒	大さじ4		

つくり方

1 エビは水洗いして、頭を取る。いっしょに背わたも取る。

2 なべに、つや煮のだしと調味料を入れてふっとうさせる。ここに、1のエビをからつきのまま入れて、1～2分サッと煮る。

3 2が冷めたら、からをむく。

4 エビのつや煮と雷白うりを、へぎ盆に盛りつける。

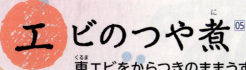

Simmered shrimp /Simmer large shelled prawn in lightly seasoned broth, and glaze at the finishing process.

Ingredients for 6 servings
- large prawn : 6

[simmering broth]
- dashi : 4 tbsps
- sake : 4 tbsps
- salt : 1 tsp
- sugar : 2 tbsps
- light soy sauce : 1 tbsp

How to make
1. Rinse large prawn with water. Remove the head and sand vein. Do not peel off the shell. /2. Pour ingredients of simmering broth into a pot and boil. Put shelled shrimp in the pot and cook for 1-2 min. /3. Peel off shells after the temperature goes down. /4. Dish up simmered shrimp and Cucumis melo on a Hegi tray.

はみだし 英訳

P86

04 What is "Shinjo" /Shinjo is the steamed or the boiled dumpling made with ground shrimp, crab, white fish or chicken and grated yam. Yam is used as the liaison. Hanpen which is the ingredient of Oden (Japanese hotchpotch) is one example of shinjo. Shinjo has soft texture and is eaten with wasabi and soy sauce like sashimi or as an ingredient of the soup. **05** Shrimp shinjo dumpling in the clear soup. Topped with sansho leaf. **06** Hanpen (soft cake of steamed fish paste).

P88-89

04 What is "Ohitashi"? /Ohitashi is the vegetables briefly boiled and dipped in broth. Typical ingredients are spinach, Japanese mustard spinach, rape blossoms and crown daisy. Squeeze water after boiling and dip in broth, or just season with soy sauce. Deep-fried foods can be used as ingredients, or ingredients can be boiled in the broth from the beginning. **05** Beautifully colored deep-fried eggplant dipped in soy sauce broth. **09 Why both sides of chopsticks are narrow?** /The reason why both edges of eating chopsticks are tapered is because one is for the gods and the other is for the people to eat. It is said by using same chopsticks and eating together between the gods and the people, good fortune can be brought in and misfortunes can be brought out. This shape of chopsticks is used at festive occasions, celebrations or something special occasions. Willow chopsticks used at the New Year is a typical example. Willow is an auspicious tree which sprouts in spring and chopsticks made by willow are long-lasting and hard to break. **10** Chopsticks for the New Year celebration

P91

08 Sake is essential for Washoku /Japan has developed its culture with rice cropping and rice has been precious food for Japanese. Sake is made from rice and it has made an important role in Japanese food culture. Sake brewing starts from steaming the rice. Mix koji and water with steamed rice and undergo fermentation to make "Moromi" which become the basis of sake. Supernatant liquid obtained after filtering moromi is sake. Yeast makes an important role during the process of rice fermentation. Each local sake brewery has passed down its own yeast through generations, and makes local sake which has unique characteristics. Sake is considered as a drink that can shorten the distance between people and the gods. Sake was offered to the gods, and after the offering they shared it for drinking at every local festival. In sake drinking parties, people used one cup together and drank by turns. Sake cup was passed around to all the members at the parties and returned again to the first. This round is called "Ikkon" People enjoyed snacks and foods after each "Ikkon." Japanese menu is called "Kondate," and it is said that kondate originates from the custom of drinking sake in ikkon style. **09** The raw material of sake is rice. Each local region grows rice which suits for making sake. **10** Spread steamed rice on trays, and lower the temperature to good enough for Koji mold to propagate. **11** Sake barrels dedicated to the shrine.

P99

12 Sit on your heels and make an elegant bow **13** How to place both hands on the floor **14 Slight bow** /Close your fingers and place your hands in front of your knees. **15 Usual bow** /Once look into the eyes of someone that you are going to bow, then bow your head slowly. **16 Polite bow** /Make a deep bow and place your both palms on the tatami floor.

P103

04 Paper lantern was hung in Kyoto to celebrate the registration of Washoku as UNESCO Intangible Cultural Heritage. **05 Many twists and turns to get through registration** /The circumstances how Washoku got intangible heritage status are as follows. Nowadays, less people eat traditional Washoku, so Japanese Chef's association of "Japanese Culinary Academy" made a proposal that Washoku should be registered as an intangible heritage. At the beginning, Japanese government did not place much value on promoting Washoku. But the movement to recover from the damage caused by misinformation of Japanese food due to the Great East Japan Earthquake in 2011, and actions by the government to promote Japanese food by Cool Japan Strategy has appeared. This is how Japanese government has become concentrating the power to the registration of Washoku as a world heritage. ＊Cool Japan strategy : A strategy to promote unique Japanese cultures such as manga, fashion, and traditional crafts to the world. **06 Registered as "Washoku" not as "Kaiseki cuisine"** /At first Japan appealed that Kaiseki cuisine is the typical Japanese food, but it is only for upper class people and not eaten widely. Korean court cuisine for aristocracy could not be registered as a world heritage, either. So Japanese government revised the strategy to register as Washoku which is widely eaten by ordinary people. **07** Beautifully decorated Kaiseki dish in autumn.

第4章
chapter 4

和食からWASHOKUへ
From " 和食 " to "Washoku"

世界にひろがる和食
Washoku spreading all over the world

和食からWASHOKUへ
世界にひろがる和食
パート1 知ろう！ 調べよう！

世界じゅうで人気の日本食 [01]

おいしくて見た目も美しく、そして健康的だとして、いまや海外で日本食がブームになっています。

● ブームは世界じゅうへ ● [02]

20世紀の終わりごろからアメリカやヨーロッパなどの先進諸国で日本食のブームが始まり、日本食を食べる外国人がふえてきました。最近ではロシアやアジア各国、そして中東などにもひろがり、ブームは世界的になってきました。

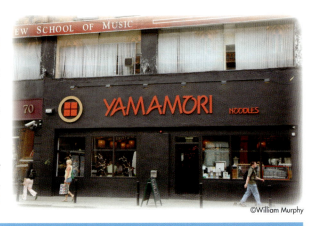

ヨーロッパのアイルランドにある日本食レストラン。麺類がメインの店だ。[03]
©William Murphy

海外における日本食レストラン* の展開状況（2013年3月）[04]

- ヨーロッパ [05] 約5500店
- ロシア [06] 約1200店
- アフリカ [07] 約150店
- 中東 [08] 約250店
- アジア [09] 約2万7000店
- オセアニア [10] 約700店
- 北アメリカ [11] 約1万7000店
- 中央・南アメリカ [12] 約2900店
- 世界合計 [13] 約5万5000店

[14] ＊日本食レストランの数は、すし・さしみなどの日本食がメニューにある店舗数。日本食専門店以外もふくまれる。　資料：「日本食・食文化の海外普及について」（農林水産省）

---

01 Washoku is popular all over the world **02** Global Washoku boom /A boom of Japanese food in European countries and the United States has begun in the late 20th century. Now, it spreads all over the world including Russia, Asia and the Middle East. **03** Japanese noodle restaurant in Ireland. **04** Number of Japanese restaurants in foreign countries (as of March 2013) **05** Europe : approx. 5,500 **06** Russia : approx. 1,200 **07** Africa : approx. 150 **08** Middle East : approx. 250 **09** Asia : approx. 27,000 **10** Oceania : approx. 700 **11** North America : approx. 17,000 **12** Central and South America : approx. 2,900 **13** Total: approx. 55,000 **14** ＊The number includes Japanese restaurants which provide Washoku such as sushi or sashimi and restaurants which are not specialized for Washoku. **15** The birthplace of Washoku /It is said that Washoku in foreign countries has appeared in the places where many Japanese descents concentrate, for example Sao Paulo in Brazil and San Francisco in the U.S. These cities became the regional

●「日本食・発祥の地」とは？ 15

海外の日本食は、移民として海外に渡った日系人が多い土地で始まったといわれています。ブラジルのサンパウロやアメリカのサンフランシスコがそうです。これらの都市は「日本食・発祥の地」となり、そこからその国じゅうにひろがっていきました。

現在、アメリカのカリフォルニア州には4000軒近い日本食レストランがあります。ニューヨーク市の中心部には700～800軒の日本食レストランが集中しているといいます。

アメリカにおける日本食レストランの増加 16

2010年は調査を始めた1992年の4.63倍にもふえている！

年	店舗数
1992	3051
1995	4086
2000	5988
2005	9182
2010	14129

州別日本食レストランの増加（上位5州） 17

太平洋岸のカリフォルニア州がとびぬけて多い！

2010年:
- カリフォルニア州 3963
- ニューヨーク州 1439
- フロリダ州 941
- ワシントン州 827
- ニュージャージー州 523

資料：「米国における日本食レストラン動向」（JETRO）

●アメリカの日本人街 18

アメリカのサンフランシスコには大きな日本人街があります。日本食レストランも多く、そのショーウィンドーには、日本のように食品サンプルがならべられています。しかし、日本人にとっては少しかわったメニューもあります。

さしみ用の船の上に、さしみとてんぷら、それにステーキが組みあわされている。ステーキではなく焼き肉なら、代表的な日本料理といえるかもしれない。 19

ヒレカツが巻きずしと組みあわされている。すしはカリフォルニアロール（→118ページ）。それでもさすがに日系人のまちのレストラン。かわってはいくも、おいしそうな日本料理だといえる。 20

Zaru Maguro をローマ字式に読んでみると、「ざるマグロ」。ざるそばの上にマグロのさしみがのっている。ざるそばもマグロのさしみも、両方ともわさびをつけて食べるので、意外においしいかもしれない。 21

海外のすしは巻きずしから

かつて、アメリカで日本食といえばすしでした。
最初にアメリカで受け入れられたすしは、どんなすしだったでしょうか。

カリフォルニアロールから発展したカラフルな巻きずし。

カリフォルニア生まれのすし

カリフォルニアロールというすしを知っていますか。カリフォルニアロールというのは、外側が酢めしで内側がのりと具（アボカドやゆでたカニの身など）になるように巻いた巻きずし*のことです。味つけにマヨネーズがつかわれたり、ごまがふりかけられたりすることもあります。

これは、1970年ごろにロサンゼルスの日本人街「リトル東京」で、日本人のすし職人が、当時生の魚介類を食べる習慣がなかったアメリカ人のために、マグロのかわりにアボカドをつかうことを思いついたのが始まりだといわれています。のりを内側に巻きこむようにしたのも、アメリカ人が黒いのりを気味悪がったからだといいます。

アボカド（半分に割ったものと丸ままのもの）。

酢めしのまわりにごまをつけたセサミロール。タレで飾っているところが、いかにも海外のすしっぽい。

* 日本の巻きずしはのりを外側にして巻く。のりを内側にして巻く巻き方は「うら巻き」とよばれる。

---

01 Roll Sushi in foreign countries 02 California Roll /California roll is a sushi which rolls nori and other ingredients inside by the vinegared rice outside. Some mayonnaise is sometimes added, or outside is coated with sesame seeds. It is said that a sushi chef in "Little Tokyo," Japantown in Los Angeles, started to use avocado instead of tuna around 1970. At that time, Americans have no custom to eat raw fish. The appearance in black of nori did not appeal to Americans, so the inside-out roll sushi which nori is rolled inside was developed. /* Traditional Japanese roll sushi is to roll outside with black nori. **03** Colorful roll sushi derived from California roll. **04** Roll sushi coated with sesame seeds. Garnishing with sauce represents a typical new-style sushi born in abroad. **05** Whole avocado and half-cut avocado. **06 Takeout Sushi** /The number of restaurants and coffee shops selling sushi has increased recently. Roll sushi like California roll were popular before, but nowadays traditional nigiri-zushi (hand-rolled sushi) and the new-

●すしのもちかえりも

最近になってアメリカでは、日本食レストラン以外のレストランやカフェでも、すしをあつかうところがふえてきました。それにともなって、以前はカリフォルニアロールなどの巻きずしが中心でしたが、本格的なにぎりずしや、アメリカ人の好みにあわせたいろいろなすしもふえています。

また、すしは日本食レストランで食べることができるだけでなく、すしのもちかえりも普及しています。スーパーマーケットでもすしが販売されていて、すしの人気はますます高まっています。

このため、中国の日本食レストランは、アメリカやヨーロッパとは逆で、はじめは、すし、さしみ、てんぷらなど、いろいろな料理を提供する店が多かったといいます。すしなどの専門店は、最近になってふえてきました。

スーパーマーケットで売られているパック入りのすし。

北京に開店したバイキング方式の日本料理店に多くの人が訪れる。

●中国の大都市では

中国では、首都の北京や、上海、広州、大連などの大都市に多くの日本食レストランがあります。北京で日本料理の店が急速にふえたのは1995年前後からです。これは、そのころから日本と中国の経済交流がさかんになってきたことが背景にあります。また中国では、「食べ放題（バイキング）」という方式が、一般の中国人客を日本食レストランによびこむきっかけとなったといわれています。

●回転ずしが東南アジアを席巻

タイの首都バンコクでは、以前は、日本食を提供するのは高級レストランでした。しかし、近年になって、日本食を提供するファミリーレストランや回転ずし店も登場し、日本食は若い世代を中心にはば広い層に受け入れられていきました。とくに2000年代に入ると、中国と同じように食べ放題方式のすし店や日本食レストランが登場し、日本食ブームに拍車をかけました。

「食べ放題」のすし店の看板。

10 以降の英訳は ➡ P150

---

type sushi that match the taste of Americans attract attention. Not only eating sushi at the restaurants but also take-outs are getting more popular. 07 Packaged sushi sold at a supermarket. 08 **Japanese restaurants in China** /There are many Japanese restaurants in Beijing, the capital of China, and Shanghai, Guangzhou, Dalian and so on. The number of Japanese restaurants in Beijing has rapidly increased around 1995. It is because the economic exchange between Japan and China has become active in this period. "All-you-can-eat system," the buffet style has also appealed to the broad range of people in China. Popular Japanese restaurants in China provide many kinds of dishes like sushi, sashimi, tempura and so on, while they provide not so many dishes in Europe and the U.S. Nowadays specialized restaurants like sushi restaurant have appeared. 09 A lot of people visit a Japanese restaurant of all-you-can-eat system newly opened in Beijing.

すしが世界で人気のわけ

「日本料理＝すし」というぐらいに、海外でのすしの人気は高くなっています。海外ではどんなすしが食べられているでしょうか。

● フルーツにぎりもある ●

そもそも「すし（にぎりずし）」とは、小さくにぎった酢めしにおもに魚介類をのせて食べるもので、江戸時代に江戸で考案された日本料理です。日本ですしというと、このにぎりずしが代表的ですが、押しずし、ちらしずし、巻きずし、いなりずしなど、多くの種類があります。こうした日本のすしと同じように、海外でもそれぞれの国の人の好みにあわせて、その国の食材をつかったさまざまなすしがつくられています。生の魚介類を食べない人たちのために、くだものをつかったすしも見られます。「フルーツにぎり」があってもおかしくはなく、いちごやキウイをのせたフルーツにぎりやマカデミアナッツの巻きずしなど、かわったメニューがつぎつぎと生みだされています。

● フランスでは日本料理がブーム ●

現在フランスでは空前の日本料理ブームで、大都市だけでなく地方の小さなまちにも、かならずといっていいほど日本料理の店があります。以前はピザと中国料理の店が多かったのですが、日本料理は「健康によい」ということで人気をよび、中国料理の店が日本料理に切りかえることも多いのです。そのため、日本料理店の多くは、日本人ではないアジア人経営の日本食レストランです。こうした店で食べられるさしみやすしは、サーモン、カリフォルニアロールが中心です。

いっぽうで、新鮮でおいしい魚が手に入るフランスでは、本格的なさしみやすしをだす日本料理店もあります。大きなまちでは、ウナギ、うどん、ラー

01 Why sushi is popular all over the world? 02 **Fruit sushi** /Sushi is a small vinegared rice ball topped with seafood. It was created in the Edo period. The most typical sushi is nigiri-zushi (hand-rolled sushi), and there are some others such as oshi-zushi (pressed sushi), chirashi-zushi (vinegared rice bowl decorated with seafood), maki-zushi (roll sushi) and inari-zushi (vinegared rice wrapped in deep-fried tofu). Each foreign country localizes sushi, using local ingredients to create new-style sushi suit to the country. There is fruit sushi for the people who cannot eat raw fish. 03 **Washoku boom in France** /Nowadays, Washoku is in a big boom in France. There are some Japanese restaurants in not only big cities but also small provincial cities. There used to be many pizza restaurants and Chinese restaurants there, but as Japanese food is getting popular as healthy food recently, some Chinese restaurants switch to Japanese. This is why most of the Japanese restaurants are managed by Asian but not Japanese. Foods served at these restaurants are salmon

パート1　知ろう！調べよう！

イタリアの日本食レストラン。サーモンとマグロのにぎりずし、サーモンとアボカドの押しずしに、枝豆や焼きとりも見える。この店には、日本のしょうゆがだされている。06

04 フランスの家庭はホームパーティーをよく開き、おしゃべりとワインと食事をたのしむ。パーティーでは、巻きずしはつまみやすいと人気がある。

05 パリにある日本料理店でにぎりずしや松花堂弁当＊を味わうフランス人。
＊松花堂弁当というのは、仕切りのついた容器にさしみやてんぷらなどの料理が美しく盛りこまれている弁当形式の会席料理のこと（→80ページ）。

●ヨーロッパの日本料理● 07

　どこの国でも、本格的な日本料理の店（日本人経営・日本人料理人）は少なく、大都市に少しあるだけです。その他のまちでは、すしといっても、マリネしたサーモンの押しずしや、うら巻き（→118ページ）など色とりどりのすしということが多いようです。最近は、居酒屋やラーメン店、回転ずしの店もできてきています。

メン（→128ページ）といった日本料理の専門店もふえています。パリのうどん屋さんでは、昼食時に行列ができるほどです。フランス料理は値段が高くて食べるのに時間がかかるので、安くて気軽に食べられるアジア料理・日本料理のランチメニューが人気をよんでいます。日本の弁当（Bento）も、ごはんと何種類ものおかずをいっしょに食べられて栄養バランスがよい上に、職場でも手軽に食べられるということで、人気がでています。パリにはBentoの店もできはじめました。

行列ができているパリのうどん屋さん。

イギリスのロンドンにできた大型チェーン店が経営する回転ずし店。08

料理が向こうからやってくると大喜びの子ども。09

07以降の英訳は→P150

---

sashimi and California roll mainly. On the other hand, as fresh and delicious fishes are available in France, there are traditional and authentic Japanese restaurants, too. Restaurants which specialize in eel, udon or ramen are appearing in big cities. Some udon restaurants in Paris are often crowded with people at lunchtime. French cuisine is expensive and takes time to eat, so eating cheaper and easier Asian and Japanese cuisines are getting popular. Japanese Bento (lunch box) is one of the trends in Paris because it is well nutrition-balanced. Bentos including variety of foods with rice are easy to eat at the office. 04 Easy-to-eat roll sushi is a popular cuisine at home parties in France. 05 French people tasting Shokado-style Bento box at a Japanese restaurant in Paris. /＊Shokado Bento is the meal box of Kaiseki cuisine with sashimi or tempura packed in a box with cross-shaped separators. 06 Japanese restaurant in Italy. Nigiri-zushi with salmon and tuna, oshi-zushi with salmon and avocado, edamame and Yakitori are served with Japanese soy sauce.

そもそも「日本料理」とは？

海外で「日本料理」とよばれるものには、すしやてんぷらだけでなく、カレーライスやハヤシライス、オムライスなどもあります。

● 日本料理・西洋料理

海外の「日本料理」は、日本でいうそれとは少しちがったイメージがあります。

海外では、カレーライス（→124ページ）やラーメン（→128ページ）なども日本料理とされています。なぜなら、それらはもともとは海外が発祥の食べ物でありながら、発祥の国のものとはかけはなれた料理となり、現在は日本じゅうでよく食べられているからです。

歴史的に見ると、「日本料理」ということばは、明治の文明開化の時代に「西洋料理」が生まれたことから、これに対してできたと考えられています。明治時代に皇室の料理を担当していた石井家の石井治兵衛・泰次郎親子は、はじめて「日本料理」ということばをつかって1898（明治31）年に『日本料理法大全』を、ついで『日本料理法大成』を出版しました。

● 洋食も日本の食文化！

明治になると日本人は、外国からやってきた人などを通して急激にヨーロッパやアメリカの文化を学びました。食文化もそのひとつでした。

はじめ西洋料理（洋食）として紹介されたヨーロッパやアメリカの料理は、まもなく日本の食と融合し、和洋折衷料理（→124ページ）が工夫されました。なかには、日本人の好みにあわず消えていったものも多くありましたが、すき焼きやオムライス、とんカツなどは、新しい料理として日本に定着しました。それらの料理は、食材、調理法、道具などをふくめ、独自の発展をしました。

洋食とは、日本で独自に発展した西洋風の料理のことをさします。こうした洋食は、もちろん純粋な日本料理ではありませんが、日本じゅうで食べられ、伝統的な日本料理とともに日本の食文化を形づくっています。

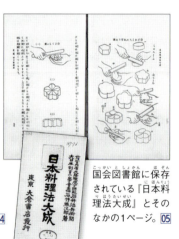

日本のカレーライスはインドにはなく、日本と同じようなラーメンは中国にはありません。スパゲッティのナポリタンもイタリアにはありません。

これらは、幕末から明治期にかけて来日した西洋人のためにつくられた料理がルーツとなり、日本で独自に発展した料理なのです。

西洋料理発祥の碑。鎖国をしていた江戸時代、唯一の開港地だった長崎。現在は喫茶室として利用されている旧グラバー邸の近くの「旧自由亭」は、日本最初の西洋料理店とされている。そのため、旧自由亭のそばに「西洋料理発祥の碑」が建てられている。

国会図書館に保存されている『日本料理法大成』とそのなかの1ページ。

●ポークカツレツからとんカツへ

とんカツをはじめてつくったのは、19世紀の終わりごろ、東京銀座にある煉瓦亭という洋食店の料理長をしていた木田元次郎だという説があります。木田は、パン粉をまぶしたうす切りの牛肉をバターでソテーするフランス料理のコトレットからヒントを得て、小麦粉・とき卵・パン粉の順につけたうす切りのぶた肉をてんぷらのようにたっぷりの油で揚げることを考案し、「ポークカツレツ」と命名したといわれています。

その後、いろいろな人がさまざまに工夫をした結果、厚みのあるぶた肉を揚げて、おはしで食べやすいようにあらかじめ包丁で切りわけ、キャベツの千切りをそえて盛りつける、現在のようなとんカツのスタイルが生まれました。

日本を訪れる外国人にもとんカツは人気がある。

外国における日本料理トップ10

海外で人気の日本食レストランを外国人旅行者の口コミをもとにランキングしたものが、トリップアドバイザーというサイトで紹介されました。トップ10とされた料理のほとんどが、すしです。このことは、外国人の多くが、日本料理といえばすしを思いうかべることをしめしています。

1位 イタリア
2位 ポルトガル
3位 アメリカ
4位 ハワイ(アメリカ)
5位 アメリカ
6位 ニュージーランド
7位 メキシコ
8位 イギリス
9位 メキシコ
10位 チリ

06以降の英訳は➡P150

---

introduced as Western cuisine and fused with original Japanese cuisine to be established as a cross of Western and Japanese cuisine. Sukiyaki, omelet with fried rice and Tonkatsu (pork cutlet) have been established as new-cuisine. This fusion of Western and Japanese cuisine has developed in a unique way including ingredients, cooking methods and cooking tools. "Yoshoku" is not the traditional Japanese cuisine, but now it is widely eaten throughout Japan and is an important element of Japanese culinary culture with traditional and authentic Japanese cuisine. The monument of "Birthplace of Western cuisine" at Jiyuu-tei restaurant in Nagasaki. Nagasaki was the only city with an open port during the national isolation in the Edo period. Jiyuu-tei restaurant just close to the Glover Residence is considered as the first Western cuisine restaurant in Japan. It is now used as a coffee house. The cooking book written by Ishii kept at the National Diet Library.

和洋折衷の日本の料理

日本のカレーライスと洋食のクリームシチュー、そして
日本のおふくろの味の代表ともいえる肉じゃがの共通点は、なんでしょうか。

● カレーの起源はイギリス？

「カレー」という名前の由来は、インドで話されているタミール語の「カリ」（ごはんにかけるスープみたいなもの）からきているといわれています（ほかにもいくつかの説がある）。ところが、

本場インドのカレーには香辛料がたっぷりつかわれているが、日本のカレーにはそれほどつかわれていなかった。

日本のカレーのルーツはインドではなく、イギリスであることは意外と知られていません。

17世紀にインドからイギリスに渡ったカレーがイギリス風のカレーとなり、明治時代初期にイギリス海軍によって日本にもちこまれました。これが、現在の日本のカレーライスの起源だと考えられています。つまり、イギリス海軍の乗組員により考えだされた、クリームシチューと同じ材料を煮て、牛乳のかわりにインドの香辛料のカレーパウダーをつかった料理が、日本の海軍に伝わり*、日本に上陸。それが独自の発展をして日本のカレーライスになったといいます。

肉や、にんじん、たまねぎ、じゃがいもなどの野菜をよく煮こんでから、「カレールー」を入れればカレーに、「クリームシチューのもと」をとかせばクリームシチューになるのは、料理の起源から考えても当然のことなのです。

＊当時、大日本帝国海軍の軍人が、同盟関係にあったイギリス海軍を参考にしてつくったのが始まりとされている。

● 海軍割烹術参考書によるレシピ

『海軍割烹術参考書』（1908年）には、つぎのように記されています。

> 初メ米ヲ洗ヒ置キ牛肉（鶏肉）玉葱、人参、馬鈴薯ヲ四角ニ恰モ賽ノ目ノ如ク細ク切リ別ニ「フライパン」ニ「ヘット」ヲ布キ麦粉ヲ入レ狐色位ニ煎リ「カレイ粉」ヲ入レ「スープ」ニテ薄トロク如ク溶シ之レニ前ニ切リ置キシ肉野菜ヲ少シク煎リテ入レ（馬鈴薯ハ人参玉葱ノ殆ンド煮エタルトキ入ル可シ）弱火ニ掛ケ煮込ミ置先ノ米ヲ「スープ」ニテ炊キ之ヲ皿ニ盛リ前ノ煮込ミシモノニ塩ニテ味ヲ付ケ飯ニ掛ケテ供卓ス此時漬物類即チ「チャツネ」ヲ付ケテ出スモノトス

これをわかりやすく記すと、つぎのとおりです。

1 米をといで、肉、たまねぎ、にんじん、じゃがいもをさいの目に切っておく。

2 ヘット（牛脂）をひいたフライパンで小麦粉をいため、きつね色になったらカレー粉を加える。

3 それにスープを入れ、うすめのとろろ汁の濃さまでのばす。

4 肉・野菜をいためて **3** に入れ、弱火で煮こむ。じゃがいもは、たまねぎとにんじんがほぼ煮えてから入れる。

5 米をスープで炊き、炊き上がったら皿に盛る。

6 **4** で煮こんだものを塩で調味し、皿に盛ったごはんにかけ、「チャツネ」などの漬物をそえて食卓にだす。

2007年に舞鶴市が発行した現代語訳の『海軍割烹術参考書』。

---

01 Washoku mixed with Western style **02** Japanese curry and rice originates from England /It is said that the origin of a name "curry" is from Tamil spoken in India. "Kari" is a soup poured over rice in Tamil. One theory says that "Kari" has transformed into "curry." It is not well known that Japanese curry originates from England and not from India. In the 17th century, the curry was brought from India to England and it has developed into English-style curry. British navy brought this to Japan in the early Meiji period. A crew of British navy made curry by adding Indian spices instead of milk during the process of making cream stew. This curry was introduced to Japanese navy at first and has developed into Japanese curry and rice. The processes of making Japanese curry and cream stew are very similar; the difference is adding curry roux or cream stew roux.

● ビーフシチューから肉じゃが

肉じゃがは、肉とじゃがいも、たまねぎ、糸こんにゃくなどを油でいため、しょうゆ、砂糖、みりんで煮こんだ肉料理です。

じつはこの肉じゃがは、日露戦争（1904～5年）のころ、京都府の舞鶴に置かれた鎮守府という海軍の組織の長官をしていた東郷平八郎が、青年時代にイギリスのポーツマスに留学していたことに関係して生まれたといわれています。

かれはイギリス海軍のビーフシチューが大好きで、帰国後、舞鶴でそのシチューを日本風にしてつくらせたといわれています。それが肉じゃがの起源（ほかにも説がある）です。そのため、舞鶴市は「肉じゃが発祥の地」を宣言しています。

ただし、広島県の呉市も、東郷が舞鶴赴任より10年前に呉鎮守府の参謀長として赴任していたことから、発祥地は同市であると主張しています。

● 海軍厨業管理教科書

1938年に刊行された『海軍厨業管理教科書』には、「甘煮」という料理名で、肉じゃがのレシピがつぎのように紹介されています。

1. なべに油を入れ、加熱する。
2. 3分後、牛肉を入れる。
3. 7分後、砂糖を入れる。
4. 10分後、しょうゆを入れる。
5. 14分後、じゃがいも・糸こんにゃくを入れる。
6. 31分後、たまねぎを入れる。
7. 34分後、終了。

分刻みに作業がおこなわれるところは、まさに軍隊です。料理ともよべないような気になりますが、そのおいしさのほどは？

舞鶴市の海上自衛隊第四術科学校に残されている『海軍厨業管理教科書』。

03 Indian curry contains many spices but Japanese curry contains less. 04 **Japanese navy recipe book published in 1908** /The recipe of Japanese curry and rice is written in the recipe book by Japanese navy (1908). /1.Wash rice. Cut meat, onions, carrots and potatoes into cubes. /2.Saute wheat flour with beef tallow till it gets browning. Add curry powder. /3.Pour soup, keep thick texture. /4.Saute vegetables in another pan and put into (3), stew over the low flame. Add potatoes at the last when onions and carrots are almost cooked. Season with salt. /5.Cook rice with soup. /6.Dish up rice and pour curry. Garnish with some pickles like chutneys. 05 Maizuru City published Japanese navy recipe book in a modern translation in 2007.

すしのつぎに人気の日本料理は?

すしがいちばん人気なら、そのつぎに人気なのはどんな料理でしょうか。
すき焼きやてんぷら、お好み焼きや焼きとりも見のがせません。

● すき焼き ● 02

すき焼きは、明治時代初期に横浜や東京などで文明開化の象徴といわれた牛なべなどから発展したものと考えられます。

なお、1963年に坂本九の歌『SUKIYAKI(原題・上を向いて歩こう)』が牛肉好きのアメリカ人のあいだで大ヒットしたことから、当時アメリカでは、すき焼きはすし以上に多くの人が知る日本料理だったことがわかります。

● てんぷら ● 03

てんぷらは、魚介類や野菜などに衣をつけて油で揚げる、代表的な日本料理です。揚げ物好きの外国人に人気の日本料理です。てんぷらは、現地の野菜や魚介類など、手に入りやすい食材をつかえば、どの国でもつくることができます。日本人はてんつゆや塩で食べますが、海外ではその国の人の好みによってケチャップやソースで食べることもあります。

てんぷらの歴史や語源については、さまざまな説がありますが、400年ほど前にポルトガル人によって長崎に伝えられ、語源もポルトガル語であるという説が、現在はもっとも有力です。

● お好み焼きは日本のピザ!? ● 04

お好み焼きは、水でといた小麦粉の生地にキャベツをまぜ、具として野菜や肉、魚介類などをのせ、鉄板の上で焼いた日本料理です。お好み焼きの起源は古く、安土桃山時代にまでさかのぼるといわれています。現在、「関西風お好み焼き」「広島風お好み焼き」など、地域によって具やつくり方はちがいますが、日本じゅうでよく食べられています。生の魚介類が食べられないため、すしがだめだという外国人もたいていは、魚介類を入れたお好み焼きは好きです。

同じく鉄板をつかう日本の料理に、客の目の前でステーキなどを焼く鉄板焼きがあります。1960年代にアメリカに渡った鉄板焼きは、「Teppanyaki」として広く親しまれています。

© Dustin M. Ramsey

---

01 What is popular Japanese food next to Sushi? 02 **Sukiyaki** /Sukiyaki is said to have developed from beef hot pot which was the symbol of Westernization movement in the early Meiji period in Tokyo and Yokohama areas. The song "Sukiyaki" sung by Kyu Sakamoto was a big hit among Americans who love beef. Sukiyaki was more popular than sushi in those days in the U.S. 03 **Tempura** /Tempura is a typical Washoku and is very popular among foreigners who love fried foods. Deep-fry vegetables or seafood with a light batter. Tempura can be made at any country by using local vegetables or seafood. Japanese people eat tempura with dipping in tempura sauce or with salt, but you can eat with ketchup or whatever you want. One of the widely accepted theories of the origin of tempura is that Portuguese brought it to Nagasaki about 400 years ago. 04 **Japanese Pizza: Okonomiyaki** /Okonomiyaki is a flat cake of batter fried on an iron plate with various ingredients like cabbage, meat and seafood. Okonomiyaki has a long

とりのから揚げと焼きとり

日本料理になれていない外国人もよく食べるのが、とりのから揚げや焼きとりです。から揚げは日本独特の料理法で、第二次世界大戦後の食料難のなか、養鶏場が多くつくられた際に考えだされた食べ方が発展したものといわれています。いっぽう焼きとりは、にわとりの肉や内臓をひと口大に切り、竹串にさして焼いた日本料理です。から揚げと焼きとりを丼に入れたごはんの上にのせた「から揚げ丼」や「焼きとり丼」を、メニューに取り入れている海外の日本食レストランも多くあります。とんカツを卵でとじたカツ丼も人気があります。

日本料理が人気のフランスでは、パーティーなどでは庭で焼きとりをすることもある。

ミソスープ好きの外国人が急増

日本料理にかかすことのできないみそ汁。だしをとった汁に、野菜やとうふ、海藻、貝など季節の食材やその地方の特産物を入れて煮て、みそをとき入れてつくります。海外で日本食レストランがふえたおかげで、みそ汁（ミソスープ）好きの外国人がどんどんふえています。
ただし、外国人が経営する日本食レストランなどでは、だしをとらず、みそをといただけの汁の場合が多いといいます。

ヨーロッパやアメリカでは、焼きとりは人気がある。

ディナーとして、みそ汁と肉じゃがをつくることもあるという、アメリカ東海岸に住むアメリカ人家庭。

08以降の英訳は→P150

---

history and it dates back to the Azuchi-Momoyama period. Each local region has its own ingredients and the way to make Okonomiyaki, and it is widely eaten throughout Japan. There is Teppan-yaki cooked on an iron plate same with Okonomiyaki. Teppan-yaki was introduced to the U.S. in 1960s and it has been popular among Americans. 05 **Kara-age (deep-fried chicken) and Yakitori** /Chicken Kara-age and Yakitori are often eaten by foreigners who are not accustomed to eating Washoku. The style of cooking Kara-age is peculiar to Japan, and it is said to be created during the period of food shortage after the World War II. In those days, many chicken farms were built. Yakitori is the dish to grill chicken meat and innards cut into one-sized bite and put on a skewer. There are many Japanese restaurants in abroad providing rice bowls topped with Kara-age or Yakitori. 06 Washoku is popular in France and some people grill Yakitori at a garden party. 07 Yakitori is popular in Europe and the U.S.

ラーメンも日本の食文化だ！

カレーライスとならんで日本の国民食ともいえるラーメンですが、その故郷は中国だと考えられています。

● 海外の食文化が根づくには ● 02

どこの国でも外国から食べ物が入ってきた場合、その国の人びとに受け入れられないか、一時的な流行で終わってしまうか、あるいはその国に根づいていくか、のいずれかです。

日本に海外の食文化が根づくには、つくり方や味が日本人の好みにあうように変化したり、食材も日本のものがつかわれるようになったりするのがふつうです。日本に根づいた海外の食文化の典型は、なんといってもラーメンです。日本に入ってきたあと、日本の南から北まで、独自の発展をしていきました。その土地の名前がついたご当地ラーメンは全国にかぞえきれないほどあります。その一部を地図で紹介しましょう。

これらはすでに、中国のラーメンとは異なる日本の食文化としてすっかり定着しています。こうしたラーメンは、世界の料理のなかで見れば、まちがいなく日本料理ということができるでしょう。

高山ラーメン 1
尾道ラーメン 20
京都ラーメン 17
博多ラーメン 21
久留米ラーメン 22
和歌山ラーメン
徳島ラーメン 19

中国語では「拉麺（ラーミエン）」 03

ラーメンということばは、中国語の「拉麺（ラーミエン）」ということばからきているという説が有力です。「拉（ラー）」には「引っぱる」という意味があります。中国では、生地を引っぱって麺をつくるのです。

日本のラーメンの麺は、いまではたいてい機械でつくります。手打ちの場合でも、うどんやそばのように生地をめん棒でのばし、折りたたんで包丁で切ります。引っぱってつくるわけではありません。ラーメンという名前だけが残ったのです。この意味でも、日本のラーメンは、日本の食文化だということができます。

01 Ramen is one of Japanese gastronomic cultures /Ramen is considered as a national dish same with curry and rice. It is supposed the birthplace of ramen is China. **02 How can the food from different culture take root?** /Localization is the key for foreign foods to take root in Japan. A typical example is ramen. After ramen was introduced from China, it has originally developed at each local region. **03 Ramyen in Chinese** /It is widely accepted that the term ramen is from Ramyen in Chinese. "Ra" means "pull" in Chinese, and Chinese Ramyen is made by pulling the dough. Most of the Japanese ramen noodles are made by a noodle machine. Hand-made dough is rolled out to a thin sheet, folded and cut into noodles. From these differences, Japanese ramen can be said to have developed as a Japanese food culture. **04 What is your favorite foreign food?** /According to the results of a questionnaire survey conducted in March 2013 by JETRO with 2,800 people from seven countries and regions (China, Hong Kong,

全国のご当地ラーメン

- 函館ラーメン
- 旭川ラーメン
- 札幌ラーメン
- 米沢ラーメン
- 喜多方ラーメン
- 佐野ラーメン
- 東京ラーメン
- 横浜ラーメン

好きな外国料理は？

2013年3月、日本貿易振興機構（JETRO）が7つの国・地域（中国、香港、台湾、韓国、アメリカ、フランス、イタリア）の合計2800人に対してアンケート調査をした結果が公表されました。「好きな外国料理は？」という質問に対して、1位は日本料理でした。このアンケートは、自分の国の料理は選んではいけないが複数回答できるという条件で実施されたといいます。いま、日本料理がブームだということは、このことからもわかりますね。

■好きな外国料理は？

- アフリカ料理
- 中東・アラブ料理
- スペイン料理
- インド料理
- メキシコ料理
- アメリカ料理
- フランス料理
- 韓国料理
- タイ料理
- イタリア料理
- 中国料理
- 日本料理 83.8%

出典：「日本食・食文化の海外普及について」
（農林水産省）

ラーメン店でラーメンを食べるアメリカ人のお父さんと女の子（アメリカ東海岸のまち）。

Taiwan, South Korea, U.S.A., France, Italy), the Japanese food was ranked No.1 to the answers of the question: "What is your favorite foreign food?" 05 graph top-to-bottom /African cuisine /Middle Eastern and Arabic cuisine / Spanish cuisine /Indian cuisine /Mexican cuisine /American cuisine /French cuisine /Korean cuisine /Thai cuisine / Italian cuisine /Chinese cuisine /Japanese cuisine 06 Father and daughter eating ramen at a ramen restaurant in the East Coast of the U.S. 07 Local ramen throughout Japan 08 Hakodate ramen 09 Asahikawa ramen 10 Sapporo ramen 11 Yonezawa ramen 12 Kitakata ramen 13 Sano ramen 14 Tokyo ramen 15 Yokohama ramen 16 Takayama ramen 17 Kyoto ramen 18 Wakayama ramen 19 Tokushima ramen 20 Onomichi ramen 21 Hakata ramen 22 Kurume ramen

日本発の新しい食文化

現代の食生活には、インスタント食品も大きな位置をしめるようになりました。とくに日本で開発されたインスタントラーメンやカニカマなどは海外でも人気が高く、広い意味では日本料理の海外進出の一端をになっています。

インスタントラーメンは日本発

世界初のインスタントラーメンは、日清食品の創業者である安藤百福が1958年につくったチキンラーメンです。その後、インスタントラーメンは世界に普及し、新しい食文化となったのです。2012年には世界全体の消費量（袋入りラーメン・カップラーメン）は、ついに1000億食を越えました。世界人口が70億人ぐらいなので、この数字がいかにすごいかがわかります。

アメリカのスーパーマーケットのたなにならぶ、日本のインスタントラーメン（上のたなには、みそも見える）。

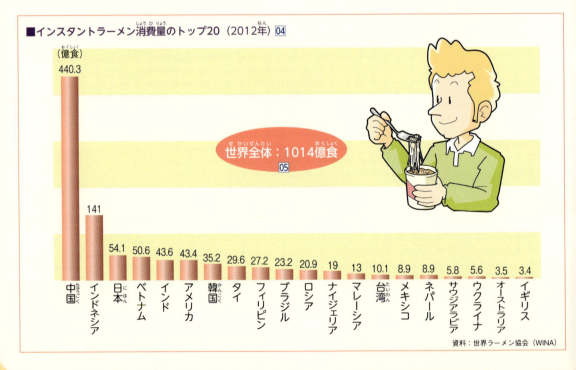

■インスタントラーメン消費量のトップ20（2012年）

世界全体：1014億食

国	億食
中国	440.3
インドネシア	141
日本	54.1
ベトナム	50.6
インド	43.6
アメリカ	43.4
韓国	35.2
タイ	29.6
フィリピン	27.2
ブラジル	23.2
ロシア	20.9
ナイジェリア	19
マレーシア	13
台湾	10.1
メキシコ	8.9
ネパール	8.9
サウジアラビア	5.8
ウクライナ	5.6
オーストラリア	3.5
イギリス	3.4

資料：世界ラーメン協会（WINA）

---

01 Newborn culinary culture generated from Japan / Ready-to-eat foods and instant foods take a big position in our modern diet. Especially instant noodles and Kanikama (imitation crab meat) developed in Japan are popular in foreign countries. These ingredients contribute to an expansion of Japanese food market in foreign countries. **02 Instant noodles born in Japan** / The world's first instant noodle is "Chicken Ramen" which was launched on the market in 1958 by Momofuku Ando, the founder of Nissin Food Products. After that, instant noodles have spread all over the world and have established a new food culture. The consumption of instant noodles in 2012 exceeded 100 billion. The world population is about 7 billion, so you can imagine how numerous it is. **03** Japanese instant noodles selling at a supermarket in the U.S. Miso is displayed on the top shelf. **04 Top 20 of the global consumption of instant noodles in 2012** (vertical axis /hundred million) (horizontal axis /China, Indonesia, Japan, Vietnam,

カニカマとは 06

カニカマというのは、1970年代に日本の水産加工メーカーが開発した、魚のすり身にカニの風味をつけたかまぼこのことです。棒状タイプのものやカニ足そっくりのものなどがあります。

カニカマは、「おいしくてヘルシーな食材」として世界各国で大ヒットし、いまではフランス、イタリア、ロシア、アメリカ、ブラジル、インドなど、世界21か国で生産されています。海外の生産量は国内の約7倍にものぼります。カニカマの世界進出をささえたのが、日本のメーカーがつくるカニカマ製造機です。

もっとも一般的な棒状タイプのカニカマ。07

機械をつかって操業しているインドのカニカマ工場。08

各国で販売されているカニカマ。フランスのカニカマは、「Surimi」という名で親しまれている。09

カニカマをおやつとして食べるフランスの子どもたち。10

India, U.S.A., South Korea, Thailand, Philippines, Brazil, Russia, Nigeria, Malaysia, Taiwan, Mexico, Nepal, Saudi Arabia, Ukraine, Australia, England) 05 World consumption total 101.4 billion 06 What is Kanikama (imitation crab meat)? /Kanikama is the steamed fish paste with crab flavor developed by Japanese seafood products manufacturer in 1970s. There are stick type Kanikama and some others which look like crab legs. Kanikama became a big hit around the world as "a tasty and healthy food," and it is produced in 21 countries all over the world today including France, Italy, Russia, U.S.A., Brazil and India. The production of Kanikama in foreign countries is about seven times larger than the production in Japan. Kanikama manufacturing machines made in Japan contribute to this world expansion. 07 Typical bar-shaped Kanikama. 08 Kanikama factory in India. 09 Kanikamas being sold all over the world. French Kanikama is known as "surimi." 10 French children eating Kanikama as a snack.

しょうゆとみそ [01]

しょうゆとみそは、いまでは世界じゅうに進出し、日本料理といえば、しょうゆ、みそをイメージする外国人は多いようです。

● 世界にひろがるしょうゆ ● [02]

日本の料理になくてはならないしょうゆは、いまでは世界じゅうでつかわれています。はじめてしょうゆが海外へでたのは1668年のこと。12たるのしょうゆを積んだオランダ船が、インド東海岸に向けて長崎港をでたのが最初だといわれています。その後、しょうゆはオランダからヨーロッパ各国へ伝えられ、たいへん貴重なものとしてもてはやされました。

現在では、世界的な日本料理ブームにより、世界各地でしょうゆの人気が高まっています。1989年当時、しょうゆの輸出は50パーセント以上がアメリカ向けでしたが、2012年には16パーセントほどとなっています。このことから、しょうゆがさまざまな国へ輸出されるようになったことがわかります。

また、しょうゆは、海外の工場でさかんに生産されています。1975年当時ですでに海外での生産量は8000キロリットルもありましたが、2011年には約20万キロリットルと、25倍にものびています。

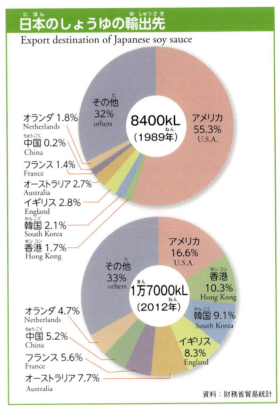

日本のしょうゆの輸出先
Export destination of Japanese soy sauce

8400kL (1989年)
- アメリカ U.S.A. 55.3%
- その他 others 32%
- オランダ Netherlands 1.8%
- 中国 China 0.2%
- フランス France 1.4%
- オーストラリア Australia 2.7%
- イギリス England 2.8%
- 韓国 South Korea 2.1%
- 香港 Hong Kong 1.7%

1万7000kL (2012年)
- アメリカ U.S.A. 16.6%
- 香港 Hong Kong 10.3%
- 韓国 South Korea 9.1%
- イギリス England 8.3%
- オーストラリア Australia 7.7%
- フランス France 5.6%
- 中国 China 5.2%
- オランダ Netherlands 4.7%
- その他 others 33%

資料：財務省貿易統計

しょうゆとテリヤキソースを売っているオーストラリアのコンビニエンスストア。[03]

しょうゆ・テリヤキソース・ぽん酢など、アジアの食材も売っているアメリカのスーパーマーケット。[04]

[01] Soy sauce and Miso [02] Soy sauce spreading throughout the world / Soy sauce is essential for Japanese food and is used widely all over the world today. The first exportation from Japan was in 1668. A Dutch ship laden with 12 barrels of soy sauce left Nagasaki port for the east coast of India. Afterwards soy sauce was introduced from Netherlands to European countries and accepted as the valuable merchandise. In 1989 over 50% of soy sauce exportation was for the United States, but in 2016 it is about 16%. This means that soy sauce is exported to other countries today. Soy sauce is also produced in factories outside Japan. Production of the soy sauce in overseas was 8,000kL in 1975 and in 2011 it grows to 200,000kL, increased by 25 times. [03] A convenience store in Australia selling soy sauce and Teriyaki sauce. [04] A supermarket in America selling Asian ingredients like soy sauce, Teriyaki sauce and ponzu sauce. [05] Soy sauce popular in foreign countries / Soy sauce in Japanese is "Shoyu." It is sometimes called as "Teriyaki" in foreign

●海外で人気のしょうゆ 05

しょうゆは英語では「SOY SAUCE」といいますが、「TERIYAKI」とよばれることも多くあります。現在では、海外のスーパーマーケットでもしょうゆを手に入れやすくなっています。

「TERIYAKI」ということばは、「肉や魚をしょうゆにひたしてから焼く料理」としてアメリカの辞書にもでています。肉料理のメニューに、「TERIYAKI」をのせているレストランもあります。

アメリカの日本食レストランの肉料理「TERIYAKI」。

●日本の食文化になくてはならないみそ 06

みそは、大豆を発酵させてつくる発酵食品で、日本各地でつくられています。原料から見ると、大豆に米麹を加えてつくる「米みそ」、大豆に麦麹を加えてつくる「麦みそ」、大豆のみを主原料とする「豆みそ」の3種類と、これらを調合した「調合みそ」があります。

みその起源は弥生時代にまでさかのぼり、古墳時代に発酵の技術が加わったとされる説や、奈良時代に中国から朝鮮半島を経て伝わってきたという説などがあります。ベトナムや朝鮮半島でも、独自の起源をもつみそがあるといわれています。

●みその輸出 07

みそは日本の代表的な調味料ですが、現在では、MISOとして海外でもよく知られるようになりました。輸出もさかんにおこなわれています。1992年のみその輸出量は2972トンでしたが、20年後の2012年には約1万トンにふえています。1992年当時は半数以上が北アメリカ（アメリカやカナダ）向けに輸出されていましたが、2012年には、アジアが輸出先の第1位となっています。また、1992年の輸出先が39か国・地域であったのに対し、2012年は47か国・地域にひろがっています。このことから、みそもしょうゆと同じように、世界各地で人気が高まっていることが見てとれます。

みその輸出先の変化
Change of Miso export destination

1992年
北アメリカ 56.4% North America
アジア 28.4% Asia
ヨーロッパ 9.8% Europe
オセアニア 4.7% Oceania
その他 0.6% others

2012年
北アメリカ 39.0% North America
アジア 40.1% Asia
ヨーロッパ 12.5% Europe
オセアニア 6.8% Oceania
その他 1.61% others

資料：財務省貿易統計

countries. Nowadays soy sauce is available at supermarkets in foreign countries. "Teriyaki" is listed in American dictionaries as "Grilled fish or meat marinated with soy sauce." Some restaurants have Teriyaki dish among the list of meat dishes. 06 **Miso is essential for Japanese food culture** /Miso is made from fermented soy beans and is produced all over Japan. It is classified into 3 types, Rice Miso, Barley Miso and Bean Miso. Origin of miso goes back to the Yayoi period, and there is a theory that fermentation technology was developed in tumulus period or introduced from China through Korean Peninsula in the Nara period. Vietnam and Korea have their own original miso. 07 **Exportation of miso** /The exportation of miso is active today. The export of miso in 1992 was 2,972 ton and it increased to 10,000 ton in 2012. In 1992 half of the export was to North America, but in 2012 Asia became the biggest export destination. In 1992 export destination was 39 countries and regions, but it increased to 47 in 2012.

日本のソースとうま味調味料

日本のソースにはどのような特徴があるでしょうか。
また、うま味調味料についてくわしく見ていきましょう。

●ウスターソースのひみつ●

日本の家庭で「ソース」とだけいった場合、たいていはウスターソースのことをさしています。

ウスターソースの名前は地名からきています。19世紀のはじめごろ、イギリスのウスターというまちの主婦が野菜や果実の切れはしを香辛料とともにつぼに入れて貯蔵していたところ、発酵してソースができていたといういわれがあるからです。

現在、世界各国でつかわれているソースは、19世紀後半にインドから伝わった製法でイギリスでつくられはじめたリーペリンソースがもとになっているといわれています。アンチョビーと、モルトビネガー（酢）に漬けこんだたまねぎやにんにく、トマトなどの野菜、多種類の香辛料を原料としてつくられています。

1900年ごろのリーペリンソース。
LEA & PERRINGS sauce in 1900s.

●日本のウスターソース●

日本のウスターソースは、イギリスの魚しょう的なソースとはちがい、イギリスから伝わったソースが独自に発展したものだといわれています。この点、カレーの起源（→124ページ）に似ています。明治時代に製造が始まった日本のソースは、たまねぎやトマトなどの野菜と、りんごなどの果実、砂糖、酢、カラメル、香辛料が主原料です。香辛料をひかえめにし、カラメルを加えることで甘味を強め、でんぷんを加えて粘度をつけているのが、日本のウスターソースの特徴です。日本にはウスターソースのほかに、粘度の高いとんカツソースや、粘度や味つけをかえたお好み焼きソースなどもあります。

もともとソースは料理のかくし味としてつかわれるものでしたが、日本では、揚げ物やお好み焼きなどにたっぷりとかけて食べるのが一般的です。とんカツなどの日本料理が海外にひろまるとともに、こうしたソースのつかい方も海外で受け入れられています。

日本では、とんカツにはとんカツソースをかけるのが一般的。
Tonkatsu is often enjoyed with "Tonkatsu sauce."

---

01 Japanese sauce and Umami seasonings **02** The secret of Worcestershire sauce / Worcestershire sauce derives from Worcester in England. The housewife in Worcester put leftover of vegetables, fruits and spices in a bottle and kept it in storage. Then it started fermentation and happened to become a sauce. It is said that sauce used all over the world derives from LEA & PERRINGS sauce made in England with the methods of Indian sauce in the 19th century. This sauce is made from anchovies, malt vinegar, pickled onions, garlic, tomatoes, other vegetables and spices. **03** Japanese Worcestershire sauce / Japanese Worcestershire sauce began to be produced in the Meiji period and its main ingredients are vegetables like onions and tomatoes, apples, sugar, vinegar, caramel and spices. The caramel is added for the sweetness, starch as a thickener, and less spices. There are sauces for Tonkatsu (pork cutlet) and for Okonomiyaki. The sauce was used as a secret seasoning originally, but in Japan, it is used as a main seasoning for

パート1　知ろう！ 調べよう！

うま味の発見 04

「うま味調味料」とは、料理に「うま味」を加える調味料のことです。「うま味」を発見したのは、明治時代後期の日本人化学者、東京帝国大学（現在の東京大学）の池田菊苗博士でした。

日本では昔から料理にこんぶだしがつかわれていました。池田博士は、味には、甘味（あまい）、塩味（しおからい）、苦味（にがい）、酸味（すっぱい）という4つの味のほかに、これらのどれにもあてはまらない第5の味があり、それがこんぶだしのおいしさのもとだと考えました。

グルタミン酸の発見につづき、かつお節にふくまれるイノシン酸、干ししいたけにふくまれるグアニル酸も、うま味のもとであることが発見されました。また、うま味成分は単独でつかうより、組みあわせてつかうほうがさらにおいしくなることがわかりました。こうして、日本の伝統的な食文化が生んだうま味は、「UMAMI」として世界じゅうに通じる共通語となりました。

いまでは、これらのうま味成分をうまく組みあわせた、いろいろな種類のうま味調味料がつくられています。

基本五味　Basic five tastes
あまい 甘味 sweet／しおからい 塩味 salty／にがい 苦味 bitter／すっぱい 酸味 sour　＋　うま味 umami

研究を始めた池田博士は、1908年、こんぶだしの主成分がグルタミン酸であることをつきとめ、その味を「うま味」と名づけました。そして、グルタミン酸を原料としたうま味調味料の製造方法を発明しました。翌年には、うま味調味料の製造が事業化され、「うま味のもと」ということから「味の素」と名づけられた調味料が発売されたのです。

世界のうま味 05

うま味が発見されたのは日本でですが、世界各地でもさまざまな形でうま味が利用されてきました。たとえば、ヨーロッパで昔からつかわれているアンチョビーも、うま味たっぷりの発酵食品です。フランス料理で基本のだしとしてつかわれているのは、フォン・ド・ヴォーです。これは牛の肉や骨と野菜を煮だしてつくったものです。ヨーロッパでよくつかわれるトマトにも、うま味が豊富にふくまれていることがわかっています。

日本では、こんぶとかつお節と干ししいたけのうま味が好んでつかわれてきましたが、ヨーロッパや中国などでは、肉や魚、野菜のうま味が利用されてきたのです。

05の英訳は→P150

---

deep-fried dishes and Okonomiyaki. **04 Discovery of Umami** /Umami seasoning is to add umami to the food. Umami was discovered by Dr. Kikunae Ikeda, a chemist and a professor of Tokyo University in the late Meiji period. Dr. Ikeda added umami as the fifth basic taste. Existing four tastes are sweet, salty, bitter and sour. Umami is the taste of kelp dashi which has been used for Japanese cooking since a long time ago. Dr. Ikeda started his research and identified that the main compound of the taste of kelp dashi is glutamic acid, and named it as umami. Later he invented the manufacturing process to make umami seasoning with glutamic acid. He succeeded in industrial production, and "Aji-no-moto" was launched on the market. Aji-no-moto means "source of umami." Followed by the discovery of glutamic acid, inocinic acid from dried bonito and guanylic acid from dried shiitake mushroom were discovered. Umami has a synergetic effect by combined together. Now, "umami" is the common word all over the world.

あらためて考える「和食」

「和食」は「日本料理」と同じく、「西洋料理(洋食)」に対応してできたことばです。「和食」についてあらためて考えてみましょう。

●和食のほうが庶民的●

「日本料理」は、1898（明治31）年発行の『日本料理法大全』(→122ページ)という本により一般化したといわれていますが、「和食」ということばが最初につかわれた文献はわかっていません。「日本料理」と「和食」のニュアンスのちがいについては、つぎのような指摘があります。

> 「日本料理といったときのイメージは、料理屋で提供される高級料理のイメージがあり、家庭食に重点を置いて日本食文化の全体を見ようとすれば、和食ということばのほうがふさわしい。」
> 出典：『和食―日本人の伝統的な食文化』（農林水産省）

●和食とは？●

家庭で食べるごはんとみそ汁に主菜がさしみや焼き魚なら、だれもが和食と感じます。食堂で食べる焼き魚定食も同じです。すしもウナギも和食。うどんやそばなどの麺類も和食のなかに入ります。また、鉄板焼きも和食と感じるでしょう。

ところが、主菜となるおかずがカレーやハンバーグ、ビーフシチューの場合はどうでしょうか。

海外のレストランではこのようなメニューは日本料理とされますが、日本人のなかには、それらを「和食」とは思わない人も多くいます。あらためて、「和食とはなにか？」を考えてみましょう。

●和食を育ててきたもの●

現在日本で食べられているあらゆる料理のなかで、なにが和食らしくしているのかを、食材、料理、栄養、もてなしの4つの要素でまとめてみましょう。

食材

「和食」で用いられる食材は、米を中心とする穀類、野菜、きのこ、魚、貝、海藻などがおもなものです。野菜は、昔から日本にある品種から明治時代以降に入ってきた西洋野菜まで、いろいろな種類のものがあります。また、日本近海に生息する魚種は約4200種類にものぼり、多種多様な方法で魚が食べられてきました。近年は、牛肉、ぶた肉、とり肉など肉類もつかわれていますが、中心となるのは魚料理です。

---

01 Re-evaluation of Washoku 02 Washoku is a humble dish /It is said that the concept and term of "Japanese cuisine" got popular owing to the description in the book: "Complete work on the method of Japanese cuisine." But it is not clear what the first document in which the term "Washoku" was described is. The difference between "Japanese cuisine" and "Washoku" is pointed out as below: *The image of Japanese cuisine is high-class food served at first-class restaurants, and Washoku is home-cooked food and covers whole gastronomic culture in Japan. Reference from "Washoku–traditional Japanese food culture."* **03 What is Washoku?** /Everybody feels it is Washoku when having home-cooked rice, Miso-shiru and sashimi or grilled fish. It is same with the set meal of grilled fish, rice and Miso-shiru at local restaurants. Sushi, eel dishes, Teppanyaki, udon and soba are Washoku, too. However, what do you think when the main dish is curry, hamburg steaks or beef stew? These dishes are considered as Washoku at the overseas restaurants but some

パート1　知ろう！調べよう！

料理 06

　和食の基本的な献立は「一汁三菜」です。ごはんを中心に、汁物1品とおかず3品（主菜1品、副菜が2品）を組みあわせた食事です。日本の食事は昔から淡白な味の穀物や野菜が中心でした。そのため、素材がもつおいしさを生かすために、だしがじょうずにつかわれました。だしは、こんぶやかつお節からとることもあれば、素材を煮こんで抽出することもあります。だしのうま味は、和食の味を決定づける大事な要素です。

もてなし 08

　「もてなし」は、主人から客への「サービス」という意味ではありません。料理をつくる人、食べる人のおたがいに対する思いやりのことです。つくる側の人は、食べる人のことを思って、旬の食材をおいしく調理し、美しく盛りつけて、その料理がいちばんおいしい状態でだします。食べる側の人も、その思いやりに気づき、「いただきます」「ごちそうさま」ということばで、感謝の気持ちをあらわすのです。

栄養 07

　ごはんを中心とした伝統的な和食は、健康的な生活を送るために理想的な栄養バランスをとりやすい食事です。ごはんでエネルギー源となる炭水化物を、動物性脂質の少ないおかずでその他の栄養素をバランスよくとることができます。主食と副食を交互に、口の中で調和させながら食べるのは、和食独特の食べ方です。うま味を生かした料理は、うす味でもおいしく食べられ、油脂をつかわずにすむので、塩分やカロリーをコントロールできます。

和食ワールドチャレンジ2013 09

　2013年12月、東京都内で、外国人による和食の世界大会「和食ワールドチャレンジ2013」（主催：和食ワールドチャレンジ2013実行委員会・農林水産省）がおこなわれました。これは、世界各国・地域で和食に取り組んでいる料理人の才能を発掘し、和食の魅力をさらに世界にひろげていくことを目的として、今回はじめて開催されました。

　今回の料理のテーマは「健康」。素材そのもののおいしさを生かし、うま味成分を活用することで、油脂の使用を減らしながら、おいしく満足感の高い料理をつくるという、和食の特徴をふまえたヘルシーでおいしい料理をいかにつくれるかがきそわれました。

07以降の英訳は➡P151

Japanese do not think so. 04 **Factors of Washoku** /What is "Washoku-like" in our daily meals? Let's re-evaluate it by four factors: ingredients, cooking, nutrition and serving hospitality. 05 **Ingredients** /Main ingredients used for Washoku are grains centering on rice, vegetables, mushrooms, fish, shellfish and seaweeds. There are many species of vegetable eaten since long time ago, and new western vegetables have been introduced after the Meiji period. The number of fish species in the seas around Japan totals 4,200, and they have been eaten in many ways. Recently, beef, pork and chicken are used but fish is the main ingredients of Washoku. 06 **Cooking** /Basic meal of Washoku is 1 Soup and 3 Dishes. 1 soup, 1 main dish and 2 side dishes are combined with the rice, the staple food. Japanese meal used to be consisted of grains and vegetables with light tastes. People made good use of dashi to bring out the tastes of ingredients. Umami of dashi is the key factor of the taste of Washoku.

和食の海外普及 [01]

いまや世界の主要都市で、日本食レストランを見かけないことはありません。日本食レストランは、和食の発信拠点ともなっています。

● 和食を正しく伝える ● [02]

世界各国にある日本食レストランは、その国の人が日本の食を味わい、日本の食文化にふれることができる場所です。食をとおして日本を理解してもらうことにつながるのです。

海外にある日本食レストランの数は、2013年3月時点で約5万5000店にのぼります（→116ページ）。しかし、これらのなかには、和食のようだけれどそうとはいえないような料理をだすところが多いといわれています。みそ汁にしても、だしをとらずに、ただみそをといただけのものだったり、素材のもち味がわからなくなるほど調味料や油脂をたっぷりとつかって調理されたものだったりします。

また、日本食でもっとも人気があるのは「すし」「さしみ」のため、生魚をあつかうときの衛生面が問題になることもあります。

そこで、日本食レストランの信頼性を高め、和食を正しく知ってもらうために、さまざまな活動がおこなわれています。そのひとつが、「日本食レストラン海外普及推進機構（JRO）」というNPO*が実施した右のような活動です。

＊NPOは、Nonprofit Organizationの略で、特定非営利活動法人（利益を目的としない社会貢献活動をおこなう市民団体）のこと。

シカゴのNRA・SHOW 2013にジャパン・

NRA・SHOWというのは、アメリカ最大規模の食関連見本市のこと。ジャパン・パビリオンの全体テーマは、和食の最大の特徴でもある「うま味」（→135ページ）。いまや世界共通語となっている「UMAMI」をアピール。[04]

---

[01] **The expansion of Washoku throughout the world** /Every big city in the world has Japanese restaurants. They are bases of promoting Washoku. [02] **Introducing Washoku correctly** /Japanese restaurants in each country are the places to introduce Japanese foods and culture. It leads to deeper understanding of Japan through the foods. The number of Japanese restaurants in foreign countries is about 55,000 as of March 2013. But not all of these restaurants provide the authentic Washoku. Some of them make miso soup without dashi or add excess oil or seasoning to foods that result in killing original tastes of ingredients. The most popular Washoku is sushi or sashimi, so the hygiene management should be observed particularly when handling raw fish. There are many activities which are carried out to enhance reliability of Japanese restaurants and the correct understanding of Washoku.

海外の料理人に生魚のあつかい方を講習 06

生魚のあつかい方を説明し、マグロの大きなブロックからさしみをつくるまでを実演。07

パビリオンを出展 03

「うま味」発見のきっかけとなったのは、こんぶだし。真こんぶ、利尻こんぶ、日高こんぶ、羅臼こんぶの実物を展示。05

海外の料理人に対する「うま味」の講習・切り方の実演 08

かつお節を実際にけずり、けずり節でかつおだしをとることを説明。

こんぶとかつお節で一番だしをとるのを実演し、味わってもらう。09

和包丁の特徴やあつかい方を説明し、野菜の切り方を実演。10

モスクワで衛生講習会を実施 11

生ものをあつかうときの手指の消毒、包丁・まな板など調理道具の衛生管理の重要性を説明。12

生魚の正しい調理方法を、実習を交えながら解説。13

03 Japanese Pavilion at NRA SHOW 2013 04 NRA SHOW is one of the biggest food exhibitions in the U.S. Japan appealed "umami", the key of Washoku there. 05 The kelp dashi became the trigger of discovery of umami. 06 Lecture on how to handle raw fish to foreign chefs 07 An explanation of how to handle raw fish and how to cut the big block fish into sashimi slices. 08 Lecture on umami and cutting demonstration 09 Shave dried bonito into flakes and make the first dashi. 10 An explanation of the characteristic of Japanese knives and the demonstration on how to cut vegetables. 11 Hygiene control seminar in Moscow 12 An explanation of washing hands with a sanitizer and the importance of hygiene control of cooking tools. 13 A demonstration of how to cook raw fish.

和食を未来へ引きつぐ

2013年12月、和食がユネスコ無形文化遺産に登録されました（→第3章102ページ）。和食を未来に引きつぐために、どんなことができるでしょうか。

● 和食があぶない ●

現代の日本人の食生活はかつてないほどのスピードで変化しています。世界じゅうの国の料理が取り入れられ、多様な食のスタイルが生まれてきました。そのいっぽうで米と魚といった日本の伝統的な和食を好む人はどんどん減っています。お正月のおせち料理やお雑煮も食べない人がふえています。郷土料理や行事の料理は、どんどん消えていっています。それどころか、和食の基本となっているごはんを食べない人も多くなってきました。

また、和食は、日本の食材をつかってつくられることに意義があるにもかかわらず、いまや日本の食料自給率は40パーセントを割ってしまっています。

こうしたなか、和食（WASHOKU）が無形文化遺産に登録されたのです。これは、まさに和食の危機のうら返しだったのです。

● 食育を推進しよう ●

和食が無形文化遺産に登録されたことを受けて、文部科学大臣は「文部科学省としても、和食が次世代に着実に継承されるよう、食育を推進したい」と語りました。

食育は、家庭・学校・地域が連携して進めていくことがたいせつです。具体的には、下のようなことが可能です。

家庭
- 幼いときから和食の献立とおいしさを体験する。
- 食の作法（おはしのつかい方、「いただきます」「ごちそうさま」）を身につける。
- 家族が食卓をかこんで食べるたのしさを知る。

学校
- 地場野菜がつかわれた給食を食べる。
- 食についての知識（栄養・自給率など）を得る。
- 調理技術・食べ物の味覚を学ぶ。

地域
- 地域の年中行事と密接にかかわる食文化を受けつぐ。
- 地域の産物を知り、郷土料理をたいせつにする。

---

01 Inheritance of Washoku to the next generation **02** Washoku is in crisis / Dietary life of modern Japanese people is changing in a high speed. Foods are introduced from all over the world to Japan and wide varieties of eating habits have been developed. On the other hand, the number of people who prefer traditional Japanese food like rice and fish is decreasing. People eat less Osechi or Zoni soup in the New Year, local foods and seasonal festive foods. Using Japanese ingredients has a great value for Washoku, but the food self-sufficiency ratio of Japan is now less than 40%. Under these conditions, Washoku was registered as UNESCO Intangible Cultural Heritage. We have to reconsider Washoku and inherit it to the next generation. **03** Promotion of Food Education / On the occasion of the registration of Washoku, the Minister of Education, Culture, Sports, Science and Technology mentioned as follows: "The Ministry of Education would like to promote the food education so that Washoku is inherited to the next generation."

「味覚の一週間」とは

「味覚の一週間」は、1990年にフランスで始まり、20年以上に渡って実施されているユニークな食育の取り組みです。当時フランスでは、子どもたちを取り巻く食文化の乱れが深刻な問題となっていました。そのため、子どものころからフランスの食文化をきちんと身につけられるように、毎年10月の第3週を「味覚の一週間」と設定したのです。

この期間、多数のシェフや食に関する職人たちが、いろいろ工夫をこらして子どもたちに味覚の基本を教えます。子どもたちといっしょに料理をつくったりもします。この取り組みはフランス全土にひろまり、国を挙げた食育活動となっています。食に関する討論会や農場の見学、有名なレストランでの食事会などさまざまなイベントが、役所や市民団体、学校、食品関連企業などによって開催されています。

日本の「味覚の一週間」

食育の一環として、2010年より日本でも10月の第4週に「味覚の一週間」の活動がおこなわれるようになりました。この期間中、日本各地の小学校やレストランなどで、五感をつかって味わうことのたいせつさや、食のたのしみを体感できるさまざまな取り組みが実施されます。

日本の「味覚の一週間」には、つぎの3つの柱があります。

- **味覚の授業** 全国の小学校で、シェフ・料理人やパティシエなどが子どもたちに味の基本や五感をつかって食べるたいせつさを教えます。
- **味覚の食卓** 「味覚の授業」に参加したシェフ・料理人のお店を中心に開催。家族や友人と会話をたのしみながら味わうたのしさを見いだします。
- **味覚のアトリエ** 協賛企業や協力組織による味覚体験イベントです。

「味覚の一週間」の授業の一環として、ブーランジェリー（パン屋さん）でパンづくりを体験するフランスの子どもたち。

「味覚の授業」のようす。上は香りを感じる授業。下はシェフによる調理実演。

The food education needs to be done in cooperation with homes, schools and local regions. School /• Eat school lunch with local vegetables. /• Learn about foods, nutrition and self-sufficiency. / • Learn about cooking methods and tastes of foods. Home /• Eat Washoku and enjoy its tastes from childhood. / • Learn good table manners. / • Experience the joy of eating with family. Region /• Inherit local festivals and food cultures. /• Respect local foods and ingredients. **What is "The Week of Taste"?** /The Week of Taste is an annual event initiated in France more than 20 years before. At that time, children's imbalanced diet was a serious problem. So they set the third week of October as The Week of Taste and started educating culture of French cuisine. In this week many chefs and people in food industries teach the basic tastes to children and cook together. These activities became a nationwide food education project today. French children taking a lesson of making bread on The Week of Taste.

和食からWASHOKUへ
世界にひろがる和食

パート2 つくろう！ 食べよう！

てんぷら・かき揚げ

衣をじょうずにつくって、サクッとしたてんぷらを揚げましょう。材料の下ごしらえはていねいにしましょう。

【材料 4人分】

<てんぷら>
- エビ …………… 8尾
- イカ …………… 4切
- キス …………… 4尾
- 小なす …………… 2個
- ししとうがらし ………… 4本
- さつまいも（5mm厚さの輪切り）… 4枚

<かき揚げ>
- 芝エビ …………… 20尾
- みつば …………… 1/3パック

<衣>★
- 薄力粉 …………… 1.5カップ
- 冷水 …………… 1カップ
- 卵 …………… 1個

★卵に冷水を加えてよくかきまぜる。そこにふるった薄力粉を加えてまぜる。まぜすぎないように気をつけること。

てんぷら

つくり方

1 エビは、頭を取りながら背わたをぬく。尾をひと節だけ残して、からをむく。

2 エビの尾の先を包丁で切りそろえて水気をとり、腹側を2～3か所、手で反対に折るようにして筋をのばす。

3 キスは水洗いし、背開きして中骨を取る。

4 小なすは、がくを切りとり、たて半分に切ったあと、切りはなさないように切りこみを入れる（末広切りという）。

5 衣をつけて、野菜は170℃、エビとエビの頭・キスは180℃の油で揚げる。

6 イカは小麦粉をうすくつけてから、衣をつけて180℃の油で揚げる。

---

01 Tempura and Kakiage (mixed vegetable and seafood tempura) /Make good batter, and deep-fry the ingredients crispy. The key point is the preparation of ingredients.

02 Ingredients for 4 servings

[Tempura]
- shrimp : 8
- squid : 4
- sillago : 4
- small eggplant : 2
- green pepper : 4
- sweet potato sliced in 5mm thickness : 4

[Kakiage (mixed vegetable and seafood tempura)]
- Shiba shrimp : 20
- Mitsuba (Japanese hornwort) : 1/3 package

[batter]★
- light wheat flour : 1.5 cups
- cold water : 1 cup
- egg : 1

★Beat eggs, add cold water and mix well. Put sifted flour into the mixture of eggs and water, mix lightly. Be careful not to over-mix.

かき揚げ 04

つくり方

1. 芝エビはからをむき、背わたを取る。

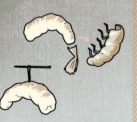

2. 1と2cmの長さに切ったみつばをボウルに入れてまぜあわせる。

3. 2に衣を入れてまぜ、おたまで180℃の油の中に入れて揚げる。

4. てんぷらとかき揚げを皿に盛る。好みで、だいこんおろしとてんつゆをそえる。

---

03 Tempura How to make

1. Remove the head and the sand vein of the shrimp and peel off shells. Keep tail and 1 segment of the shell next to the tail. /2. Cut off the edge of the tail in a good shape; remove wetness of the body; press 2 or 3 points of abdominal side to the opposite side with fingers to elongate the flesh. /3. Wash sillago, then cut and open from the back and remove the backbone. /4. Cut sepals off the eggplant and cut them into half lengthwise. Make several cuts from the top just below the calyx to the bottom. /5. Coat with batter and deep-fry vegetables in 170℃ oil, shrimp and sillago in 180℃. /6. Coat squid with the wheat flour lightly then coat with batter and deep-fry in 180℃.

04 Kakiage (mixed vegetable and seafood tempura) How to make

1. Peel off shells and the sand vein of Shiba shrimp. /2. Cut Mitsuba into 2cm length and mix with the shrimp. /3. Add appropriate amount of batter to (2) and put into 180℃ oil with a ladle and deep-fry. /4. Dish up with grated daikon and dipping sauce.

ドラゴンロール [01]

スライスしたアボカドがまるでドラゴンのように見える巻きずし！
酢めしをのりの外側にして巻く、
海外で人気の「うら巻き」の仕方を覚えましょう。

【材料 4本分】[02]

焼きのり……4枚	サニーレタス……4枚
エビてんぷら……8本	マヨネーズ……適量
<厚焼き卵 1本>	とびこ……適量
卵……3個	アボカド……2個
砂糖……大さじ2	レモン汁……適量
塩……少々	ごはん……3合
うすくちしょうゆ……小さじ1/2	<合わせ酢>
	酢……60mL
	砂糖……25g
	塩……5g

[02] Ingredients for 4 servings
- nori(toasted laver) : 4 sheets
- shrimp tempura : 8

[Japanese thick omelet]
- egg : 3
- sugar : 2 tbsps
- salt : a little
- light soy sauce : 1/2 tsp

- red leaf lettuce : 4 leaves
- mayonnaise : adequate amount
- flying fish roe : adequate amount
- avocado : 2
- lemon juice : adequate amount
- rice : 3 rice cups (540mL)

[sushi vinegar]
- rice vinegar : 60mL
- sugar : 25g
- salt : 5g

[01] **Dragon Roll Sushi** /Sliced avocado looks like a dragon. Roll sushi with the rice on the outside; inside-out roll sushi is called "Uramaki." Uramaki is popular in abroad.

[03] How to make
1. Transfer freshly cooked rice to a wooden container, pour blended sushi vinegar. Mix quickly and cool the rice by waving a fan. /2. Make Japanese thick omelet and some shrimp tempura. /3. Place the cling-film on the whole surface of the bamboo rolling mat and put nori cut into 3/4 size. Spread 1/4 of the rice on nori. /4. Spread flying fish roe on the whole surface of the rice and turn over the layer of nori-rice-flying fish roe on the film. /5. Put red leaf lettuce, shrimp tempura, egg omelet and mayonnaise on nori. Lift the mat using your fingers and make a roll. /6. Peel off the skin of avocados, cut them into half

パート2 つくろう！食べよう！

つくり方 03

1. 炊きたてのごはんを飯台にあけ、合わせ酢をまわしかける。手早くまぜたあと、うちわであおいで冷ます。

2. 厚焼き卵をつくる（つくり方は右）。142ページの要領でエビてんぷらをつくる。

3. 巻きす全体にラップをかけ、3/4に切ったのりを置く。1の酢めしの1/4量を取り、のりの上にひろげる。

4. 3の酢めしの上全体にとびこをしきつめ、のりをもってうら返す。

5. 4の上に、サニーレタス、エビてんぷら、厚焼き卵、マヨネーズをのせて、のり巻きの要領で巻いていく。

6. アボカドの皮をむき、半分に切って種を取り、うすくスライスする。色がかわらないようにレモン汁を少しかけ、ラップの上にならべる。

7. 6の上に5をのせて、巻きすでおさえて形をととのえる。

8. ラップをしたまま包丁で切る。ラップをはずして、皿に盛りつける。

厚焼き卵をつくろう 04

① 卵を割りほぐし、分量の調味料を入れてよくかきまぜる。

② 卵焼き器をよく熱して、油をひく。①の卵液の1/3量を一気に流し入れ、中火で焼く。

③ 半熟状態になったら、手早く巻いていく。

④ 卵を手前によせ、油をふくませたクッキングペーパーで卵焼き器をふく。

⑤ 卵を向こう側によせ、残りの半量の卵液を流し入れる。

⑥ 卵を少しもち上げて、卵液が全体に流れるようにする。

⑦ 卵液が半熟状態になったら、手早く巻いていく。同じようにして残りの卵液も焼く。

---

lengthwise and remove the seed. Slice avocados thinly and pour lemon juice to prevent discoloration, then place them on the film as same width with nori. /7. Put (5) roll on (6) avocado. Make a good shape by using a mat. /8. Cut with the film and remove it when dishing up.

04 How to make Atsuyaki Tamago (Japanese thick omelet)
1. Beat eggs and mix with seasonings. /2. Heat the egg omelet pan well and pour oil. Pour 1/3 of egg liquid and heat over medium fire. /3. Roll the egg quickly by using chopsticks when it gets half-cooked. /4. Pull rolled egg on your side and grease the pan with oil-saturated paper. /5. Put the rolled egg to the opposite side and pour egg liquid on your side. /6. Lift the egg omelet a little bit and spread the egg liquid to the whole pan./7. Roll the egg quickly when it gets half-cooked, repeat (2)-(6).

焼(や)きとり

手(て)で串(くし)をもって食(た)べられる焼(や)きとりは、海外(かいがい)でも人気(にんき)。
材料(ざいりょう)が均一(きんいつ)に焼(や)けるように、串(くし)のさし方(かた)を工夫(くふう)しましょう。

01 Yakitori (grilled chicken) /Yakitori can be eaten directly from skewers. The tip is to put skewers so that meat cooked evenly.

02 Ingredients for 4 servings
- chiken leg : 1
- chiken liver : adequate amount
- Welsh onion : 1

[sauce for Yakitori]
- soy sauce : 140mL
- sake : 30mL
- sugar : 1 tbsp
- mirin : 100mL
- starch dissolved with water : adequate amount
- salt and pepper : adequate amount
- lemon : adequate amount

パート2 つくろう！食べよう！

【材料 4人分】
- とりもも肉 ……… 1枚
- とりレバー ……… 適量
- 長ねぎ ……… 1本
- <焼きとりのタレ>
  - しょうゆ ……… 140mL
  - 酒 ……… 30mL
  - 砂糖 ……… 大さじ1
  - みりん ……… 100mL
  - 水ときかたくり粉 ……… 適量
  - 塩・こしょう ……… 適量
  - レモン ……… 適量

つくり方

1 とりもも肉はひと口大に切る。とりレバーはひと口大に切り、しばらく流水につける。

2 長ねぎは2cmの長さに切る。

3 焼きとりのタレの調味料をなべに入れ、弱火でしばらく煮る。最後に水ときかたくり粉でとろみをつける。

4 とりもも肉と長ねぎを交互に串にさす。もも肉だけをさす串もつくる。とりレバーも串にさす。

5 4の串の半量は、塩・こしょうをふってから焼く。

6 残りはそのまま焼き、七〜八分焼けたら、3のタレをつけて焼く。かわいたら再度タレをつける（2〜3回くり返す）。

7 焼けたら皿に盛り、レモンをそえる。

水ときかたくり粉

料理にとろみをつけるとき、かたくり粉やコーンスターチなどのでんぷんをつかいます。でんぷんは、水とともに加熱するとかたまる性質があるからです。

<じょうずにとろみをつけるコツ>
- かたくり粉は同量〜2倍量の水でとかす。
- かたくり粉はすぐに沈殿するので、煮汁に入れる前に再度よくかきまぜる。
- 水ときかたくり粉は、かならず煮汁が煮立った状態のときに入れる。
- 水ときかたくり粉を「の」の字をえがくようにまわし入れ、素早くかきまぜる。
- 好みのとろみになるまで、少しずつ入れてはまぜるをくり返す。

04の英訳は⇒ P151

How to make
1. Cut a chicken leg and liver into bite-sized pieces. Rinse pieces of liver with running water. /2. Cut the Welsh onion into 2cm length. /3. Put the sauce ingredients of Yakitori into a pan: soy sauce, sake, sugar and mirin, and heat it over low flame. Add starch with water at the end to thicken the sauce. /4. Make 3 types of chicken skewers. Type 1 is to put pieces of chicken leg and Welsh onion on skewers alternately. Type 2 is to use chicken meat only, and type 3 is to use chicken liver only. /5. Season half of the skewers with salt and pepper before grilling. /6. Grill the rest of the skewers without sauce at the beginning. Spread sauce when they are almost cooked. Spread sauce again when the surface get dried. Repeat grilling and spreading sauce for 2 or 3 times. /7. Dish up and garnish with sliced lemon.

カツ丼

海外で丼物は人気がありますが、なかでもカツ丼はいちばん人気です。
たまねぎの甘みを生かした丼つゆが、おいしさのひけつです。

Katsudon (pork cutlet on a bowl of rice) /Katsudon is the most popular rice bowl with topping. The sweetness is given to the sauce by onion.

Ingredients for 4 servings
- pork loin : 4 slices
- egg : 4
- onion : 2
- Japanese hornwort(Mitsuba) : 18 pieces
- wheat flour : adequate amount
- beaten egg : adequate amount
- fresh bread crumbs : adequate amount
- salt and pepper : adequate amount
- rice : adequate amount

[sauce]
- dashi : 3 cups
- soy sauce : 1 cup
- mirin : 1 cup
- sugar : 2 tbsps

パート2 つくろう！食べよう！

【材料 4人分】

ぶたロース	4枚
卵	4個
たまねぎ	2個
みつば	18本
小麦粉	適量
とき卵	適量
生パン粉	適量
塩・こしょう	適量
ごはん	適量
<丼つゆ>	
だし	3カップ
しょうゆ	1カップ
みりん	1カップ
砂糖	大さじ2

つくり方

1. ぶた肉は筋切りをし、塩・こしょうする。小麦粉、とき卵、生パン粉の順につける。これを4枚つくる。

2. たっぷりの油で、1を色よく揚げ、食べやすい大きさに切っておく。

3. たまねぎは半分に切り、1cmぐらいの厚さに横に切っておく。

4. 丼つゆのだしと調味料をなべに入れ、3のたまねぎを加えて半煮え状態にしておく。

5. 親子なべ（→153ページ）に4の丼つゆの1/4量を入れ、2のカットしたとんカツをのせて火にかける。

6. 5に軽くほぐした卵を流し入れる。

7. 6にみつばをのせ、ふたをしてサッと火を通す。

8. 親子なべをゆすり、なべに卵がくっついていないことを確認し、ごはんをよそった丼に流し入れて仕上げる。

たまねぎの切り方 <たてに切る・横に切る>

たまねぎは、料理によって、たてに切る場合と、横に切る場合があります。
たまねぎをたてに切ると、熱がよく通り、煮くずれしやすくなります。逆に、たまねぎを横に切ると、熱を加えても煮くずれしにくくなります。また、たまねぎ特有の辛み成分がぬけて甘みがでやすくなります。それで、カツ丼につかうたまねぎは、横に切ることが多いのです。

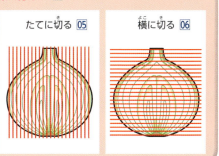

たてに切る　　横に切る

04以降の英訳は ➡ P151

How to make

1. The preparation of the pork. Make small cuts against the grain and season with salt and pepper. Coat pork with the wheat flour, beaten egg and fresh bread crumbs in this order. /2. Deep-fry pork with plenty of oil. Cut them into good size of amount to eat. /3. Cut onions into halves, then slice them crosswise into 1cm width. /4. Pour dashi, sauce ingredients and the onion into a pan, and heat. Turn off the heat when the onion gets half-cooked. /5. Transfer 1/4 of (4) sauce and the onion to a shallow pan, put (2) pork cutlets and heat. /6. Pour lightly beaten egg. /7. Put some Mitsuba on the top, cover with a lid and lightly cook. /8. Dish up on the top of rice in the bowl.

はみだし英訳

P119

10 Sushi-go-round is a big trend in Southeast Asia
Japanese restaurants in Bangkok, Thailand used to be exclusive ones, but nowadays casual dining restaurants and sushi-go-round (kaiten-zushi) restaurants began to serve Washoku. Japanese foods became popular among younger generations mainly. In the 2000s, all-you-can-eat type sushi restaurants have appeared in Bangkok, and Washoku boom is sparked off.
11 Signboard of buffet sushi restaurant.

P121

07 Japanese cuisine in Europe
Authentic Japanese restaurants managed by the Japanese owner or the Japanese chef are few. There are only some in the big cities. Most of the Japanese restaurants serve rather new-style sushi with marinated salmon and inside-out roll sushi. Nowadays Japanese style bars (Izakayas), ramen restaurants and sushi-go-round restaurants have appeared.
08 Sushi-go-round restaurant in London managed by the large chain restaurant.
09 A happy child seeing the food rotating on the conveyor.

P123

06 Pork Cutlet is transformed to Tonkatsu
It is said that Motojiro Kida from Western-Japanese restaurant, Rengatei is the first chef who made Tonkatsu. Kida was inspired from French dish Cotelette that is butter sauted thin slice of beef coated with bread crumbs. He made deep-fried thick slice pork coated with flour, beaten egg and bread crumbs, and named "Pork cutlet."
Afterwards Tonkatsu of similar style with present-day was created. It is to deep-fry thick pork slice, cut in a good size easily eaten with chopsticks and garnish with shredded cabbage.
07 Tonkatsu is popular among tourists visiting Japan.
08 Top 10 ranking Japanese food in foreign countries/A site of Tripadvisor announced top 10 ranking Japanese food for foreign tourists. The most popular dish is sushi.
1st Italy, 2nd Portugal, 3rd U.S.A., 4th Hawaii (U.S.A.), 5th U.S.A., 6th New Zealand, 7th Mexico, 8th U.K., 9th Mexico, 10th Chile

P125

06 The origin of Nikujaga is Beef stew/Nikujaga is a typical Japanese Mom's dish and is a braised dish with meat, potatoes, onion, konnyaku seasoned with soy sauce, sugar and mirin.
It is said that Nikujaga has a deep connection with the commander in chief of a navy base in Maizuru, Kyoto, Heihachiro Tōgō who studied in Portsmouth, England in his younger days.
Tōgō loved beef stew of British navy, and he ordered to make this arrange to Japanese style at the navy base when he came back to Japan. This is the origin of Nikujaga. So Maizuru is considered as the birthplace of Nikujaga.
07 Japanese navy cooking book published in 1938
Recipe of Nikujaga
1. Pour oil into a pot and heat.
2. Add beef 3 min later.
3. Add sugar 7 min later.
4. Add soy sauce 10 min later.
5. Add potatoes and konnyaku 14 min later.
6. Add onion 31 min later.
7. Finish cooking after 34 min.
All the process worked out to the minute is exactly like the army.
08 Recipe book kept in the Maritime Self-Defence Force in Maizuru City.

P127

08 Rapid increase of foreigners who like Miso-shiru
Miso-shiru (miso soup) is essential to Washoku. Cook seasonal vegetables, tofu, seaweeds or shellfish in dashi and add miso. As the number of Japanese restaurants in abroad is increasing, Miso-shiru is getting popular among foreigners. But some Japanese restaurants managed by foreigners serve miso soup just mixing miso with water and not using dashi.
09 An American family in the East Coast makes Miso soup and Nikujaga for dinner.

P135

05 Umami taste in the world/Umami was discovered in Japan but each country has its own way to make the most of umami. For example, the anchovy eaten in Europe since long time ago is a fermented food rich with umami. French basic soup stock "fond de veau" is an extract which is rich with the essence of beef, bones and vegetables. Tomato which is popular in Europe is found to be the source of umami. Umami from the kelp and dried bonito have been used in Japan. But meats, fishes and vegetables were used as umami ingredients in Europe and in China.

P137
07 Nutrition
Washoku is well balanced in nutrition. The rice is carbohydrates and is a source of energy. Balanced nutrition with low animal fat can be obtained from other dishes. Eat rice and side dishes in turns and mix the tastes inside the mouth. The foods focused on umami can be enjoyed even with light taste. As they do not need to use fat, it is easy to control the amount of salt and calorie.

08 Hospitality
Hospitality does not mean just the service from the host to the guests. It is to have consideration for each other, both who make meal and who eat. The person who makes meal prepares foods with seasonal ingredients, dishes up beautifully and serves at the best timing. The eaters show their gratitude by the words "Itadakimasu" or "Gochisosama" for the hospitality.

09 Washoku World Challenge Competition 2013
Washoku cooking competition for foreign chefs, sponsored by Ministry of Agriculture, Forestry and Fisheries was held on December 2013. This aims to discover talented foreign chefs who make Washoku within Japan or in foreign countries, and to appeal Washoku all over the world.

P141
09 "The Week of Taste" in Japan
Japan has started The Week of Taste as a part of the food education from 2010 in the 4th week of October. During the period many events are held to enjoy tasting with five senses and cooking by themselves.
There are 3 initiatives of The Week of Taste.
Class of the Taste /Chefs or patissiers lecture the basic tastes and the importance of eating with 5 senses.
Dining and Tasting /Children have pleasant experience with eating and talking with families and friends at the restaurants.
Tasting event /A tasting seminar or event organized by sponsored companies.

10 The lesson of tastes to feel the sense of smell and flavor, and cooking demonstration by the chef.

P147
04 Katakuriko (potato starch) dissolved with water
Potato starch or corn starch is added as a thickener, because starch with water coagulates by heating.
A tip to thicken with Katakuriko:
- Dissolve Katakuriko with same or twice times the amount of water.
- Katakuriko is easily precipitate in the water, so mix again before adding to the soup.
- Add Katakuriko when soup is boiling.
- Pour small amount of Katakuriko into the soup in a shape of circle, mix quickly.
- Add Katakuriko by degrees and mix, repeat this process to your pleasant thickness.

P149
04 How to cut onion.
Cut lengthwise or cut crosswise
Cutting onion into lengthwise or crosswise depends on the food to cook. Lengthwise cut onion is easily to be cooked and fall apart while cooking. Crosswise cut onion do not easily fall apart while cooking. Moreover, the pungent taste is deteriorated and the sweetness is given. That is why the onion for Katsudon is cut crosswise to add sweetness.
05 Cut lengthwise
06 Cut crosswise

和食の調理道具 01

おろし金 02
だいこんやしょうが、根わさびなどをすりおろすときにつかう。

飯台 03
すしめしをつくるときにつかう木製のおけ。「半切（飯切）」ともよぶ。

巻きす 04
細くけずった竹を糸で編んだもの。のり巻きなど、食材を巻いて形づくるときにつかう。

すりばち・すりこぎ 05
ごまをすったり、材料をまぜあわせてなめらかにしたりするときにつかう。あたりばち・あたり棒ともいう。

こし器 06
だしなど液体をこすための、目のこまかいふるい。馬のしっぽの毛をつかったこし器（写真のもの）やステンレス製のものなどがある。

---

01 Cooking tools for Washoku 02 Grater to grate daikon, ginger or wasabi etc. 03 Wooden container for vinegared rice. 04 Bamboo rolling mat to make sushi rolls or something to make a roll. 05 Mortar and pestle to make smooth paste. 06 Strainer for liquid. There are strainers for which horse tails are used, or made by steel. 07 Square shaped egg omelet pan. 08 Shallow pan for egg-bound chicken or egg-bound cutlet. Approximately 16cm in diameter. 09 Measuring spoon and cup 10 Table spoon: tbsp 15mL 11 Tea spoon: tsp 5mL 12 Measuring cup 200mL 13 Rice cup for measuring rice 180mL 14 Cooking terms of Washoku 15 Aeru: dress prepared vegetables or ingredients with seasonings, miso sauce, sesame sauce, vinegar sauce and so on. 16 Aku wo toru: skim off the scum during boiling or simmering process. If leaving the scum as it is unpleasant smell remains or the food tastes bad. 17 Aranetsu wo toru: cool down the food from very hot condition. 18 Otoshi buta: drop-lid for simmering. The broth will be served all around the

卵焼き器 07
卵焼き専用のなべ。写真のような正方形のものと、長方形のものがある。

親子なべ 08
直径16cm前後の浅いなべ。親子丼やカツ丼などをつくるときにつかう。

計量スプーン・カップ 09
大さじ 15mL 10
小さじ 5mL 11
計量カップ 12
200mL
※米の計量には、180mL（1合）のカップをつかう。 13

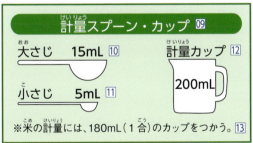

和食の料理用語 14

15 あえる 下ごしらえをした野菜や魚介類などに、調味料やみそだれ、ごまだれ、合わせ酢などをまぜあわせること。

16 アクをとる 食材をゆでたり煮たりしたときに浮いてくるあわ（これをアクという）をすくいとること。アクをそのままにすると、料理にくさみが残り、味や見た目が悪くなる。

17 あら熱をとる アツアツの状態からほどほどの熱さまで冷ますこと。

18 落としぶた なべよりひとまわり小さいふた。落としぶたをして煮物をすると、煮汁がまんべんなくまわり、味がよくしみる。

19 飾り包丁 なすやしいたけ、魚などの表面に、包丁で切り目を入れること。見ばえをよくし、火の通りや味のしみこみをよくする。

20 酒塩 酒に塩を少しまぜあわせたもの。きのこや魚、とり肉などの下ごしらえや、焼き物の仕上げに味をととのえるためにつかわれる。

21 霜降り 魚介類や肉などをサッと熱湯に通して冷水にとり、中身は生で表面は白く霜が降りたような状態にすること。

22 立て塩 海水と同じくらいの濃度の塩水のこと。水1カップに塩小さじ1が目安。立て塩は生ぐささをとる効果があり、貝の砂ぬきや魚介類を洗うときなどにつかう。きゅうりのうす切りを立て塩に漬けてしんなりさせるなど、野菜の下ごしらえにもつかう。

23 湯通し 材料のくさみや油気をとったり、うま味をとじこめたりするために、サッと熱湯をかけたり、熱湯にくぐらせたりすること。

---

ingredients by using drop-lid, and they are cooked easily. 19 Kazari bocho: decorative cuts applied on the surface of the ingredients for beautiful presentation and easy cooking. 20 Sakajio: seasoning with sake and salt. It is used for preparation of mushrooms, fish and chicken, or finishing process of the grilled dish to make a taste. 21 Shimo furi: preparation of seafood and meat. Parboil the ingredients and then soak in iced water. The inside is raw and the outside is slightly cooked, so the outside looks white like frost. Shimo furi means becoming frosted in Japanese. 22 Tatejio: salted water almost the same salt concentration with the sea water. About 1 cup water and 1 tsp of salt. It has an effect to remove the bad smell of seafoods. Used for removing the sand of shellfish or washing seafoods. Used for the preparation of vegetables, too. Make sliced cucumber tender texture by soaking in salted water. 23 Yudōshi: parboil or pour hot water to ingredients to remove bad smell or excess oil. This process is good to keep umami inside the ingredients, too.

さくいん

INDEX

あ行

青森県	Aomori Pref.	52, 64
秋田（秋田県）	Akita (Akita Pref.)	48, 49, 52
揚げびたし		88
揚げ物	fried dish	27
預け鉢	Azukebachi	81, 88, 89
厚焼き卵	Atsuyaki Tamago (Japanese thick omelet)	11, 144, 145
アナゴ	conger eel	88, 110, 111
アボカド	avocado	118, 121, 144, 145
海女	female skin diver	61, 65
甘酢	sweetened vinegar	74
アメリカ	America (the U.S., U.S.A.)	116, 117, 118, 119, 120, 122, 126, 127, 129, 130, 131, 132, 133, 138
合わせ酢	Awasezu vinegar	37, 42
アンコウなべ	anglerfish hot pot	52
安藤百福	Momofuku Ando	130
イカのすし	squid sushi	64
イカめし	Ika-meshi (squid stuffed with rice)	47, 70
イギリス	England	121, 124, 125, 130, 132, 134
池田菊苗	Kikunae Ikeda	135
石狩なべ	Ishikari Nabe	47, 52
伊勢エビ	Ise-ebi lobster	60, 61
いため煮	braised dish	26
イタリア	Italy	102, 121, 123, 127, 131
一汁三菜	1 Soup and 3 Dishes	10, 11, 18, 30, 34, 38, 82, 83, 84, 85, 86, 88, 95, 104, 105, 137
一番だし	first dashi (first soup stock)	14, 15, 86
いちょう切り	quarter slice	23
糸づくり	Itozukuri (thin strip slice)	24
茨城県	Ibaraki Pref.	52
いろどり野菜	herb and vegetable garniture	29
岩国ずし	Iwakuni-zushi	62, 63
岩国れんこん		63
イワシのごま漬け	salted sardine with sesame	58
岩手県	Iwate Pref.	45
インスタントラーメン	instant noodles	130
インド	India	122, 124, 130, 131, 132, 134
潮汁	Ushio-jiru (clear soup)	11, 18, 19
うすくちしょうゆ	light soy sauce	21
ウスターソース	Worcestershire sauce	134
うす刃包丁	Usuba knife	22
うどん	udon	120, 121, 128, 136
うま味	umami	11, 14, 15, 18, 19, 20, 21, 25, 26, 27, 39, 85, 134, 135, 137, 138, 139, 153
うま味調味料	umami seasoning	135
梅わん	sweet red bean soup	69
うら巻き	Uramaki (inside-out roll sushi)	118, 121, 144
衛生管理	hygiene control	139
栄養	nutrition	137
江戸前ずし	Edomae-zushi	65
愛媛（愛媛県）	Ehime (Ehime Pref.)	66, 67
大阪府	Osaka Pref.	65
おかず	okazu (dishes eaten with rice)	10, 30
岡山県	Okayama Pref.	65, 74
お好み焼き	Okonomiyaki	126, 134
折敷	Oshiki (tray)	82, 83, 84, 92, 93
押しずし	oshi-zushi (pressed sushi)	62, 64, 65, 120, 121
おせち	Osechi	8, 45, 85, 140
（お）膳	tray (table)	82, 94, 95
落としぶた	drop-lid	26, 36, 41, 71, 153
おはし	chopsticks	24, 30, 32, 33, 68, 76, 83, 86, 89, 92, 93, 123
おひたし	Ohitashi	40, 88
おもてなし（もてなし）	Omotenashi (hospitality)	67, 68, 80, 81, 83, 84, 95, 98, 99, 136, 137
おやき	Oyaki (Japanese stuffed dumpling)	56, 57, 72
親子なべ	shallow pan	149, 153
おろし金	grater	152
（お）わん	bowl	30, 47, 82, 83, 86, 92, 93, 106, 107

か行

『海軍割烹術参考書』	Japanese navy recipe book	124
『海軍厨業管理教科書』	Japanese navy cooking book	125
会席料理	Kaiseki（会席）cuisine	80, 95, 103
懐石料理	Kaiseki（懐石）cuisine	80, 81, 82, 83, 95, 99
回転ずし	sushi-go-round	119, 121
鏡もち	Kagami-mochi (round rice cakes)	9, 90
香川県	Kagawa Pref.	44
カキ	oyster	44, 51, 52, 53
かきたま汁	egg drop soup	19
柿の葉ずし	Sushi wrapped with persimmon leaves	65
飾り切り	decorative cuttings	97
飾り包丁	decorative cuts	25, 40, 96, 97, 109, 153
かつお節	dried bonito	14, 15, 16, 135, 139
カツ丼	Katsudon (pork cutlet on a bowl of rice)	127, 148, 149
かつらむき	Katsura-muki cutting	97
カニカマ	Kanikama	131
から揚げ	Kara-age	127
カリフォルニアロール	California roll	117, 118, 119, 120
カレーライス	curry and rice	122, 124

日本語	ローマ字/英語	ページ
かんぴょう	Kanpyo	17
乾物	dried food	16, 17
菊だいこん	chrysanthemum shaped daikon	97
木の芽	Kinome (sansho leaf)	29, 86
基本五味	basic five tastes	135
牛刀	gyuto	22
牛なべ	beef hot pot	126
京都府	Kyoto Pref.	45
郷土料理	local foods	43, 44, 46, 47, 48, 49, 50, 54, 56, 57, 58, 59, 60, 62, 63, 64, 65, 66, 67, 68, 70, 72, 74, 76, 140
魚しょう	fish hishio	21
きりたんぽ	Kiritampo	48, 49
クールジャパン戦略	Cool Japan Strategy	103
くし形切り	wedge slice	23
クリームシチュー	cream stew	124
けずり節	shaved dried bonito	16, 139
麹	koji	21, 91
麹菌	koji mold	20
香辛料	spice	124, 134
紅茶	black tea	100
小口切り	thin round slice	23
こし器	strainer for liquid	152
五色	5 Colors	29, 80
個食	each member of the family eat what they want	105
孤食	eating alone	105
粉食	eating meal made with wheat flour	105
ご当地ラーメン	local ramen	129
ごはん	gohan (rice)	10, 11, 12, 13, 30, 31, 34, 83
ごはん茶わん	(gohan) rice bowl	30, 31
こぶじめ	Kobujime	85
五法	5 Methods	80
ごまあえ	Goma-Ae	11
米	rice	12, 13, 91, 105
米みそ	Rice Miso	20, 133
こんぶ	kombu (kelp)	14, 15, 16, 135, 139

さ行

日本語	ローマ字/英語	ページ
酒塩	seasoning with sake and salt	153
サケ	salmon	45, 47, 50, 55
酒の肴	nibbles for sake	90
笹だんご	Sasa-dango	55
さざ波づくり	sazanami zukuri (surface wavelet slice)	24, 37
さしすせそ	Sa, Shi, Su, Se, So	27
さしみ	sashimi	24, 51, 80, 85, 97, 117, 120
さしみ包丁	Sashimi knife	22
砂糖	sugar	27, 42
三方	Sampo	90
三枚おろし	three fillets slice	23, 109
塩	salt	18, 19, 20, 21, 27, 94
塩仕立て	clear soup with salt	18
塩引きザケ	salted and aged salmon	55
塩焼	grill with salt	25
滋賀県		64
卓袱料理	Shippoku cuisine	68, 69, 76, 95
島根県	Shimane Pref.	44
霜降り	parboil ingredients and then soak in iced water	110, 153
じゃっぱ汁	Jappa-jiru soup	52
主菜	main dish	10, 11, 30, 34, 38
旬	seasonal ingredient	10, 11, 28, 80, 81, 96, 99
松花堂弁当	Shokado bento (meal box)	80, 121
精進料理	Shojin cuisine	94
しょうゆ	soy sauce	9, 18, 19, 20, 21, 27, 121, 125, 132, 133
しょうゆ仕立て	clear soup with soy sauce	18
食育	food education	102, 140, 141
食材	ingredient	136
食事作法	table manner	30, 31, 92
食ばし	chopsticks for eating	89
食料自給率	food self-sufficiency ratio	140
しょっつる	Shottsuru	21, 49
しょっつるなべ	Shottsuru Nabe	49, 52
しらたき	Shirataki (devil's tongue noodles)	41, 42
汁(物)	soup	10, 11, 18, 30, 34, 38, 84
汁わん	soup bowl	83, 84, 85, 93
ジンギスカン	Genghis Khan Barbecue	46, 47
信州そば	Shinshu soba	57
しんじょう	Shinjo	86, 88, 106
酢	vinegar	27
吸口	topping	86
吸地	soup	86, 106, 107
吸物	soup	86
末広切り		142
すき焼き	Sukiyaki	122, 126
すし	sushi	64, 65, 117, 118, 119, 120, 121, 123
酢の物		37
すまし汁	Sumashi-jiru (clear soup)	19
すりばち	mortar	35, 152
すり身	fish paste	131
ずんだもち	Zunda mochi	51
西洋料理	Western cuisine	122
節句	seasonal festival	8, 9, 12
背開き	open from the back	142
千切り	thin strip slice	23
禅宗	Zen (sect)	81, 94, 98
煎茶	Sencha (green tea)	98, 100, 101

千利休　Sennorikyu　　　　　　　　　　　　　98
雑煮　Zoni (soup)　　　　　　　　8, 9, 44, 45, 51
そぎづくり（うすづくり）　usuzukuri (thin slice)　　24

た行

タイ　Thailand　　　　　　　　　　　21, 119, 130
タイ（魚）　(red) sea bream　　　19, 24, 66, 68, 85
大饗料理　Daikyo cuisine　　　　　　　　　　　94
タイそうめん　somen noodles with sea bream　　66
炊き合わせ　Takiawase　　　　　　　88, 89, 110
武田信玄　Shingen Takeda　　　　　　　　　　52
だし　dashi　　　8, 11, 14, 15, 16, 18, 19, 94, 135, 137
手綱こんにゃく　rope shaped konnyaku　　　97
立て塩　salted water (almost the same salt concentration with the sea water)　　　　　　　　112, 153
たで酢　Tadesu vinegar　　　　　　　　　　　96
伊達政宗　Masamune Date　　　　　　　　　51
食べ放題（バイキング方式）　all-you-can-eat　119
卵焼き器　egg omelet pan　　　　　　　145, 153
たんざく切り　rectangular slice　　　　　　　23
筑前煮　Chikuzen-ni　　　　　　　　　　10, 26
千葉（千葉県）　Chiba (Chiba Pref.)　　58, 59, 64
茶室　tea ceremony room　　　　　　81, 98, 99
茶せん　whisk　　　　　　　　　　　　81, 99
茶の湯　tea ceremony　　　　　81, 82, 95, 98, 99
茶わん　yunomi (tea bowl)　　　　　99, 100, 101
茶わん蒸し　Chawan-mushi (savory steamed egg custard)　　　　　　　　　　　　　　27, 29
ちゃんこなべ　Chanko Nabe　　　　　　　　53
中国　China　　　　　21, 98, 119, 128, 130, 133
調味料　seasoning　　　　　　　　　　　　27
ちらしずし　chirashi-zushi (vinegared rice bowl decorated with seafood)　　　　　　　80, 120
つくばい　Tsukubai (wash basin in Japanese gardens)　99
つみれ　minced ball　　　　　　　　　　　35
手こねずし　Tekone-zushi　　　　　　　　　65
鉄板焼き　Teppanyaki　　　　　　　　126, 136
出刃包丁　Deba knife　　　　　　　　　22, 23
照焼　Teriyaki　　　　　　　　　25, 36, 133
てんぷら　tempra　　　　　　　　　126, 142
東京都　Tokyo Pref.　　　　　　　　45, 53, 65
東郷平八郎　Heihachiro Togo　　　　　　　125
土佐酢　Tosazu vinegar　　　　　　37, 42, 112
土手なべ　hot pot (cooking)　　　　　51, 52, 53
富山県　Toyama Pref.　　　　　　　　　　　65
取りばし　chopsticks for serving　　　87, 89, 95
とんカツ　Tonkatsu (pork cutlet)　　122, 123, 134
とん汁　pork miso soup　　　　　　　　　　39

な行

長崎県　Nagasaki Pref.　　　　　　44, 68, 69, 76
長崎ちゃんぽん　Nagasaki champon noodles　69
長崎てんぷら　Nagasaki tempura　　　　　　69
長野（長野県）　Nagano (Nagano Pref.)　56, 57, 72
なます　Namasu dish　　　　　　　　　　　85
生なれずし　Namanare-zushi　　　　　　　　64
奈良県　Nara Pref.　　　　　　　　　　　　65
なれずし　Nare-zushi　　　　　　　　　　　64
南蛮漬け　Namban-zuke　　　　　　　　　69
ナンプラー　Nam pla　　　　　　　　　　21
新潟（新潟県）　Niigata (Niigata Pref.)　　54, 55
にぎりずし　Nigiri-zushi　　　64, 65, 119, 120, 121
肉じゃが　Nikujaga (braised beef and potato)　　　　　　　　　　　　　　　　41, 125, 127
煮魚　simmered fish　　　　　　　　　　　26
二番だし　second dashi (second soup stock)　14
煮びたし　stewed vegetable with a mild broth　26, 88
煮干し　dried sardine　　　　　　　　14, 15
日本酒　sake　　　　　　　　　　　　　　91
日本食レストラン　Japanese restaurant　116, 117, 119, 120, 121, 138
日本人街　Japantown　　　　　　　　117, 118
日本茶　Japanese tea　　　　　　　　　　100
日本料理　Japanese cuisine　　120, 121, 122, 123, 126, 127, 128, 129, 136
二枚おろし　two fillets slice　　　　　　　109
煮物わん　simmered food bowl　　81, 86, 87, 106
ヌックマム　Nuoc mam　　　　　　　　　21
ねじり梅　Japanese apricot shaped carrot　　97
野沢菜漬け　Nozawana pickles　　　57, 72, 73
のっぺ　Noppe soup　　　　　　　　　54, 55

は行

配膳　place dishes　　　　　　　　　　　　30
羽釜　metal pot with a thick wooden lid　　　12
鉢盛料理　Hachimori cuisine　　　　　　66, 67
八寸　Hassun (nibbles for sake)　　　　　90, 112
バッテラ　Battera　　　　　　　　　　　　65
花切りしいたけ　shiitake mushroom with flower cuts　97
花ばす　flower shaped lotus　　　　　　　　97
ハマグリ料理　Hamaguri clam dishes　　　　60
早ずし　Haya-zushi　　　　　　　　　　　64
はらこめし　Harako (salmon roe) rice bowl　50, 51
ばらずし　Bara-zushi　　　　　　　　　65, 74
半月切り　half moon slice　　　　　　　　　23
飯台　wooden container　　　　　　　145, 152
番茶　Bancha　　　　　　　　　　　　101

日本語	English	ページ
PFCバランス	PFC balance	11
ビーフシチュー	beef stew	125
ひきずり	Hikizuri (Nagoya cochin chicken hot pot)	53
醬	hishio	21, 94
比内地どり	Hinai chicken	49
兵庫県	Hyogo Pref.	53
平づくり	Hirazukuri (thick slice)	24
広島県	Hiroshima Pref.	44, 53
フォン・ド・ヴォー	fond de veau	135
フカの湯ざらし	boiled shark	67
福井県	Fukui Pref.	44
福岡県	Fukuoka Pref.	53
副菜	side dish	10, 11, 34, 38
ふくさし	blowfish sashimi	63
ふくちり	blowfish hot pot	53
ふくめん	Fukumen	67
ぶたの角煮	simmered pork	69, 76
太巻きずし	Futomaki-zushi	64
フナずし		64
ブラジル	Brazil	130, 131
フランス	France	120, 121, 127, 131, 141
フルーツにぎり	fruit sushi	120
ふろふきだいこん	simmered daikon	96
文化遺産	cultural heritage	104, 105
文明開化	Westernization movement	122, 126
へぎ盆	Hegi tray	90, 113
弁当	Bento	121
ほうじ茶	Hojicha	101
包丁	knife	22, 23, 35, 36
ほうとう	Houtou noodle	52
干ししいたけ	dried shiitake mushroom	14, 15, 94, 135
ぼたんなべ	wild boar hot pot	53
北海道	Hokkaido Pref.	45, 46, 47, 51, 52, 70
本膳料理	Honzen cuisine	95

ま行

日本語	English	ページ
巻きす	bamboo rolling mat	145, 152
巻きずし	maki-zushi	118, 119, 120, 144
マグロ	tuna	117, 118, 121, 139
マスずし	trout sushi	65
松阪肉	Matsusaka beef	61
抹茶	Matcha	81, 98, 99, 101
松葉ゆず	pine needle shaped Yuzu citrus	86, 97
豆みそ	Bean Miso	20, 133
三重(三重県)	Mie (Mie Pref.)	60, 65
「味覚の一週間」	The Week of Taste	141
水炊き	chicken hot pot	53
水ときかたくり粉	Katakuriko (potato starch) dissolved water	147
みそ	miso	18, 20, 27, 127, 130, 133
みそ仕立て	miso soup	18, 84
みそ汁(ミソスープ)	Miso-shiru (miso soup)	15, 19, 18, 127, 136, 138
宮城(宮城県)	Miyagi (Miyagi Pref.)	45, 50, 51, 52
みりん	mirin	25, 42, 85, 125
麦みそ	Barley Miso	20, 133
向付	Mukozuke	81, 83, 85, 87
蒸し物	steamed dish	27
めしわん	rice bowl	82, 83, 85, 93

や行

日本語	English	ページ
焼きとり	Yakitori (grilled chicken)	121, 127, 146
焼き物	grilled dish	80, 81, 86, 87, 88, 89, 108
焼物	ceramic	85
山口(山口県)	Yamaguchi (Yamaguchi Pref.)	53, 62
山梨県	Yamanashi Pref.	52
幽庵焼	Yuan-yaki	25, 87, 108
ユウガオ	Yugao gourd	17
ゆず	Yuzu (citrus)	58, 86, 97
湯通し	parboil	67, 71, 153
ユネスコ無形文化遺産	UNESCO Intangible Cultural Heritage	102, 103, 140
洋食	Yoshoku (cross of Western and Japanese cuisine)	122, 123
ヨーロッパ	Europe	116, 119, 121, 122, 127, 132, 133, 135

ら行

日本語	English	ページ
ラーメン	ramen	121, 122, 128, 129, 130
落花生	peanuts	59
乱切り	rolling cut	23, 39
利休ばし	Rikyu chopsticks	83, 89
両細	both tapered edges	89
緑茶	green tea	100
ロシア	Russia	116, 130, 131
六方むき	hexagonal cut	97

わ行

日本語	English	ページ
若竹汁	bamboo shoot soup	19
若竹煮	simmered bamboo shoot with wakame seaweed	96
和歌山県	Wakayama Pref.	65
輪切り	round thick slice	23
和食ワールドチャレンジ2013	Washoku World Challenge Competition 2013	137

英語さくいん — INDEX

A
- Akita (Akita Pref.) ... 48, 49, 52
- all-you-can-eat ... 119
- America (the U.S., U.S.A.) ... 116, 118, 119, 122, 126, 127, 129, 130, 131, 132, 133
- anglerfish hot pot ... 52
- Aomori Pref. ... 52, 64
- Atsuyaki Tamago (Japanese thick omelet) ... 11, 144, 145
- avocado ... 118, 121, 144, 145
- Awasezu vinegar ... 42
- Azukebachi ... 81, 88, 89

B
- bamboo rolling mat ... 144, 152
- bamboo shoot soup ... 19
- Bancha ... 101
- Bara-zushi ... 74, 78
- Barley Miso ... 20, 133
- basic five tastes ... 135
- Battera ... 78
- Bean Miso ... 20, 133
- beef hot pot ... 126
- beef stew ... 136, 150
- Bento ... 121
- black tea ... 100
- blowfish hot pot ... 53
- blowfish sashimi ... 78
- boiled shark ... 67
- both tapered edges ... 89
- bowl ... 13, 30, 31, 33, 70, 73, 74, 75, 82, 86, 92, 93, 95, 107, 110, 112, 148, 149
- braised dish ... 26
- Brazil ... 116, 131

C
- California roll ... 117, 118, 121
- ceramic ... 82, 85
- Chanko Nabe ... 52
- Chawan-mushi (savory steamed egg custard) ... 27
- Chiba (Chiba Pref.) ... 58, 59, 64
- chicken hot pot ... 53
- Chikuzen-ni ... 11, 26
- China ... 21, 98, 119, 128, 130, 133
- chirashi-zushi (vinegared rice bowl decorated with seafood) ... 80, 120
- chopsticks ... 24, 30, 31, 32, 33, 82, 87, 89, 92, 93, 114, 150
- chopsticks for eating ... 89
- chopsticks for serving ... 89
- chrysanthemum shaped daikon ... 97
- clear soup with salt ... 18
- clear soup with soy sauce ... 18
- conger eel ... 88, 110, 111
- Cool Japan Strategy ... 114
- cream stew ... 124
- cultural heritage ... 104, 105
- curry and rice ... 122, 124, 125

D
- Daikyo cuisine ... 94
- dashi ... 8, 11, 14, 15, 16, 18, 19, 94, 135, 137
- Deba knife ... 23
- decorative cuts ... 40, 97, 109, 153
- decorative cuttings ... 97
- dried bonito ... 14, 15, 16, 42, 86, 135, 139
- dried food ... 16, 17, 94
- dried sardine ... 9, 15, 59
- dried shiitake mushroom ... 11, 14, 15, 94, 135
- drop-lid ... 26, 36, 41, 71, 152

E
- each member of the family eat what they want ... 105
- eating alone ... 105
- eating meal made with wheat flour ... 105
- Edomae-zushi ... 65
- egg drop soup ... 19
- egg omelet pan ... 145, 152
- Ehime (Ehime Pref.) ... 66, 78
- England ... 124, 131, 134, 150
- Europe ... 116, 119, 122, 127, 132, 150, 151

F
- female skin diver ... 61, 65
- first dashi (first soup stock) ... 14, 86, 139
- fish hishio ... 21
- fish paste ... 44, 114, 131
- 5 Colors ... 28, 29, 80
- 5 Methods ... 80
- flower shaped lotus ... 97
- fond de veau ... 150
- food education ... 103, 140, 141, 151
- food self-sufficiency ratio ... 140
- France ... 120, 121, 127, 131, 141
- fried dish ... 27, 135
- fruit sushi ... 120
- Fukui Pref. ... 44
- Fukumen ... 67
- Fukuoka Pref. ... 53
- Futomaki-zushi ... 64

G
- Genghis Khan Barbecue ... 46, 47
- gohan (rice) ... 10, 11, 12, 30, 31, 34, 83
- Goma-Ae ... 11
- grater ... 152
- green tea ... 98, 100
- grill with salt ... 87
- grilled dish ... 80, 81, 86, 87, 88, 89, 108
- gyuto ... 22

H
- Hachimori cuisine ... 66, 67
- half-moon slice ... 23
- Hamaguri clam dishes ... 60
- Harako (salmon roe) rice bowl ... 50, 51
- Hassun (nibbles for sake) ... 90, 112
- Haya-zushi ... 64
- Hegi tray ... 91, 113
- Heihachiro Tōgō ... 150
- herb and vegetable garniture ... 29
- hexagonal cut ... 97
- Hikizuri (Nagoya Cochin chicken hot pot) ... 53
- Hinai chicken ... 49
- Hirazukuri (thick slice) ... 24
- Hiroshima Pref. ... 44, 53
- hishio ... 21, 94
- Hojicha ... 101
- Hokkaido Pref. ... 45, 46, 47, 51, 52, 70
- Honzen cuisine ... 94, 95
- hot pot (cooking) ... 51, 52, 53
- Houtou noodle ... 52
- hygiene control ... 139

I
- Hyogo Pref. ... 53
- Ibaraki Pref. ... 52
- Ika-meshi (squid stuffed with rice) ... 47, 70
- India ... 124, 131, 132, 134
- ingredient ... 137
- instant noodles ... 130
- Ise-ebi lobster ... 60, 61
- Ishikari Nabe ... 47, 52
- Italy ... 121, 129, 131, 150
- Itozukuri (thin strip slice) ... 24
- Iwakuni-zushi ... 62
- Iwate Pref. ... 45

J
- Japanese apricot shaped carrot ... 97
- Japanese cuisine ... 80, 121, 122, 123, 126, 129, 136, 150
- Japanese navy cooking book ... 150
- Japanese navy recipe book ... 125
- Japanese restaurant ... 116, 117, 119, 120, 121, 127, 138, 150
- Japanese tea ... 100
- Japantown ... 117, 118
- Jappa-jiru soup ... 52

K
- Kagami-mochi (round rice cakes) ... 9
- Kagawa Pref. ... 44
- Kaiseki（会席）cuisine ... 80, 95, 114
- Kaiseki（懐石）cuisine ... 80, 81, 82, 83, 95, 99
- Kanikama ... 131
- Kanpyo ... 17
- Kara-age ... 127
- Katakuriko (potato starch) dissolved water ... 151
- Katsudon (pork cutlet on a bowl of rice) ... 148, 151
- Katsura-muki cutting ... 97
- Kikunae Ikeda ... 135
- Kinome (sansho leaf) ... 29, 86, 114
- Kiritampo ... 48, 49
- knife ... 22, 23
- Kobujime ... 85
- koji ... 21, 114
- koji mold ... 20
- kombu (kelp) ... 14, 16, 135, 139
- Kyoto Pref. ... 44

L
- light soy sauce ... 21
- local foods ... 43, 44, 46, 47, 48, 49, 50, 54, 55, 56, 57, 58, 59, 60, 62, 64, 66, 68, 70, 72, 74, 76, 78, 141
- local ramen ... 129

M
- main dish ... 10, 11, 31
- maki-zushi (roll sushi) ... 17, 64, 118, 120, 121, 144, 150
- Masamune Date ... 50, 51
- Matcha ... 81, 98, 99, 101
- Matsusaka beef ... 61
- metal pot with a thick wooden lid ... 13
- Mie (Mie Pref.) ... 60, 65
- minced ball ... 35
- mirin ... 25, 42, 85, 87, 108, 146, 150
- miso ... 18, 20, 42, 130, 133, 150

Term	Pages
miso soup	18, 84
Miso-shiru (miso soup)	10, 14, 15, 18, 30, 44, 52, 136, 138, 150
Miyagi (Miyagi Pref.)	45, 50, 52
Momofuku Ando	130
mortar	35, 152
Mukozuke	81, 82, 84, 85, 87

N

Term	Pages
Nagano (Nagano Pref.)	56, 57, 72
Nagasaki Pref.	44, 68, 69, 76
Nagasaki champon noodles	78
Nagasaki tempura	69
Nam pla	21
Namanare-zushi	64
Namasu dish	85
Namban-zuke	69
Nara Pref.	78
Nare-zushi	64
nibbles for sake	90
Nigiri-zushi	64, 118, 120, 121
Niigata (Niigata Pref.)	54, 55
Nikujaga (braised beef and potato)	38, 41, 150
Noppe soup	54, 55
Nozawana pickles	57, 72
Nuoc mam	21
nutrition	151

O

Term	Pages
Ohitashi	114
Okayama Pref.	74, 78
okazu (dishes eaten with rice)	10
Okonomiyaki	126, 134, 135
Omotenashi (hospitality)	69, 81, 83, 98, 99, 137, 151
1 Soup and 3 Dishes	10, 11, 34, 38, 82, 83, 84, 86, 88, 95, 104, 105, 137
open from the back	143
Osaka Pref.	78
Osechi	8, 9, 140
Oshiki (tray)	82
oshi-zushi (pressed sushi)	63, 64, 78, 120, 121
Oyaki (Japanese stuffed dumpling)	56, 57, 72
oyster	44, 51, 52, 53

P

Term	Pages
parboil	67, 70, 153
peanuts	59
PFC balance	11
pine needle shaped Yuzu citrus	86, 97
place dishes	30
pork miso soup	39
parboil ingredients and then soak in iced water	153

Q

Term	Pages
quarter slice	23

R

Term	Pages
ramen	121, 122, 128, 129, 130, 150
rectangular slice	23
(red) sea bream	19, 24, 66, 67, 68, 69, 85
rice	12, 13, 104, 114
rice bowl	30, 31, 50, 51, 82, 84, 86, 93, 120, 127
Rice Miso	20, 133
Rikyu chopsticks	82, 89
rolling cut	23, 39
rope shaped konnyaku	97
round thick slice	23
Russia	116, 131

S

Term	Pages
Sa, Shi, Su, Se, So	42
sake	114
salmon	45, 47, 50, 78
salt	18, 19, 20, 21, 42, 94
salted and aged salmon	78
salted sardine with sesame	58
salted water (almost the same salt concentration with the sea water)	153
Sampo	91
Sasa-dango	55
sashimi	24, 51, 80, 85, 97, 117, 121
Sashimi knife	22
sazanami zukuri (surface wavelet slice)	24, 37
seasonal festival	8
seasonal ingredient	11, 28, 80, 81, 96, 99
seasoning	42
seasoning with sake and salt	153
second dashi (second soup stock)	14
Sencha (green tea)	98, 100, 101
Sennorikyu	99
shallow pan	149, 152
shaved dried bonito	16, 139
shiitake mushroom with flower cuts	97
Shimane Pref.	44
Shingen Takeda	52
Shinjo	88, 106, 114
Shinshu soba	57
Shippoku cuisine	68, 69, 95
Shirataki (devil's tongue noodles)	41, 42
Shojin cuisine	94
Shokado bento (meal box)	80, 121
Shottsuru	21, 49
Shottsuru Nabe	49, 52
side dish	10, 11
simmered bamboo shoot with wakame seaweed	96
simmered daikon	97
simmered fish	26
simmered food bowl	81, 86, 87, 106
simmered pork	69, 76
somen noodles with sea bream	66
soup	10, 11, 18, 29, 30, 31, 34, 35, 38, 39, 84, 86, 106, 107, 114
soup bowl	82, 84, 86, 92, 93
soy sauce	9, 18, 19, 20, 21, 42, 121, 132, 133, 150
spice	124, 125, 134
squid sushi	64
steamed dish	27
stewed vegetable with a mild broth	27
strainer for liquid	152
sugar	42
Sukiyaki	123, 126
Sumashi-jiru (clear soup)	19
sushi	64, 65, 117, 118, 119, 120, 150
Sushi wrapped with persimmon leaves	78
sushi-go-round	150
sweet red bean soup	69
sweetened vinegar	74

T

Term	Pages
table manner	30, 92
Tadesu vinegar	96
Takiawase	88
tea ceremony	80, 95, 98, 99
tea ceremony room	80, 98, 99
Tekone-zushi	65
tempra	126, 142
Teppanyaki	127, 136
Teriyaki	25, 36, 132
Thailand	21, 131, 150
The Week of Taste	141
thin round slice	23
thin strip slice	23
three fillets slice	23, 109
Tokyo Pref.	45, 52, 65
Tonkatsu (pork cutlet)	123, 134
topping	86
Tosazu vinegar	37, 42, 112
Toyama Pref.	65
tray (table)	94, 95
trout sushi	65
Tsukubai (wash basin in Japanese gardens)	99
tuna	117, 118, 121
two fillets slice	109

U

Term	Pages
udon	121, 136
umami	11, 14, 19, 21, 25, 26, 27, 85, 135, 137, 139, 150, 151, 153
umami seasoning	135
UNESCO Intangible Cultural Heritage	102, 103, 114, 140
Uramaki (inside-out roll sushi)	118, 144, 150
Ushio-jiru (clear soup)	11, 19
Usuba knife	22
usuzukuri (thin slice)	24

V

Term	Pages
vinegar	42

W

Term	Pages
Wakayama Pref.	78
Washoku World Challenge Competition 2013	151
wedge slice	23
Western cuisine	122
Westernization movement	122, 126
whisk	81, 99
wild boar hot pot	53
wooden container	144, 152
Worcestershire sauce	134

Y

Term	Pages
Yakitori (grilled chicken)	121, 127, 146
Yamaguchi (Yamaguchi Pref.)	53, 62
Yamanashi Pref.	52
Yoshoku (cross of Western and Japanese cuisine)	122, 123
Yuan-yaki	25, 108
Yugao gourd	17
yunomi (tea bowl)	99, 100, 101
Yuzu (citrus)	58, 86, 87, 97

Z

Term	Pages
Zen (sect)	81, 94, 98
Zoni (soup)	8, 9, 44, 45, 51
Zunda mochi	78

■監修

服部 幸應（はっとり ゆきお） YUKIO HATTORI

1945年、東京都生まれ。学校法人服部学園・服部栄養専門学校理事長・校長。医学博士／健康大使。農林水産省「日本文化の世界無形遺産登録に向けた検討会」委員。テレビでもおなじみの食の探求者。食育の普及活動に精力的に取り組み、内閣府「食育推進会議」、農林水産省、厚生労働省、文部科学省の食に関する委員を歴任。農林水産省「農山漁村の郷土料理百選」選定委員会の委員長もつとめた。(公社)全国調理師養成施設協会会長。著書には『食育のすすめ』(マガジンハウス)、『世界の五大料理基本事典』(東京堂出版) などが、児童書には『はじめての食育』全6巻 (岩崎書店)、『元気が出る！世界の朝ごはん』全5巻 (日本図書センター) などがある。

服部 津貴子（はっとり つきこ） TSUKIKO HATTORI

フランス及びスイスの料理学校へ留学ののち、服部流家元に就任。現在、そのほかに家元会および服部栄養料理研究会会長、学校法人服部学園常任理事をつとめる。農林水産省林野庁の特用林産物の普及委員、国際オリーブ協会アドバイザーなどとしても活躍し、兄・服部幸應氏とともに服部学園を拠点として食育の普及活動をおこなっている。著書に『おいしい！食育講座』(同友館) が、監修には『世界遺産になった食文化』全4巻 (WAVE出版) などがある。服部幸應氏との共著には、『はじめての食育』全6巻 (岩崎書店)、『元気が出る！世界の朝ごはん』全5巻 (日本図書センター) などがある。

◆英訳

山本 真希（インターナショナル・カルチャーエクスチェンジ・ジャパン）
MAKI YAMAMOTO (International Culture Exchange Japan)

編 集　こどもくらぶ（石原　尚子）
制 作　株式会社エヌ・アンド・エス企画（長江　知子、尾崎　朗子）
校 正　くすのき舎、英文／河原　昭

■料理撮影　黒部　徹

■イラスト　荒賀　賢二

■協力
学校法人服部学園・
服部栄養専門学校
服部栄養料理研究会

■服部学園・協力スタッフ
西澤　辰男（日本料理教授）
平塚　未来（日本料理教授）
森　寛貴、青木　健一、高橋　紗和子

■取材・写真協力
服部学園フランス事務局、西村真由美

■写真提供
服部栄養料理研究会、秋田県、宇和島市観光協会、男鹿なび、岡山県、霧島酒造株式会社、滋賀県、信州・長野県観光協会、千葉県、長崎市、新潟県観光協会、広島県観光協会、北海道観光連盟、三重県観光連盟、宮城県観光課、山口県観光協会、鈴木酒造店、高野山別格本山一乗院、（一社）舞鶴観光協会、(株)キタカタ、「味覚の一週間」実行委員会、トリップアドバイザー、(株)ヤナギヤ、日本食レストラン海外普及推進機構、和食ワールドチャレンジ2013実行委員会、mac morrison、Kazuko Hohki、野口晃一郎、ディヴッドソン・舞子、
©sq00920、©marucyan、©longtaildog、©joymsk、©kazoka303030、©paylessimages、©kilala、©kattyan、©norinori303、©安ちゃん、©akiyoko、©イガちゃん、©monjiro、©Reika、©Tsuboya、©promolink、©rikaw、©k817、©Botamochy、©kim、©chihana、©jkq_foto、©Lichtrevier、©Jaimie Duplass、©z10e、©jedi-master、©Ruslan Olinchuk、©promolink、©Andrey Starostin、©photosomething、©M.studio - fotolia.com

What is 和食 WASHOKU?

2016年7月15日　初版第1刷発行　〈検印省略〉

定価はカバーに
表示しています

監 修 者　服 部 幸 應
　　　　　服 部 津 貴 子
編　　者　こどもくらぶ
発 行 者　杉 田 啓 三
印 刷 者　金 子 眞 吾

発行所　株式会社 ミネルヴァ書房
607-8494 京都市山科区日ノ岡堤谷町1
電話 075-581-5191／振替 01020-0-8076

©こどもくらぶ, 2016　印刷・製本 凸版印刷株式会社

ISBN978-4-623-07739-7
NDC596/160P/25.7cm
Printed in Japan